AF477960

Music and the Making of Middle-Class Culture

Music and the Making of Middle-Class Culture

A Comparative History of Nineteenth-Century Leipzig and Birmingham

Antje Pieper

University of Birmingham

palgrave
macmillan

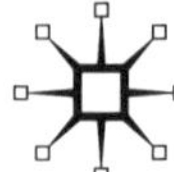

First published 2008 by
PALGRAVE MACMILLAN
Houndmills, Basingstoke, Hampshire RG21 6XS and
175 Fifth Avenue, New York, N.Y. 10010
Companies and representatives throughout the world

PALGRAVE MACMILLAN is the global academic imprint of the Palgrave Macmillan division of St. Martin's Press, LLC and of Palgrave Macmillan Ltd. Macmillan® is a registered trademark in the United States, United Kingdom and other countries. Palgrave is a registered trademark in the European Union and other countries.

ISBN-13: 978–0–230–54513–7 hardback
ISBN-10: 0–230–54513–0 hardback

This book is printed on paper suitable for recycling and made from fully managed and sustained forest sources. Logging, pulping and manufacturing processes are expected to conform to the environmental regulations of the country of origin.

A catalogue record for this book is available from the British Library.

Library of Congress Cataloging-in-Publication Data

Pieper, Antje, 1976–
    Music and the making of middle-class culture:a comparative history of
    19th-century Leipzig and Birmingham/Antje Pieper.
        p.   cm.
    Originally presented as the author's thesis: Ph.D., University of
    Birmingham, 2005.
    Includes bibliographical references (p.) and index.
    ISBN 0–230–54513–0 (alk. paper)
    1. Music—Social aspects—Germany—Leipzig—History—19th
    century.   2. Music—Social aspects—England—Birmingham—
    History—19th century.   3. Leipzig (Germany)—Intellectual life—
    19th century.   4. Birmingham (England)—Intellectual life—19th
    century.   I. Title.
    ML3916.P54 2008
    306.4′842094249609034—dc22

2008011809

10   9   8   7   6   5   4   3   2   1
17   16   15   14   13   12   11   10   09   08

Printed and bound in Great Britain by
CPI Antony Rowe, Chippenham and Eastbourne

In memory of
Michael Butler

Ich verlange in allem Leben, Möglichkeit des Daseins, und dann ist's
gut; wir haben dann nicht zu fragen, ob es schön, ob es hässlich ist, das
Gefühl, dass was geschaffen sei, Leben habe, stehe über diesen beiden,
und sei das einzige Kriterium in Kunstsachen.

Georg Büchner's Lenz, 1835

Contents

List of Figures, Graphs and Tables

Figures

Graphs

Tables

Acknowledgements

This book is based on my PhD thesis, submitted to the School of Historical Studies, University of Birmingham, in 2005. I would like to thank a number of people who made my postgraduate research a rewarding and thoroughly enjoyable experience. First of all, I owe a great debt to my supervisor, John Breuilly, who guided me throughout the process. I have benefited greatly from his expertise and experience; at the same time he always encouraged me to explore and pursue my own ideas of historical inquiry. I am particularly grateful for the initiation into the arcane mysteries of cricket that was the topic of many fruitful tea breaks. I would also like to thank my examiners, David Hill (Birmingham) and Simon Gunn (Leicester) for their constructive criticisms. The same is also true for Nigel Fortune, Peter Marsh, Amanda Cadman and Hugh McLeod whose comments on an earlier draft proved invaluable.

During 4 years of postgraduate study, I have been lucky to meet and work with a number of remarkable people present within the Schools of Humanities and Historical Studies. The friendships forged with Sania Reddig, Thomas Schmidt-Lux, Joel Love, Katie Wright, Matthew Edwards and Alan Suter sustained me with good humour throughout my research. I also wish to express my deep gratitude to Francesca Carnevali, Elaine Fulton, Deborah Jewson, Graeme Murdock, Matthew Hilton, Christina Pössel, Noelle Plack and Alex Mold.

A special mention is reserved for Michael Butler who inspired in me a love of literature. His belief in, and ability to convey, the humanising qualities of literature made him one of the rarest individuals I am ever likely to meet. My dedicating this book to him is a small measure of my appreciation for his enduring support and affectionate generosity without which this study – and so much else – would not have come so rapidly to fruition.

I am grateful to my partner Simon Blakey for his timely arrival in my life; above all, for his love, understanding and seemingly endless patience in explaining to me the importance of thermodynamics. Finally, my love to our little boy Theodore, whose unwitting assistance in sleeping so well surprisingly allowed me to finish this book on time.

Introduction

This book focuses on the nineteenth-century middle class in two industrial centres – Birmingham and Leipzig. More specifically, it concerns the ways and means by which the middle class of each town fashioned a cultural ideal as well as the institutions through which this ideal could be visibly and audibly expressed. Naturally, a cultural ideal is the product of a combination of factors and to explore its ramifications would require an analysis of a whole range of subjects covering ethical standards, religious, philosophical and educational ideals, literary and artistic preferences as demonstrated through poetry, novels, theatre plays, art exhibitions and architectural constructions, and much more. Thus, although the focus in this book is on music, reference to other cultural phenomena has to be made wherever necessary; indeed, music and the role it played within middle-class culture can often only be properly understood by reference to wider contexts, such as those offered by aesthetics or religion. Indeed, the aesthetic legacy inherited by the early nineteenth century categorically insisted that music could not exist by itself, let alone as mere entertainment. As in the other arts, therefore, music was imbued with norms and values which furthered and assured its association with didactic or edifying purposes, thus playing a role in the education and refinement of the bourgeoisie. As such, the focus on music in this study must be seen within the wider context of bourgeois culture. Neither the sole emphasis on particular compositions nor the study of specific institutions would have sufficed here.

To that end, this book proposes to work on a tripartite model which comprises firstly, a study of the religious, philosophical and aesthetic foundations of cultural practices in Britain and Germany; secondly, the ways in which those ideas about cultural practices were represented in the print media; and thirdly, how those cultural practices were realised in the dominant musical institutions of the two towns – the Gewandhaus in Leipzig and the Triennial Festival in Birmingham. There are two reasons behind this: firstly, the study of each institution continually tests the validity and legitimacy of wider national developments and *vice versa*. Secondly, it allows transnational comparative analysis to be undertaken: whilst the study of the Gewandhaus and the Triennial Festival might tell us something about themselves, such as their musical preferences, this would, in turn, only make sense within wider national contexts be these religious, philosophical or aesthetic. Given that the wider contexts are not the same, the institutions' reaction to cultural change, though potentially similar in appearance, will not have shared a similar impetus or have the same underlying purpose. A straight comparison might thus be futile, even misleading. Only after each institution has been placed within its own national context, can transnational comparison be undertaken. In that way, the similarities and differences in the ways and means by which the middle class availed themselves of the opportunities afforded by the public concert can be more fruitfully assessed.

Leipzig and Birmingham

The choice of Birmingham and Leipzig for comparison can be justified by a number of circumstances. Generally, both towns are representative of a new type of urban élite to whom a sense of collective identity and worth was, in many ways, more focused on the public cultural sphere than it was for any other social groups. Older, more traditional, élites expressed their distinctiveness in institutions and practices intrinsically linked to their own group identity, for example, clergy to the churches, the gentry and nobility to their country houses and leisure pursuits, workers to their trade unions and radical clubs. The upper classes thus focused on leisure and the lower classes perforce on work. Whilst the middle class also focused on work – in their case, of course, through the application of mental effort and entrepreneurial skills to the pursuit of wealth rather than physical labour – it was impossible for them to valorise either leisure (absence of work) or work (absence of leisure) alone. Rather, it was principally through culture – their art and science associations, galleries, libraries and public concerts – that they could visibly create and express their own distinctiveness. Thus, in both towns, middle-class culture was characterised by a particular ethos, norms and values that differentiated it from anything hitherto known that marked indelibly the age of the bourgeoisie. Although entirely different in origin and character, these norms and values impacted on Leipzig's musical culture in the same way that they did on Birmingham's. Thus, even though German music enjoys such universal dominance in our concert culture today, this fact should not lead the contemporary observer to overestimate its importance outside Germany and Austria, or, conversely, to underestimate other musical traditions (including Britain's) during the nineteenth century. As far as Birmingham in the 1860s was concerned, the cultural worth of Britain's musical tradition was positively celebrated, even deemed superior to anything hitherto known. The reasons for this are related to emergent cultural expectations which had little or no relevance to Leipzig's concert tradition (and *vice versa*).

There are also discernible similarities in the political and economic spheres of the two towns. Both expanded in size and reputation through the work of a successful entrepreneurial élite that dominated the social, political, economic and increasingly cultural spheres. Both towns lacked gentry or aristocratic social and cultural networks, which meant that neither was tied to a particular dominant cultural tradition. Both acquired cultural eminence when one of Europe's finest musicians of the early nineteenth century – Felix Mendelssohn – was appointed to head both music cultures during the 1830s and 1840s: in Birmingham as conductor at the Triennial Festival and in Leipzig as musical director at the Gewandhaus. The choice of the Gewandhaus and the Triennial Festival for comparison can be justified on the grounds that within their local confines, they were *the* élite cultural institutions. Although in both towns a number of other cultural institutions such as art galleries, museums, subscription concerts and so on were available, both the Triennial Festival and the Gewandhaus remained *the* flagship cultural enterprise. Both were instantly and recognisably associated with their respective towns. In that sense, they are functionally equivalent institutions and allow a fruitful comparative analysis to be undertaken. A further reason behind the choice of public concerts is that both were founded roughly at the same time during the late eighteenth century, which meant that both the Gewandhaus and the Triennial Festival grew out of the respective religious, philosophical and aesthetic doctrines that were prevalent at that time. Again, this circumstance is conducive to the comparative nature of this book.

Structure of the Book

For all their similarities, Birmingham and Leipzig naturally exhibited major differences. These are considered in Chapter 1, which provides a short introduction to the towns' demographic, religious, economic and political characteristics. Conclusions drawn from that will help to establish a framework within which the meanings and functions of culture in each town can be ascertained. These, in turn, provide a rationale for the ways and means in which a particular music culture could be established. A brief introduction to the history of the Gewandhaus and the Triennial Festival concludes this chapter. Chapter 2 considers the rise of cultural diversity out of the Enlightenment. The guiding principle here is that culture is a variable construct which crystallised to meet the challenges posed by the rise of urban society. This variation will be studied through an analysis of the religious, philosophical and aesthetic ideas that had developed during the Enlightenment. Chapter 2 concludes with an analysis of Leipzig's and Birmingham's music journals and daily press reports, because the print media helped to establish a symbiotic relationship between ideas and institutions that embodied them. Once established, the combination of ideas and institutions influenced the formation of distinct public spheres which, in turn, required and promoted particular beliefs and assumptions about what constitutes culture. These assumptions form the background to Chapter 3. By way of empirical analysis, this chapter demonstrates the ways in which these assumptions found clear expression in the choice of repertoires, attitudes to composers and conductors (the presence of Felix Mendelssohn in both towns offers a particularly fortunate opportunity for comparison), architectural styles of concert halls and behavioural norms during concert attendance. The symbiotic link between the press and the concert is further demonstrated through the journal's influence in the making of canons – the nucleus of cultural ideals. In Leipzig at least, the potency of bourgeois cultural ideals as developed by mid-century can be demonstrated by way of contrasting Gewandhaus practices with the idealism and revolutionary spirit which fuelled a generation of artists that participated in the tumultuous events of 1848/1849.

Chapter 4 spans the second half of the nineteenth century during which traditional assumptions about middle-class culture were challenged by a torrent of mid-century philosophical and aesthetic developments (Schopenhauer, Arnold, Nietzsche) on the one hand, and changes in religion (increasing secularisation), the economy (surge in industrial and commercial productivity), society (soaring population increase) and politics (increasing nationalism) on the other. Again, an analysis of repertoires, new concert halls (i.e., Leipzig's New Gewandhaus) as well as press reports on musicians and conductors will provide supporting empirical evidence. Chapter 5 introduces the final challenge to bourgeois assumptions about culture and canonised musical standards. This challenge above all took the form of relativism – a concept that permeated the arts as much as the sciences. By promoting the dissolution of single-value systems, it struck at the core of middle-class culture. The chapter will also deal with arguably the greatest challenge to middle-class culture, namely, the outbreak of the First World War. The expectations placed upon music in particular to contribute to the wider war effort sorely tested the exclusivity of a culture that until then had been the preserve of the urban élite. An analysis of their responses to this challenge concludes this chapter.

Primary and Secondary Sources

As far as primary sources are concerned, the collections of repertoires were crucial. For Birmingham, these can be found, excellently preserved, in the Special Collection unit which is part of the University of Birmingham Library. As far as Leipzig is concerned, Alfred Doerffel in his *Geschichte der Gewandhausconcerte zu Leipzig 1781–1881* (Leipzig: 1884) provided an extensive appendix of all composers (in alphabetical order) and their compositions performed at the Gewandhaus until 1881. Eberhard Creuzburg in his *Die Gewandhaus-Konzerte zu Leipzig 1881–1931* (Leipzig: 1931) compiled a list of all concerts in chronological order, providing the primary material for the remaining decades relevant to this study. The second most important source of primary information was the criticism voiced in music journals and daily newspapers. So far as British music journals – *The Harmonicon, The Musical Examiner, The Musical Times, The Musical World, The Quarterly Musical Magazine and Review* – are concerned, they are kept in store in the Music Library at the Barber Institute of Fine Arts in the University of Birmingham. Although occasional volumes are missing, on the whole, they provide abundant insight into cultural attitudes and expectations over the time span covered. As for daily newspapers – *Aris's Birmingham Gazette*, the *Birmingham Post* and *Birmingham Journal* – they are available on microfilm in the Local Studies Department at Birmingham's Central Library. With very few exceptions, their coverage is continuous and complete. Given that Leipzig was provided for with numerous music journals from the beginning, little research on music in the daily newspapers was undertaken. I have concentrated on the various music journals – *Allgemeine Musikalische Zeitschrift, Die Musik, Musikalisches Wochenblatt, Neue Zeitschrift für Musik, Signale für die Musikalische Welt* – all of which can be found in a specially designated music library located within Leipzig's *Stadtbibliothek*. Almost every music journal printed in Germany (and some originating in England, France, Scandinavia and Russia) is kept there.

General information concerning the Gewandhaus and the Festival, such as entrance tickets, advertising posters, architectural plans and letters of complaint, can be found in the *Stadtarchiv* in Leipzig as well as in the Local History Section of Birmingham's Central Lending Library. Unfortunately, neither archive possesses minutes or protocols related to Festival/Gewandhaus proceedings. Some compensation for this gap is afforded by letters sent to the Board and Committee by either artists or local luminaries. In addition, diaries of local industrialists, businessmen and their spouses reveal at least a minor, yet fascinating insight into individual attitudes and tastes. Such documents are of course only of limited value when more common ideals and attitudes are to be assessed, but they are nevertheless helpful as far as observations and descriptions of concerts and artists are concerned.

The choice of secondary sources reflects both an interest in interdisciplinary research and a firm belief that historical reality cannot be separated into conventionally watertight categories. The centre of this study is the middle class, a class whose cultural identity as expressed by literature, poetry, drama, music and art was influenced by political, economic, aesthetic, social and religious conditions, at both local and national levels. As a result, the analysis of Leipzig's Gewandhaus and Birmingham's Triennial Festival necessarily extended beyond the study of social and cultural history into other disciplines such as religious history, German studies, sociology, philosophy and aesthetic, as well as, of course, historical musicology.

In sum, there are five types of study from which this book has benefited. The first concerns the social history of music and public concerts as demonstrated by William Weber's *Music and the Middle Class* (1979), Walter Salmen *Das Konzert: Eine Kulturgeschichte* (1988), Carl Dahlhaus' *Nineteenth-Century Music* (1989) and Christina Bashford/ Leanne Langley's *Music and British Culture 1785–1914* (2000). The second group concentrates on the literary and aesthetic treatment of music during the late eighteenth and early nineteenth centuries. Of note are Enrico Fubini's *Geschichte der Musikästhetik von der Antike bis zur Gegenwart* (1997) and Sigfried Bimberg's *Handbuch der Musikästhetik* (1979). Whilst their work is characterised by the more abstract concerns of *Geistesgeschichte* (history of ideas), more recent studies, such as Celia Applegate's *Music and German National Identity* (2002), concentrate more on specific sociopolitical concerns such as the rise of nationalism in Germany's emergent musical tradition during the early nineteenth century.

The third group concerns the social histories of the British and German middle class. The different academic traditions of two countries itself highlight interesting methodological peculiarities. Whilst the doyens of nineteenth-century German history, particularly Gordon A. Craig, James

Sheehan, Thomas Nipperdey, tend to focus on wider national developments, British historians – Leonore Davidoff, Catherine Hall, R. J. Morris, Theodore Koditschek, for example – focus more on particular cities. This might be due to Germany's political, religious and cultural particularism, which makes the study of Germany's wider history through the history of its urban centres a less than fruitful enterprise. The two exceptions are, of course, the *Bürgertum* project led by Jürgen Kocka at the University of Bielefeld during the late 1980s and the *Stadt und Bürgertum* project led by Lothar Gall in Frankfurt am Main. Owing to a still divided Germany, however, both projects were only able to consider urban centres in the Federal Republic (hence exclude Leipzig). The latter project, in particular, focused on 15 specific towns with each historian producing a monograph on his/her case study, each having employed a similar set of techniques and concepts, something which led to accusations of a 'factory approach' to history. British historians, by contrast, have typically concentrated on specific urban centres, for example, Leeds, Manchester, Liverpool, Bradford and Birmingham. Their work demonstrates that a more individualistic approach is a fruitful method of tackling the history of the British middle class. The approach taken here constitutes a compromise: whilst Leipzig's and Birmingham's middle classes serve as my case studies, both are firmly placed within their wider national frameworks as far as political, social, philosophical, aesthetic and artistic developments are concerned. By doing so, the study of the urban centres continually tests the validity and legitimacy of wider national developments and *vice versa*.

The fourth and fifth research fields concern the works of Germanists (Eliza Butler, Friedrich Sengle and Peter Uwe Hohendahl) and sociologists (Jürgen Habermas and Pierre Bourdieu), respectively. In the case of Sengle and Hohendahl, their assessment of literature is firmly placed in a historical context in which artistic production was influenced by the socio-political and aesthetic ideas of the time. Habermas and Bourdieu created master narratives on the development of classes, taste and social distinctions. However, whilst Habermas concentrates on the development of a bourgeois public sphere as a cultural market, Bourdieu turns his attention principally to cultural practice as a way of helping to differentiate social classes.

My approach is to draw on the expertise of all these research fields. Each discipline deals with the past, but each brings its individual emphasis and offers insights from its own particular angle. Thus, a working knowledge of aesthetic foundations laid down by Hume and

Kant, Schiller and Coleridge, Arnold and Nietzsche, is essential to understanding the immediate purpose attributed to music by Birmingham's and Leipzig's bourgeois patrons. Similarly, the research undertaken by musicologists and Germanists offers insights into the literary and musical productions during a time that witnessed the rise and consolidation of the middle class – the main patrons of art in the period I cover. My argument is that only a more comprehensive treatment that takes account of the above can do full justice to the complexities of bourgeois music culture as it evolved during the eighteenth and nineteenth centuries. A history of music that fails to take into account, for example, basic aesthetic ideas, religious stipulations and resultant concepts of cultural propriety must necessarily overlook important causal factors. By recognising the interdependence of these related interdisciplinary fields, this book aims to advance our understanding of the public concert as a major aspect of the formation of bourgeois culture, thus the middle class itself.

1
Introducing the Towns

Introduction

Writers of town annals customarily emphasise the most prominent manifestations of local achievement. More often than not, these include the core industries which inform the public perceptions of a town as held by insiders as well as outsiders. Ardently reiterated and romanticised in annual 'visitor' guides, such perceptions help to transmute a town into some kind of living organism which breathes and grows until it eventually attains a distinct civic identity. Throughout the nineteenth century, the public perception of Birmingham, at home and abroad, rarely deviated from the following description:

> The men of Birmingham prefer to be known as citizens of one of the busiest, most ingenious, industrious, and prosperous of English towns... [...] The visitor, therefore, must take Birmingham for what she is – the seat of a great and constantly increasing population, trained to habits of steady industry, to the improvement of manufacturers; offering, in a thousand varied forms, illustrations of human ingenuity almost beyond belief – presenting, indeed, the spectacle of a vast community who combines in one place the industries which in other countries are spread through a hundred towns; and whose fame has been carried by their works through all the earth.[1]

It was thus her manufacturing achievements, her industrial ingenuity, the boast that she harboured a thousand trades, but also the city's tradition of nonconformism and political radicalism, that had informed the public perception of Birmingham. Alongside this extraordinary cultural and industrial mix was the list of luminaries upon whose achievements this reputation rested: industrial inventors such as James Watt, Matthew Boulton, Joseph Priestley, Samuel Clegg, William Small and William Murdock; prominent manufacturing families such as the Cadburys, Kenricks, Sturges, Chamberlains, Tangeys; and radical and liberal political reformers such as Thomas Attwood, Richard Muntz, John Bright, the Rev R. V. Dale, the Rev George Dawson and the greatest scion of the Chamberlain family, Joseph. Seminal to the growth and development of Birmingham, these men naturally dominate the civic annals.

Leipzig's reputation also rested primarily on its industry, particularly its publishing houses, printers and inventors of printing technology. The sheer increase in the number of publishing houses, whose combined output by the end of the eighteenth century amounted to 20 per cent of all books printed in Germany, meant that by the beginning of the nineteenth century Leipzig had taken the lead in this field, surpassing Frankfurt, Germany's traditional publishing city.[2] Publishing houses such as Breitkopf & Härtel, Brockhaus, Teubner and Reclam spread Leipzig's reputation throughout Germany. Beyond industry, however, Leipzig's status also rested on its university (founded in 1409) which had always been described as a magnet for aspiring academics and professionals from all over the German territories as well as on the pre-eminence of its graduates, for example, Gottfried Wilhelm Leibniz, Johann Gottlieb Fichte, Friedrich Leopold von Hardenberg (Novalis) and Leopold von Ranke.[3] The combination of these factors produced a perception of Leipzig's inhabitants – its scholars, civil servants, book traders and publishers and merchants – which conformed to the ideal of the enlightened *Bürger*:

> Leipzigs Bürger regten die fleißigen Hände, die Industrie und der Verkehr zog in ihre Mauern...; Leipzigs Bewohner waren der Kunst und Wissenschaft hold, und auf ihren hohen Schulen strebte der Flügelschlag des Geistes mächtig empor. Bürgertreue, Erfüllung der Berufspflichten und geistige Bildung geben unserer Stadt noch jetzt ein hohes Interesse und lassen manche Schattenseiten, wie sie jeder Ort bietet, vollends in das Dunkel treten.[4]

Regardless of the public perception of the two towns, however, Birmingham and Leipzig share one important similarity: both had grown from minor market and trading towns into successful industrial, political and cultural urban centres. This growth was largely due to the commitment displayed by an entrepreneurial bourgeois élite whose civic ideals and norms would inform the institutional development of each town. Thus, the rise of the urban élite was synonymous with the rise of the towns themselves, including their socio-cultural infrastructure.

In order to achieve their ascent to social, cultural and even political dominance, the middle class of both towns depended to varying degrees (but with the same exigency in assuring the existence of civic society along with its values, beliefs and ideals) on emergent networks of voluntary associations. The 'old world' offered no opportunity for the new bourgeois ideals to unfold and no platform for communal discussion and action.[5] Public opinion – a conglomerate of shared values – required institutional foundations, a network of relationships within which the sharing could take place.[6] Divorced from old corporate institutions such as the Church and the guilds, the new British and German voluntary associations served to form as much as disseminate an emergent public opinion. The increasing numbers of associations, giving rise to ever more dense networks of social interaction, effectively allowed for the dissemination of a distinctly bourgeois social and cultural identity on a local, even national level. As such they formed the socio-cultural epicentre of civic life. As Davidoff and Hall have argued:

> ... [the] network of associations redefined civil society, creating new arenas of social power and constructing a formidable base for middle-class men. Their societies provided opportunities for the public demonstration of middle-class weight and responsibility; the newspaper reports of their events, the public rituals and ceremonials designed for their occasions, the new forms of public architecture linked to their causes.[7]

These new social organisations were based on a voluntary coming-together of like-minded individuals and were, from the outset, informed by a particular interest, be that philanthropic, artistic, scientific or educational. It was essential that the object of concern of a particular voluntary association was kept separate from politics, economics and religion.[8] In this way, they could serve as a meeting point and neutral platform, bridging divisions caused by religious/political allegiances and economic competition. By introducing formal constitutions, statutes, membership requirements and, most importantly, public visibility and accountability, associations began to acquire an independent function within a newly ordered bourgeois society. The endowment of prestige and status further established a profile of bourgeois reputation which depended not on birth but on the individual's educational credentials, mercantile competence, financial respectability and public commitment.[9]

In principle, the civic landscapes of both towns were dominated by these associations. Where differences are discernible, they can be found in the level of efficacy, longevity as well as in the ethos, which they espoused. These phenomena, in turn, depended on a confluence of factors such as the relative antiquity of towns, the level of population increase and corresponding degree of social cohesion, political and religious homogeneity/partisanism, the nature of dominant industries, even an awareness of established local traditions. The institutional composition of the public sphere in Leipzig, a small but established Saxon town with a modest population increase during the first half of the nineteenth century, inevitably developed differently from that of Birmingham, a relatively insignificant market town during the seventeenth century, which grew to become one of the most important and populous manufacturing centres during the late eighteenth and early nineteenth centuries. By sketching the characteristics of the towns' public sphere, this chapter hopes to provide a rationale both for the public perceptions of themselves and for the nature of their socio-cultural institutions (including their musical establishments).

Leipzig

Despite its fifteenth-century university, Leipzig was a small and relatively insignificant market town for most of its early existence. In the seventeenth century, it still had the appearance of a medieval town with a town wall surrounding the town centre – something which was hardly conducive to the image expected from outwardly orientated trading centres. The general perception was that one might visit Leipzig but would reside in *Elb-Florenz* – the Saxon capital and royal residence – Dresden.[10] This perception survived well into the nineteenth century by which time, of course, Leipzig had prevailed over the destruction caused by two wars, which apart from devastating large parts of the town's infrastructure, severely impeded its population growth and town expansion. The first impediment was caused by the Seven Years War and the second by the Napoleonic Wars, particularly Napoleon's defeat in October 1813 in Leipzig at the hands of the Russians, Prussians and Austrians. On this occasion, the villages surrounding Leipzig and large parts of its *Vorstädte* (suburbs outside the town walls) as well as 60 surrounding villages were devastated, causing population levels to drop or at best to stagnate. Thus, between 1794 and 1820, a space of 26 years, the number of inhabitants had, on paper, increased by a mere 7000 – from 32,000 to just over 39,000. Only during the 1820s did the situation become normal again, that is, once the trade fairs and publishing industry had recovered.

Between 1834 and 1843, a space of 8 years, population numbers had increased by 8000 – from just over 46,000 to 54,000.[11]

As Graph 3.1 demonstrates, Leipzig's population growth accelerated during the late 1840s and 1850s but dramatically only during the 1860s and 1870s, with its population increasing to 66,700 in 1851 (an increase of 12,700 in 8 years), to 74,000 in 1862 (an increase of 10,000 in 11 years), to 91,800 in 1867 (an increase of 17,000 in 5 years) and to 170,000 in 1885 (an increase of 78,200 in 18 years). In 1889, 17 suburbs had been absorbed into the town, which accounts for the phenomenal rise in the population census taken in 1892. With that incorporation, Leipzig became the fourth largest town in Germany after Hamburg, Munich and Berlin. With regard to the first few decades of the nineteenth century, however, this belated population increase had a profound effect on the relatively inclusive nature of Leipzig's public sphere. This becomes evident when the demographic background of those citizens gaining the *Bürgerrecht* in Leipzig, which was achieved by showing evidence of private property, is highlighted.[12] For example, out of 50 merchants gaining the *Bürgerrecht* between 1830 and 1839, 28 were of Leipzig origin compared with 18 who had migrated from other towns and four who were foreigners.[13] Two-thirds of all factory owners gaining the *Bürgerrecht* between 1830 and 1849 were also of Leipzig origin; the remaining third came from outside Saxony.[14] Until large-scale industrialisation set in during the late nineteenth century, Leipzig's industrial élite thus remained relatively contained. This meant that Leipzig's public sphere could maintain a relatively high degree of social cohesion.

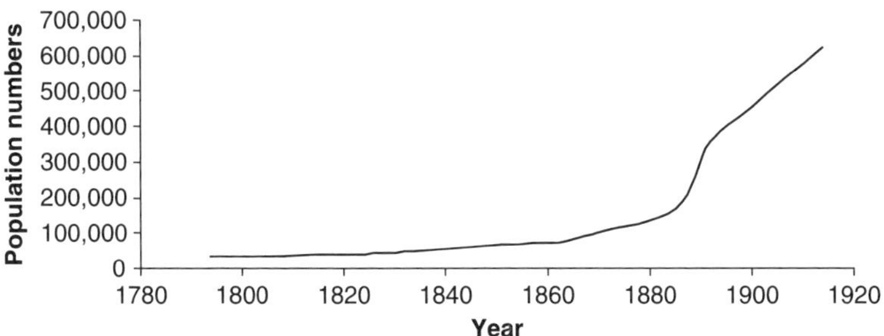

Graph 1.1 Population Growth in Leipzig

This social cohesion of Leipzig's urban élite was further helped by long-established traditions, whether historic, mythical, academic, religious, social or military, and these provided readily available points of reference. These might include, for example, the thirteenth-century churches of St Thomas and St Nikolai, both of which adopted Lutheranism in 1539 – Leipzig's dominant religious denomination ever since. Leipzig's position as a Protestant stronghold was reinforced during the late seventeenth century when around 60 Huguenot families settled in the Saxon town to escape royal persecution following the revocation of the *Edict of Nantes* under Louis XIV. Unlike the (predominantly peasant) Huguenots settling in neighbouring Brandenburg, their counterparts settling in Leipzig were mainly tradesmen and merchants.[15] Organised in the *Reformierte Gemeinde*, that is, followers of the Reformed Church founded by Calvin and Zwingli, they were given equal burgher status to the Lutherans in 1811 – the Catholics had already achieved such equality in 1807 – a move that highlighted their influence and importance within Leipzig's social, political and economic spheres.[16] The overall ascendancy and dominance of Lutheranism remained, however, uncontested.

The two wars were also important points of reference and crucial to Leipzig's social cohesion. In the wake of Napoleon's defeat in 1813,[17] for example, buildings lay destroyed and typhus raged. At a time when Leipzig numbered just over 30,000 inhabitants, more than 125,000 dead soldiers lay scattered around the town and another 30,000 wounded soldiers were housed in schools, churches and public buildings, which served as hospitals. These events gave Leipzig's inhabitants – wealthy and poor alike – a sense of collective memory and history. The *Völkerschlacht* (Battle of the Nations) of 1813 made Leipzig renowned in European history. Its importance to the repertoire of symbolic references was quickly recognised; the *Wartburg* Festival of 1817, for example, combined the victory at Leipzig with the 300th anniversary of the Reformation. As such, it entered the annals of Germany's early nationalist movement, granting Leipzig – the relatively small Saxon town – an unprecedented status within the burgeoning history of the Germany nation.

The importance of the fifteenth-century university to Leipzig's reputation has been alluded to above. Claims to educational pre-eminence, which commonly result from the existence of such time-honoured institutions, were further embellished with the dominance of the publishing and book trade within Leipzig's economic sphere. Whilst in 1797, for example, 12 publishing firms and 20 book shops were registered, their numbers had increased to 82 and approximately 200, respectively, by the early 1830s.[18] The number of new publications increased similarly: whilst in 1700, 200 new works appeared annually, by 1770, it was 300, and by 1800 the number had risen again to 1000 per year.[19] As such, Leipzig began to surpass Frankfurt as the leading publishing town; it commanded and dictated market and pricing policies.[20] Culturally, of course, the *book* evoked notions of erudition and sophistication, not just within the local confines but throughout and beyond the German territories. The patronage extended to such literary notables as Ernesti, Oeser, Sulzer, Gellert or Wieland by Leipzig's publishing houses invoked an *Elitenbewusstsein* [consciousness of one's élite status] since Leipzig's economic strength and reputation were so closely associated with the bourgeois ideals of education, virtue and cultural refinement.

Such an association was consolidated during the 1830s when, owing to the rise of the daily press, the increasing educational needs of its bourgeoisie and a rise in both political and trivial literature, particular publishing houses – Brockhaus, Teubner, Reclam, Wigand, Breitkopf & Härtel – became household names. These anchored Leipzig's luminaries firmly within Germany's economic sphere, a move which was further aided by Saxony's entry into the German Customs Union (*Deutscher Zollverein*[21]) in 1834.[22] The heightened importance of Leipzig's manufacturing, trading and publishing industries to Leipzig's wider reputation during the 1830s meant that their right to political representation could no longer be ignored.[23] Fulfilling their part in the defeat of the popular protests in 1830 – a revolutionary uprising inspired by the July Revolution in France and led mainly by proletarian and artisan groups – Leipzig's bourgeoisie, following negotiations with the royal government, carried out its reform proposals for the formation of Leipzig's first municipal council (*Stadtverordnetenversammlung*) which comprised 60 representatives. At the same time, traditional administrative powers such as the Magistracy were suspended.

All these developments, taking place a decade before Leipzig experienced its first profound population increase, mainly impinged on an inclusive circle of Leipzig's most prominent burghers. Within this circle, a comparatively high degree of social cohesion prevailed, something which proved conducive to the maintenance of common interests, be these of an economic, social or political nature. Visible manifestations of this can be found in Leipzig's rapidly growing networks of voluntary associations since the late eighteenth century. The table below lists some of them founded during the eighteenth and early nineteenth century (Table 1.1).[24]

The numbers alone are telling. More important perhaps is the fact that each of these associations was dominated by an exclusive circle of

Table 1.1   Leipzig's Voluntary Associations, 1764–1837

1764	Academie der Bildenden Künste [art]
1765	Leipziger Ökonomische Gesellschaft [economics]
1774	Fürstliche Jablonowskische Societät der Wissenschaften [natural sciences]
1784	Philologische Gesellschaft [language]
1798	Griechische Gesellschaft [Greek language and culture]
1814	Historisch-Theologische Gesellschaft
1816	Kameralistische Gesellschaft [administrative]
1817	Exegetische Gesellschaft [religion]
1818	Naturforschende Gesellschaft [natural science]
1821	Juristische Gesellschaft [law]
1823	Exegetisch-Dogmatische Gesellschaft [religion]
1824	Sächsischer Verein zur Erforschung vaterländischer Alterthümer [local treasures]
1826	Lateinische Gesellschaft [Latin]
1828	Gesellschaft für deutsche Sprache und Literatur [German language and literature]
1829	Medizinische Gesellschaft [medicine]
	Polytechnische Gesellschaft [science]
1834	Vertraute Gesellschaft [philanthropic]
1837	Leipziger Kunstverein [art]

merchants, traders, bankers, scholars and industrialists engaging in the political, economic, social or cultural affairs of the town. An example was the Leipzig Art Association (*Leipziger Kunstverein*) which was founded in 1837 by Carl Lampe and Hermann Härtel and provided a platform for artistic debates. Hermann Härtel, co-owner of Leipzig's major publishing house, was an active member of Leipzig's *Liedertafel*, publisher of Leipzig's weekly music journal and a member of the Gewandhaus Board of Directors. This Board included other high-ranking industrialists such as Gustav Harkort (owner of an iron-melting factory), a director of the *Leipziger Bank* as well as a main shareholder of the Leipzig-Dresden Railway Company. Carl Lampe and Gustav Moritz Claus, both directors of the *Leipziger Kunstverein*, were also shareholders of the latter. Another example is the *Vertraute Gesellschaft*, an association founded to support impoverished artists, artisans and orphans. It was headed by its secretary Jacob Bernhard Limburger, a silk merchant, town councillor, co-founder of Leipzig's Singing Academy and one of the longest serving members of the Gewandhaus Board of Directors. By 1834, the *Vertraute Gesellschaft* was led by a Board consisting of 16 directors, six of whom were members of, or related to members of, the Gewandhaus Board of Directors and were town councillors before or/and after 1830.[25] During the 1830s and 1840s, the majority of Gewandhaus Board members were engaged in public office, controlling the affairs of the town, be these related to finance, town improvement, poor relief or the organisation of the commemoration of Napoleon's defeat.[26]

Birmingham

From the late eighteenth century and throughout the nineteenth century, Birmingham was a haven of economic freedom. While middle-class settlers were attracted by the economic opportunities, rural labourers and farmers found refuge and employment in workshops and warehouses, and were sometimes able to achieve moderate success on their own. Constant immigration as well as natural population increase meant that Birmingham grew from being a relatively insignificant market town during the seventeenth century to being the fourth largest town after Liverpool, Manchester and London during the 1830s. Later still, just before the outbreak of First World War, Birmingham rose to become England's 'second city'. This staggering growth is plotted by the graph below (Graph 1.2).[27]

Just as Leipzig's (comparatively) stagnant population brought with it a specific social-cultural arrangements, so Birmingham's continual rise in population numbers brought with it its own set local peculiarities. A prominent outcome of this large-scale immigration into Birmingham was the increase in the variety of trades and industries. Table 1.2 shows

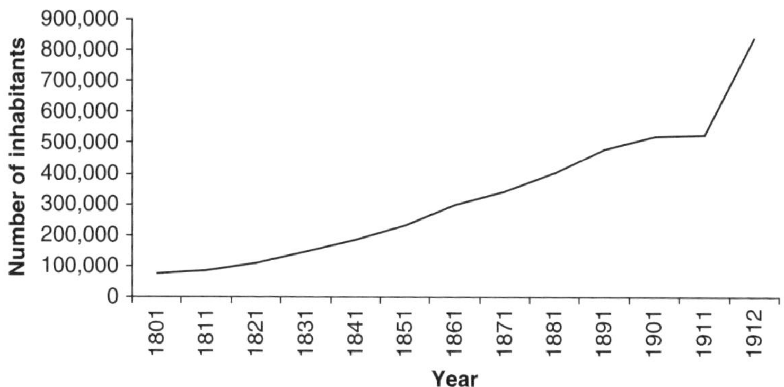

Graph 1.2   Population Growth in Birmingham

Table 1.2   Birmingham's Manufacturers and Professions

Profession	1780	1816/1817	1846/1847
Brassfounders	23	90	170
Diesinkers	29	25	55
Nail manufacturers	0	20	35
Surgeons	0	40	95
Physicians	2	7	18
Surveyors	0	9	55
Architects	0	4	20
Solicitors/Attorneys	0	40	105
Engineers	0	5	40

a selection of Birmingham's manufactures and professions in 1780 and their numerical increase by 1816 and 1846, respectively.[28]

Unlike Manchester with its gigantic textile industries, Birmingham's manufacturing sector developed along a workshop basis, employing highly skilled craftsmen engaged in specialist manufacture. In times of economic crises, this variety of trades, the lack of dependence on heavy industries and a reliance on individual skill rather than large capital investment proved advantageous as Birmingham was spared the devastating consequences brought about by the fluctuations of international commerce.[29] At the same time, however, the lack of a single, dominant industry narrowed the scope for initiative.[30] There was no type of industry which could be used as a catalyst for political and social action by representatives sharing the same business interests. This was compounded by the fact that during the first half of the nineteenth century at least, Birmingham did not possess an outstandingly wealthy, oligarchic élite. Until the second half of the nineteenth century, Birmingham's workshop-based economy simply could not produce such wealthy individuals of bourgeois background when compared to the cotton and mining magnates in Manchester, the woollen magnates in Leeds, the iron and steel tycoons in Sheffield and shipping entrepreneurs in Liverpool (or indeed the publishing moguls of Leipzig). As a result, there was, for example, no Birmingham equivalent of the Manchester-based Anti-Corn Law League which was mainly represented by textile magnates. Instead, Birmingham was defined by a variety of interest groups with each posing different demands and carried by a middle class which, even during the 1840s, was still new and disorganised.

A second effect of Birmingham's rapid population increase was that during the early nineteenth century, at least, its reputation was not built upon long-established traditions and shared notions of the past. The preoccupation with the present rather than the past meant that Birmingham's merchants, industrialists and traders did not yet share a sense of common bond, a sense of belonging and local pride. Apart from a comparatively small élite of indigenous inhabitants, the general population shared no common history and as yet could not be identified through peculiar habits or accents specific to the Midland town. Rather, it presented a comprehensive selection of English, even British, habits, traditions and accents. The subsequent lack of social coherence became the hallmark of Birmingham. Although open to newcomers, Birmingham's social constitution appeared depersonalised in character, its inhabitants largely detached from one another.

This detachment was enhanced by Birmingham's religious diversity, a third product of Birmingham's staggering population increase. Famous for being a bastion of radical nonconformism, the first chapels and meeting houses were founded following the *Declaration of Indulgence* in 1672 which entitled nonconformists to congregate in their own places of worship. Throughout the eighteenth and early nineteenth centuries, nonconformism prospered as the graph below (Graph 1.3) may demonstrate.[31] Even though, according to the religious census of 1851, Anglicanism, with 51 per cent, ranked proportionally higher than nonconformism with 49 per cent, it was members of dissenting chapels and meeting houses who exercised the greatest influence upon Birmingham's political and economic spheres.[32] This was despite, or perhaps because of, the inequalities nonconformists had to suffer in English society, as was

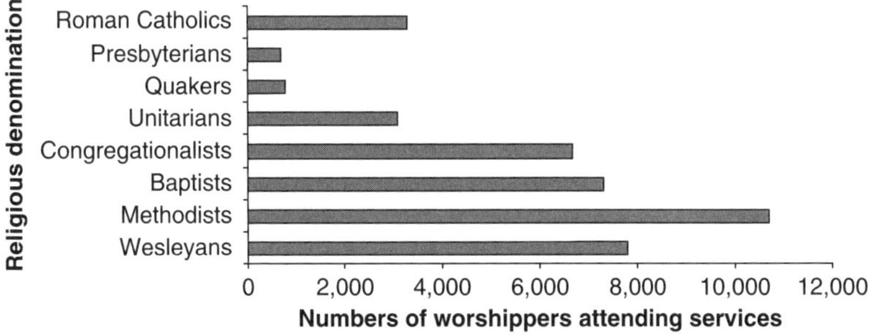

Graph 1.3   Nonconformism in Birmingham in 1851

exemplified by the exclusion from public office of all those who rejected the Oath of Supremacy and Allegiance to the Sovereign or refused to receive Communion according to Church of England convention (in force until 1829).

Apart from the obvious conflict between the established and nonconformist groups, Birmingham's religious landscape was further complicated by the fact that the two most influential denominations, the Quakers (represented by the Cadburys, Bakers, Goodricks, Lloyds and Sturges) and the Unitarians (represented by the Kenricks, Chamberlains, Martineaus, Beales and Rylands), were themselves uniquely distinctive.[33] Unitarians were conspicuous both by their often scientifically orientated theological beliefs which included the refusal to accept the Doctrine of the Trinity and the Divinity of Christ. In Birmingham, their existence was also associated with a history of sturdy radicalism, particularly the riots of 1791, which involved their most famous minister, Joseph Priestley.[34] Quakers, by contrast, remained distinctive by their appearance, lifestyle and religious organisation which had long dispensed with traditional liturgies, creeds, ecclesiastical authority, ordained ministers, consecrated places of worship and the sacraments. If the Methodists – the most numerous amongst Birmingham's nonconformists – with their appeal to religious sentiment through more enthusiastic approaches to the scriptures, preaching and singing, combined with a leaning on Anglican traditions are taken into the equation as well, the preconditions for religious cacophony is plainly established.

Thus, whilst Leipzig's religious identity was fairly homogenous and rarely questioned, Birmingham's multi-denominationalism invoked a religious atmosphere which was constantly and intensely heated, with each denomination with its own religious and liturgical conventions being at odds with the others. Given that membership of a particular religious denomination corresponded with a specific political allegiance (Anglican/Tory; Dissent/Liberal), Birmingham's multi-denominationalism also led to openly partisan discourse on political matters fought over with equal force by Tories, Whigs and Liberals alike. This, combined with a considerable degree of social anonymity and lack of oligarchic leadership, proved to be the greatest impediment to social cohesion.

This lack of unity might have contributed to the fact that until the founding of the Birmingham Midland Institute (BMI) in 1854, Birmingham's voluntary associations proved ephemeral. The Philosophical Institution, proposed in 1800, the Mechanics' Institute and Artisans'

Library (1825), the Polytechnic Institution (1843) and the Literary and Scientific Institute (1852), were all superseded by the BMI which, through its 'literature and science classes, public lectures, musical and archaeological sections, became one of the most successful of all similar institutions'.[35] Yet, compared to other educational institutions, such as the Mechanics Institutes in Glasgow (1823), Manchester (1824) and many other cities, Birmingham's establishment of the Midland Institute was rather belated.

This delay was also symptomatic of Birmingham's political development. Up until the early nineteenth century, the medieval seats of authority such as the courts of the Manor, the Court Baron and the Court Leet – all self-governing bodies whose members were selected largely from amongst the gentry – continued to hold their sway over Birmingham's administration.[36] The Improvement Act of 1769, by which Parliament handed over local responsibilities to 50 Street Commissioners had, by the early nineteenth century, produced little more than a gentrified oligarchy of the wealthiest ratepayers who chose new members through personal acquaintance rather than election. The advent of the *Birmingham Political Union for the Protection of Public Rights* (BPU) founded in 1829 by Thomas Attwood following heightened interest in parliamentary representation and local government since the French wars, thus seemed timely. National pressure resulted in the 1832 Reform Act which made Birmingham a parliamentary borough, returning two MPs, Thomas Attwood and William Scholefield, to the House of Commons.[37] The first elections under the 1832 Reform Act produced a Whig–Liberal government which was in favour of reforming local government and in 1835, Lord John Russell secured his Municipal Corporations Act, by which the Crown granted charters on the petition of the inhabitants to elect a council that in turn could elect the mayor.[38]

Yet, despite these liberal successes, the traditional system of local governance, particularly the Street Commissioners, had not seen their offices abolished, which meant that local authority was still divided between the Council and several local bodies. This fragmented jurisdiction began to cause paralysis in dealing with everyday problems, a great number of which were exposed by the Rawlinson Report of 1849.[39] The 1851 Health Improvement Act which followed finally abolished the offices held by the Street Commissioners and referred all local powers to the Corporation. For the first time, Birmingham's Town Council was given complete control over roads, lighting, sewers, drainage, sanitation, all public buildings, properties and markets. As a financial authority, it was able to levy an improvement rate so as to implement policies efficiently. Yet, despite the unifying powers now granted to Birmingham, the town council 'made depressingly little use of them [...] which partly accounts for the lull between 1851 and 1868'.[40] Owing to the power of the economy party intent on keeping the municipal rate to a minimum, Birmingham began to fall behind other provincial towns so far as educational and health issues were concerned. Whilst Manchester, for example, took advantage of the Museum and Library Act of 1850 and opened its first Free Library in 1852, Birmingham managed to follow suit only in 1861 with the opening of its own Free Library.[41] Birmingham also trailed behind northern towns so far as health and sanitation were concerned. It merely looked on, as in 1860 Glasgow's Corporation supplied its citizens with four times as much water as Birmingham obtained by private enterprise, and again in 1867 when the Manchester Improvement Act, following pioneering research, provided a framework for national slum-clearance legislation. While Liverpool and London had already appointed Medical Officers of Health in 1847 and 1848, respectively, Birmingham did so only in 1872.[42]

By then, of course, Birmingham's *coeur de lion*, Joseph Chamberlain, had risen to the highest ranks of civil administration, becoming mayor in 1873, a Member of Parliament in 1876 and a member in Gladstone's Cabinet in 1880.[43] On a national level, Chamberlain's campaign for protectionism (or 'Free Trade within the Empire') meant that 'Birmingham now raised the flag of the Empire, [just as] Manchester had hoisted the banner of universal peace' during the free trade agitation 50 years previously.[44] On the local level, Chamberlain transformed the city: gas and water were municipalised, a Medical Officer of Health was employed, a Council House replaced older and disjointed Public Offices, administrative and technical personnel quadrupled, sanitation was addressed through the establishment of a Drainage Board, paving and street lighting were taken care of and six public parks were acquired.[45] A new building for the Public Reference Library, destroyed by fire in 1879, was set up and the government of the Free Grammar School reorganised so that it would become more representative of the city. The greatest transformation was in the shape of Corporation Street which had been cleared of vast areas of slums and back-to-back yards following the powers conveyed by Disraeli's Artisans' Dwelling Act of 1875. The Corporation Consolidation Act of 1883, which had further unified the operative powers of the Town Council, extended its administrative authority and opened the floodgates for ever increasing national legislation (the Technical Instruction Act of 1891, the Education Act of

1902 and the various Health, Housing, Insurance and Factory Inspection Acts passed between 1906 and 1914) as well as various local Acts which either confirmed or gave special authority for a specific undertaking. This included the new Municipal Art Gallery and Central School of Art (1885), the Law Courts (1887), a new building for the Technical School (1895), new municipal houses (1890), a University (1900), the tramways (1903–1914), the Elan Valley Water Scheme which supplied Birmingham with Welsh water (1904), the Bishopric (1905) and the extension of the municipal boundaries which paved the way for a Greater Birmingham (1911).[46]

The comparison between the first and second half of the nineteenth century shows how Birmingham's civil administration leapt from a town council, seemingly unwilling or unable to produce any significant improvements, straight to the political emergence of Joseph Chamberlain during whose term of office, legislation appeared an inexorable force setting in motion one improvement scheme upon another. The sheer number of institutions created under Chamberlain's mayoralty implies that Birmingham had clearly missed out on the golden age of voluntary associations which, in other towns, had done so much promote the founding of art galleries, libraries, scientific institutions and schools. To a large extent, this apparent lack of commitment on the part of Birmingham's wealthier population was in fact related to the peculiar nature of Birmingham's public sphere. To recap, the dramatic rise in population numbers since the late eighteenth century impeded the rise of common bonds and shared histories. These in turn generated social fragmentation, obscurity and anonymity. The increase of trades and industries operating on a comparatively small-scale meant that no dominant industry, hence no pressure group which could spearhead campaigns for political, social or civic improvement, emerged. This lack of common interests was further encumbered by Birmingham's multi-denominationalism which, during a time of heightened religious fervour, was bound to hamper mutual cooperation.

Whilst this disparity severely debilitated the success of voluntary associations which were usually aimed at particular ends such as educational, physical or mental improvement, it was the realm of culture which, by itself, could alleviate the pressures caused by socio-cultural differences. To be sure, similarly to culture, voluntary associations too were supposed to be able to transcend political and religious differences and thus provide platforms for communication and interaction. However, as the brief survey of Birmingham's public sphere has shown, this was not always the case. However, even in Birmingham, different findings appear as soon as the cultural aspect is included in the equation. This is because culture differed from voluntary associations in one important aspect: it could bestow upon the middle-class notions of erudition, virtuous conduct, sentimental aptitude and moral refinement. These notions could, of course, be found within individual gatherings – whether in the churches, chapels or voluntary associations – but given the specificity of the occasion, the numbers required to affect anything resembling public participation, could not be achieved in this way. Only culture with its unifying properties was able to include all citizens equally because the values espoused were not specific to one particular religion but could be commonly appreciated by all those participating. Within Leipzig's fairly homogeneous *Bürgertum*, by contrast, culture did not perform such an overt and outwardly orientated function. There were no obvious religious and political divisions to bridge, no common social bonds to forge and no deficiencies in industrial prestige to compensate for. Most institutional needs were catered for by an elaborate network of voluntary associations. The result was that, rather than being purpose-orientated, culture took on an existence of its own; it fulfilled no other purpose than to provide respectable 'entertainment' for Leipzig's bourgeoisie. A glance at the institutional development of Leipzig's and Birmingham's premier musical establishments demonstrates this difference.

The Origins of the Triennial Festival and the Gewandhaus

Neither Birmingham nor Leipzig was culturally dominated by networks of aristocratic patronage which, traditionally, could have procured the services of professional composers and musicians. Rather, the prime employers of musicians were the town itself, the Church and, in the case of Leipzig, also the university. All of these patrons used music for functional rather than cultural or recreational purposes. Changes to the musical infrastructure, however, occurred in both towns during the course of late eighteenth century, when a rising class of traders, merchants and professionals came to the fore as consumers of culture.

In Birmingham, concerts and small-scale music meetings were held in its churches, chapels, Assembly Rooms and theatres. Larger productions of operas and oratorios were held at various theatres with Birmingham's church organists and choir masters directing musical performances. Thus, Barnabas Gunn, organist at St Philip's, between 1715 and 1730, began to promote musical entertainment at Moor Street theatre, an association which was further cemented by succeeding generations of organists such as William St Thunes (employed between 1733 and 1735), John Eversman (1735–1765) and Jeremiah Clarke (1765–1803).[47] The association between St Philip's Church and Moor Street theatre was again seen during the Triennial Festival when morning performances were held in the Church and evening performances at Moor Street theatre. During the 1760s, the performance of oratorios on three successive days either in September or October was first arranged by Richard Hobbs, organist and choir master at St Martin's Church.[48] This chronological pattern would later serve as a timeframe for the Triennial Festival. The large choirs required for the performance of oratorios were drawn from a musical club known as the Musical and Amicable Society (MAS; 1762) – an amalgamation of St Philip's Church and St Bartholomew's Chapel choirs – directed by James Kempson, a member of St Philip's Choir and choir master at St Bartholomew's. It was through this choir that the social benefits of public music-making were first realised when the MAS collected subscriptions 'for forming a fund for assisting members who might, in case of illness, require aid'.[49] The philanthropic benefits of public music-making were, however, only properly realised after the Seven Years War, during which hostilities between Britain and France in colonial America had proved detrimental to Birmingham's economic well-being. As a response, Kempson formed the *Oratorio Choral Society*. Resolved to cultivate public singing on a larger scale, their first Music Meeting took place at St Bartholomew's Chapel on Christmas Day, 1766. All profits arising from the events were distributed to the 'aged and distressed housekeepers' of the town. The success of the first performance encouraged repeats on an annual basis.[50]

Apart from these annual charitable Christmas concerts, Kempson was also involved in forging a link between his Musical Society and the General Hospital which without donations from Kempson's music meetings, might never have reached completion (at least not in the eighteenth century). The General Hospital was instigated by John Ash, a physician, in 1765. Initial subscriptions for its erection were insufficient, and construction work was suspended a year later, the Hospital Committee having fallen heavily in debt. A last attempt to raise funds was made in 1768, by appointing a committee to conduct musical entertainment, and the first concert took place in the same year. The success of this concert encouraged further events and the Hospital was finally opened in 1779, the year following the second Music Meeting. The next Meeting was held in 1780 and, after the 1784 Festival, the committee agreed to stage it triennially. Initially for 3 days every 3 years,[51] oratorios were to be performed for the benefit of public charity during the morning sessions held at St Philip's while a selection of instrumental and vocal music was given as musical entertainment during the evening sessions held at a local theatre.[52] Tickets could be purchased for either the stalls or the galleries, each being priced at a different level. This meant that personal wealth could buy places within the social hierarchy of the middle class, as one could tell who was who by the colour of the programme or the concert ticket, which visibly demonstrated where the individual could afford to sit.[53] Concert attendance was thereby rendered a status commodity, as reserved seats in the more private and visible galleries were considerably more expensive than unreserved seats on the more crowded floor.

These external mechanisms were fixed and provided the scaffolding of the Festival which lasted for more than a century. The internal workings, however, inevitably changed with time. The first profound change took place with the appointment of a new committee director, Joseph Moore, whose appointment was important in the sense that he was not professionally related to any of Birmingham's churches or chapels. Rather, Moore was a representative of the new middle class. Sent to Birmingham to be trained in diesinking, by then a profitable trade in the town, he entered into a partnership in the button trade which led to his financial independence. The partnership led also to the acquaintance of Matthew Boulton at whose instigation Moore founded the Gentlemen's Private Concerts in 1799.[54] It was in the same year that the General Hospital board – consisting of William Small, Matthew Boulton and Samuel Galton – asked for his assistance. By the time Moore got involved with the Hospital, the Festival had already suffered its first setbacks due to falling attendance. One of the first changes Moore subsequently introduced was to abandon most of the heavy oratorio repertoire which had been blamed for declining profits. Sacred music was to be limited to Handel's *Messiah*, Haydn's *Creation* and a selection of excerpts mainly composed by Handel. On top of that, the orchestra and chorus were enlarged, as performers were now engaged from London, Oxford, Norwich, Canterbury and from the Worcester and Lichfield Choirs as well as the Lancashire Choral Societies of Manchester and Liverpool.[55] By 1834, the choir consisted of 184 singers (compared with 30 in 1780).[56] In all, under Moore's astute management, it was not just receipts and profits that increased, but perhaps more importantly, Birmingham's cultural reputation, which now exceeded that of the Festivals of Lichfield, Wolverhampton, Bridgnorth and Walsall. In all, the progress and transformations made under Moore were indicative of a town whose reputation in the industrial sphere had extended beyond the British shores; a corresponding degree of cultural esteem was evidently regarded essential to the attainment of a vibrant public sphere. Choices, particularly in the repertoire, had to be made and these generally corresponded to contemporary middle-class values.

Birmingham's cultural ascent was further cemented with the opening of the Town Hall which, with the help of public subscriptions, was opened in 1834. Bar one or two exceptions, the Festival was no longer divided according to musical performances, as both morning and evening performances were held there. Pride in the Triennial Festival as the largest of all provincial festivals seemed visibly justified by the Town Hall, and Birmingham's cultural aspirations were confirmed by the appointment of one the most eminent and well-known musicians of his time, Felix Mendelssohn, to the post of Festival conductor in 1837. His presence bestowed upon Birmingham a cultural reputation that could be carried beyond the shores of Britain, confirming Birmingham's place on the European cultural map. With Mendelssohn as its embodiment, the Festival had developed to be the most important of its kind. The attainment of such enormous cultural accomplishments (especially when compared to the town's rather modest musical origins) meant that Birmingham's middle class found public confirmation of its cultural worth.

Leipzig's public music culture, by contrast, originated in two *Collegia Musica*. The first was founded by Georg Philipp Telemann in 1702[57] and the second by Johann Fasch in 1708. In both, students from the university gathered once or twice a week to rehearse and perform predominantly contemporary secular music, displaying their youthful spirit at academic ceremonies and evening concerts for visiting dignitaries.[58] During the eighteenth century, the *Collegia* gave up their academic and exclusive character and turned semi-public, catering for an ever-growing mercantile public. In a move away from this university-led arrangement, Leipzig's bourgeois élites built upon the foundations of the *Collegia Musica* and founded the 'Grand Concerts' (also popularly called '*Kaufmannskonzerte*' [merchant concerts]) in 1743. A *Direktorium* (Board of Directors) consisting of 12 merchants, headed by Leipzig's mayor Wilhelm Müller, was set up. The Board took it upon itself to manage all organisational aspects of the concerts: it engaged principal music directors, soloists and orchestral musicians and decided upon the repertoire. To finance the concerts, subscriptions were offered to cover the entire season. These concerts marked the beginnings of modern concert life in Leipzig.

Following the severe disruptions caused by the Seven Years War (1756–63), the concerts were resumed. From 1771, they were under the musical directorship of Johann Adam Hiller – a composer of *Singspiele*, editor of a weekly musical newspaper and founder of the *Musikübende Gesellschaft* (1775), an association consisting of dilettante and professional musicians who performed around 30 concerts a year.[59] This music association was to come to the rescue when the Grand Concerts came to an end in 1778 due to financial difficulties brought about by an obsolete administration and a fall in the level of subscriptions.[60] Following the demise of the Grand Concerts, Hiller's ensemble staged the first of the *Leipziger Konzerte* in August 1781. Similar to the Grand Concerts, the *Leipziger Konzerte* were organised around a Board of Directors, consisting of six scholars and six merchants. To mark the new era, a new concert venue was provided by way of converting the vacant room above the cloth floor in the so-called Gewandhaus into a concert hall.[61] This was achieved in 1781, and it is from that time onwards that the *Leipziger Konzerte* became popularly known as the *Gewandhauskonzerte*. Led by Johann Gottfried Schicht since 1784, the concerts were conducted by Johann Philip Christian Schulz since 1810. He, in turn, was succeeded in 1827 by Christian August Polenz, the last *Kapellmeister* before the arrival of Felix Mendelssohn in 1835. From Schicht's appointment during the late eighteenth century, the Gewandhaus witnessed a steady increase of instrumental music, particularly during the 1810s, resulting in Leipzig being commonly perceived as one of the major cultural centres of contemporary music. As was increasingly evident at Birmingham's Triennial Festival, the Gewandhaus repertoire similarly mirrored contemporary cultural sentiments. The subsistence of instrumental, rather than vocal music, points towards interesting questions as to how this could be achieved.

As in Birmingham, confidence in the town's cultural achievements reached its pinnacle when the Gewandhaus Board approached Mendelssohn, then director at the Lower Rhine Festival, to accept the post as *Gewandhauskapellmeister*.[62] This he did in 1835. As was to be the case later in Birmingham, the work he performed as *Kapellmeister* not only corresponded with dominant notions of artistic propriety, his cultural authority further helped to consolidate them into a clearly defined canon. When Mendelssohn died in 1847, all energies were focused on the protection of his cultural legacy. In the Gewandhaus, for the next 40 years, an obligation to continuity became the highest priority which meant that artistic and cultural stagnation was allowed to inch its way into Leipzig's premier event. No successor could be found who was equal in stature to Mendelssohn. Only few were willing to forfeit their own artistic authority in order to ensure Mendelssohn's legacy. Niels Gade, for example, resigned in 1848. Julius Rietz, *Kapellmeister* at the *Leipziger Stadttheater* since 1847, teacher at the Conservatoire and director of the *Singakademie*, resigned in 1852. The English composer and friend of Mendelssohn, William Sterndale Bennett, was invited but refused the offer. Robert Schumann offered to take the job but was turned down. The 1852/1853 season was conducted in turns by Niels Gade and Ferdinand David. In the following year, David took over but resigned at the end of the 1854 season. Julius Rietz agreed to man the Gewandhaus rostrum until 1860 when he resigned for the second time and moved to Dresden. Finally, some stability was achieved with the appointment of Carl Reinecke who remained at the Gewandhaus until 1895. During this time, Leipzig entered its most conservative era yet as the traditional repertoire, first introduced by Schicht and promoted by Mendelssohn, was fervently maintained. An important event during Reinecke's reign was the construction of the second Gewandhaus which opened in 1884. The arrival of Arthur Nikisch following Reinecke's dismissal in 1895 was greeted with a sigh of relief. The incestuous mediocrity and cultural frailty which had crept in during the last 30 years or so had become a source of dismay even amongst the most conservative of listeners. Nikisch combined traditional concepts of cultural respectability with artistic progress. Being averse to modern French music and the second Viennese School represented by Schönberg, Webern and Berg, Nikisch nevertheless transformed the Gewandhaus repertoire by including composers such as Wagner, Bruckner and Tchaikovsky. As such, the Gewandhaus entered the First World War healthier than it had been since Mendelssohn's death.

In Birmingham too, Mendelssohn's death was a great source of concern to the maintenance of Birmingham's cultural well-being. His *Elijah* sensation in 1846, marking the height of Birmingham's cultural prestige thus far, meant that Birmingham was compelled to produce continuous cultural triumphs. This was commonly presumed to be achievable through the commissioning of new works with the underlying hope that a new *Elijah* could be discovered. A suitable replacement as Festival conductor was found in 1849 in the Italian Michael Costa, who would retain his post until his death in 1884. Having been the director of the Royal Italian Opera at Covent Garden (which he founded in 1846), the Philharmonic Orchestra (1846–1853 and 1855–1868) and the Sacred Harmonic Society (since 1848), he had demonstrated the artistic credentials that Birmingham sought in their artistic directors.

Perhaps due to the progress made by the Triennial Festival, the second half of the nineteenth century 'saw a great advancement in the development of Birmingham's own resources both chorally and instrumentally'.[63] This found expression in the formation of numerous musical societies such as the *Apollo Glee and Musical Society* in 1842 which celebrated English composers such as Webbe, Horsley and Calcott. Similar motives led to the formation of the *Birmingham Amateur Harmonic Association* (1855–1889) which aimed at giving Birmingham's amateur singers and instrumentalists an opportunity to rehearse and perform on a regular basis. Similarly concerned with orchestral music was the *Birmingham Philharmonic*, founded in 1870, and the *Flute Society*, a private club of amateur flautists with a library of sheet music and literature, which was founded in 1871 and lasted until 1950. The *Birmingham Musical Union* (1863) was particularly concerned with chamber music and the *Clef Club*, founded in 1881, with the study and practice of vocal and instrumental music.[64] The two most prominent musical associations were the Harrison Concerts, which were introduced in 1853, but only reached wide popularity during the 1870s, and the Birmingham Festival Choral Society which, as the name suggests, was associated with the Triennial Festival. Until 1916, Harrison's concerts were held four times a season, exploiting the traditional vocal repertoire, on the one hand, and introducing instrumental music such as that by Schubert, Bach, Grieg, Schumann and Brahms, on the other.[65] A great novelty surrounding Harrison's concerts were the guest appearances of Manchester's Hallé Orchestra (first introduced to Birmingham in 1875), the Queens Hall Orchestra (first appearance under Henry Wood in 1904), the London Symphony Orchestra (since 1905 under Edward Elgar, but later under Arthur Nikisch) and the New Symphony Orchestra under Landon Ronald in 1908 and 1911. Each in turn introduced notable soloists such as Joseph Joachim, Hans von Bülow, Charles Hallé and Percy Granger to Birmingham audiences.[66]

By far the greatest musical association in the town was the *Birmingham Festival Choral Society*, which by the 1850s had achieved a towering reputation. Its origins can be traced back to 1808 when Joseph Moore founded the *Choral Society of the Town*, which by 1811 became known as the *Birmingham Oratorio Choral Society*. This society provided skilled singers for the Triennial Festival chorus under the directorship of Thomas Munden. With the appointment of William Stockley, the *Birmingham Festival Choral Society* came to operate under its own management – no longer depending on the Triennial Festival Committee. With membership increasing to 200 in 1859 compared to 70 in 1855,[67] three (later four) subscription concerts per year were successfully reinstated under the directorship of a chorus master and a conductor, which over time included the likes of Sir Henry Wood, Sir Thomas Beecham and Sir Adrian Boult. To support his choralists, William Stockley endeavoured to provide his choir with a band of instrumentalists, an aim he achieved in 1856. In

1873, he formed Birmingham's first orchestra which existed and performed independently of choirs and festivals. With the new orchestra, he launched a series of orchestral concerts, each of which consisted of a complete symphony, one or two classical overtures, smaller orchestral pieces and 'vocal items as far as possible arranged to correspond with the classical character of the instrumental'.[68] It was in Stockley's concert series (which he directed until 1897) that Edward Elgar, then a violinist in this orchestra, was first provided with the opportunity to introduce some his own compositions.

Although, following Costa's death, calls for English conductors[69] came to the fore, the reign of well-known foreign conductors was continued at the Festival with the appointment of the Austrian Hans Richter. Like Costa, Richter's list of artistic appointments, which included the National Theatre in Pest, the Vienna Court Opera (*Hofoper*) and the Vienna Philharmonic, was impressive. Real progress was also made following Stockley's resignation from both the Festival Choral Society and the Birmingham Orchestra in 1897. Whilst the former withered within 2 years of his resignation, the latter, at least for a short while, revolutionised Birmingham's concert life under the directorship of George Halford. Backed by members of notable local families such as the Cadburys, Dixons, Kenricks, Martineaus, Perkins, Rowlands, Rylands and Chamberlains, the concert series (lasting from October to March) increased from four to ten per season and reduced vocal music to a minimum. In this way, Halford introduced something of a continental subscription concert series into Birmingham's cultural life. Concentrating on contemporary symphonic works by British as well as continental composers, Halford created a musical spectrum which began with and ended with Saint-Saëns, Liszt, Brahms, Bruch, Chopin, Wagner, Tchaikovsky, Dvořák, Delibes, Debussy, Smetana, Borodin and Bruckner. Of particular note is Rachmaninov's Second Piano Concerto which was introduced to Birmingham in 1903,[70] as well as the performance of all the Beethoven symphonies during the 1904/1905 season.

Unfortunately, however, Halford's rather daring endeavours fell short of appreciative audiences and his comparatively bold series came to an end in 1907.[71] Suffering from the same predicament, Birmingham-born Charles Swinnerton Heap's annual series of (strictly instrumental) chamber concerts at the *Birmingham and Midland Institute*, which included string quartets by contemporary composers, also failed to catch on. The decline of both Halford's and Heap's concert series was, however, in stark contrast to Max Mossel's chamber music venture, held in the Grosvenor

Rooms of the Grand Hotel. Here, Mossel employed a number of well-known soloists of the day and presented a repertoire which consisted of a mixture of instrumental and vocal music – songs, glees and folk tunes. Mossel also organised the highly successful and popular *Promenade Concerts* at the Theatre Royal, which ran for 3 weeks in May or June from 1905 until 1914. Thus, it was not that the consumers of culture did not exist but that they were not tuned to much of the music on offer. The outbreak of First World War further destabilised Birmingham's rather fragile cultural sphere in that it heralded the end for most of Birmingham's concert ventures. As mentioned before, Halford's Concerts had been consigned to memory since 1907 and Harrison's concert series ended in 1916. The last of the Triennial Festivals was held in 1912 – its demise being of particular interest: some have blamed higher taxation, others the imminence of war and conscription. Still others blamed the balance sheet since, although more money was taken in, the expenditure was devouring most of it at the expense of charity. Although each, no doubt, contributed their part to the demise, the principal reasons must be sought somewhere else.

Conclusion

In Birmingham, it was the churches and chapels – their organists and choir masters – which first provided musical entertainment. The association of public music-making with a clearly defined philanthropic mission, whether the raising of public relief funds or the financing of a hospital, set the format out of which the Festival later grew. In that way, the Festival contained a type of culture that could transcend individual loyalties and unite Birmingham's mercantile populace which was politically and religiously divided. This was done by grounding its culture on traditional values based on religiously inspired morality and charity. The Gewandhaus, by contrast, did not seek such overt expression of practical values: Leipzig's fairly homogeneous *Bürgertum* did not see culture as a means of bridging obvious religious and political divisions or of forging common social bonds. These were already established by Leipzig's socio-economic constitution. Thus, rather than being purpose-orientated, the Gewandhaus was geared primarily towards the provision of regular and respectable, that is, edifying, musical 'entertainment' for Leipzig's mercantile class.

Whilst the *raison d'être* and ethos of both cultural institutions were conditioned by the socio-cultural constitution of the towns in question, both types of public concert were equally reliant on the exigencies of an emergent middle-class identity. In both cases, such formations of identity were rooted in norms and values that were formed during and after the Enlightenment and provided the rising middle-class consciousness with clearly defined ideas regarding the nature of art and public culture. The study of these is the subject of the next chapter.

Notes

1. *Cornish's Stranger's Guide Through Birmingham* (Birmingham: W. Cornish, 1913), p. 3.
2. C. C. C. Gretschel, *Leipzig und seine Umgebung* (Leipzig: F. Fleischer, 1982 [1836]), p. 184.
3. Under Napoleonic rule, the universities of Halle and Wittenberg were merged, leaving the University of Leipzig as the foremost Town University in Saxony.
4. Gretschel, *Leipzig*, p. v. 'Leipzig's burghers moved their willing hands, industry and trade moved into the town ...; Leipzig's inhabitants were well-disposed towards the arts and sciences, and in her higher schools the spirit's beat of wings strove upwards mightily. Burgher loyalty, fulfilment of professional commitments and intellectual/spiritual education bestow high interest upon our town even now and allow for the shady side, as exists in every place, to retreat completely into darkness.' (The 'shady side' refers to the 1830 uprisings.)
5. T. Nipperdey, *Deutsche Geschichte 1800–1866* (Munich: Beck, 1983), p. 267.
6. J. J. Sheehan, *Germany History 1770–1866* (Oxford: Oxford University Press, 1998 [1989]), p. 145.
7. C. Hall, L. Davidoff, *Family Fortunes: Men and Women of the English Middle Class 1780–1850* (London: Routledge, 2002 [1987]), p. 416.
8. The historian to argue this point most strongly is R. J. Morris in his 'Voluntary Societies and British Urban Élites', *The Historical Journal*, 26/1 (1983). This article influenced many subsequent writings on Voluntary Associations.
9. T. Maentel, 'Zwischen weltbürgerlicher Aufklärung' in D. Hein, A. Schulz (eds), *Bürgerkultur im 19. Jahrhundert: Bildung, Kunst und Lebenswelt* (Munich: Beck, 1996), p. 152.
10. I. Bergfeld, *Leipzig: Eine Kleine Stadtgeschichte* (Erfurt: Suttonverlag, 2002), p. 34.
11. J. E. Kneschke, *Leipzig seit 100 Jahren: Säcularchronik einer werdenden Grossstadt* (Leipzig: Selbstverlag, 1868), p. 458.
12. *Bürgerrecht*: the right to claim burgher status by providing evidence of private property and adequate financial funds.
13. S. Schötz, *Städtische Mittelschichten in Leipzig während der bürgerlichen Umwälzung 1830–1870* (Leipzig: Unpublished PhD, 1985), p. 125.
14. Schötz, *Städtische Mittelschichten*, p. 166.
15. K. Middell, *Hugenotten in Leipzig: Streifzüge durch Alltag und Kultur* (Leipzig: Leipziger Universitätsverlag, 1998), p. 21. In 1700, they founded the *Reformierte Gemeinde* (Reformed Church) in Leipzig. A building was purchased from the King of Saxony in 1702 which served as a church until 1899, when a purpose-built church was erected.

16. H.-J. Sievers, *In der Mitte der Stadt: Die Evangelisch-reformierte Kirche zu Leipzig von der Einwanderung der Hugenotten bis zur Friedlichen Revolution* (Leipzig: Evangelische Verlagsanstalt Leipzig, 2000), p. 41. Of particular renown was Carl Heinrich Reclam, whose publishing house was one of the largest in Leipzig, and the Dufour family, particularly Jean Marc Albert Dufour-Feronce, a fifth generation silk merchant, who was involved in the financing of the Dresden-Leipzig Railway as well as the region's coal industries. From 1834 until 1836, he was only the second Reformed member of Leipzig's town council. Then, of course, there was Felix Mendelssohn (baptised 1816) and his wife, Cécile Jeanrenaud, a French Huguenot from Frankfurt, who became members of the local Reformed Church.

17. On 18 October 1806, Leipzig, officially allied to Prussia, was occupied by French troops. Regarded as the main goods 'depot' for English manufacturing goods (three-quarters of all English produce directed at the German market came through it), Leipzig was made to suffer, particularly its trade fairs, through the continental blockade. Publishing too was financially hit by the occupation as Napoleon had imposed a 50 per cent tax on books printed in the German territories and entering the French market. (Merchants turned to the French as their main trading partners, which, however, backfired when the Russians decreed in 1813 that no French goods were allowed onto German markets.) Forced financial contributions to the French war effort and the occasional public burning of illegal English produce no doubt increased animosities against Napoleon. When Napoleon's aim to defeat the Prussians, Austrians, Russians and Swedes in separate battles failed, the Prussian Kaiser occupied Leipzig's surrounding villages awaiting the final conflict. Victory effectively ended Napoleon's reign in Saxony.

18. Kneschke, *Leipzig seit 100 Jahren*, p. 399.

19. D. Gleisberg, *Merkur und die Musen: Schätze der Weltkultur aus Leipzig. Eine Ausstellung aus der Deutschen Demokratischen Republik im Künstlerhaus Wien, 21.9.1989–18.2.1990* (Vienna: Das Künstlerhaus, 1989), p. 91.

20. At the local trade fair, Leipzig's publishing bourgeoisie ended the century-old practice by which goods were exchanged for goods. Instead, goods were now exchanged for cash without the opportunity to return unsold books.

21. Tariffs existing between Saxony, Prussia, Bavaria, Würtemberg, Hessen and Thuringia were abolished.

22. Besides the publishing industry, Leipzig's economic sphere was also well-served by the manufacture of textile and its varied constituents. Following the abandonment of guild restrictions during the late eighteenth century, Leipzig's merchants and traders began to organise artisan traders such as millers, smiths, dressmakers, goldsmiths and weavers. With it, they promoted Leipzig's reputation as a major manufacturing and trading centre for the dressmaking, shoemaking and wig-making industries. As Leipzig's bourgeoisie was provided with the latest fashion accessories, the Saxon town proved worthy of the title of 'Little Paris'. Similar to the publishing industry, Leipzig's involvement with fashion was conducive to its claim to industrial respectability.

23. According to medieval tradition, the local council (*Rat*) comprised Leipzig's wealthiest élite as well as the Royal Council (*Kurfürstliches Amt*) and representatives of the University. Between them, they shared the administrative powers

that governed the town. During the Napoleonic wars of 1813, a bourgeois movement consisting of local business men emerged, which, through agitation, aimed at gaining a share in local politics. Proposals for reform regarding the formation of a town council, however, fell short of the movement's expectations as the royal government in Dresden granted the bourgeois committee merely an advisory role. Fourteen communal representatives sworn into office in 1817 were not elected by Leipzig's bourgeois élite but chosen by the royal government in Dresden. As the local powers of the magistrates were hardly altered, the representative committee, widely regarded as existing in the shadow of the Magistracy, was continually undermined. See, H. Zwahr, *Revolution in Sachsen – Beiträge zur Sozial- und Kulturgeschichte* (Köln, Weimar, Wien: Böhlau Verlag, 1996), p. 63.

24. Data derived from Gretschel, *Leipzig*, pp. 336–339.
25. Carl Friedrich Gruner, Christian Gottlob Frege, Johann Wilhelm Gross, Jacob Bernhard Limburger, Gustav Moritz Clauss, Johann Rudolf Gruner.
26. A. Doerffel, *Geschichte der Gewandhausconcerte zu Leipzig 25 November 1781 bis 25 November 1881* (Leipzig: Breitkopf & Härtel, 1884). Doerffel provides a complete list of members serving on the Gewandhaus Board of Directors. During the period under review, all of them were members of the town council.
27. Numbers taken from *Illustrated Stranger's Guide to Birmingham* (Birmingham: R. Wrightson, 1913), p. 23.
28. Figures taken from *The Birmingham Directory* 1816 and 1846 and *The Birmingham, Wolverhampton, Walsall, Dudley, Billston and Willenhall Directory* 1780.
29. A. Briggs, *History of Birmingham, Volume 2: Borough and City 1865–1938* (Oxford: Oxford University Press, 1952), p. 5.
30. P. Marsh, *Joseph Chamberlain: Entrepreneur in Politics* (New Haven and London: Yale University Press, 1994), p. 13.
31. Graph constructed from the 1851 religious census. Data derived from C. Gill, *History of Birmingham, Vol 1: Manor and Borough to 1865* (Oxford: Oxford University Press, 1952), p. 374. The religious census only counted people who actually went to Church on this particular Mothering Sunday. On this Sunday people in service were usually expected to return to their home churches. In Birmingham, a mere 61,000 (36 per cent) attended religious services – resulting in accusations of an unusual degree of secularism. The results are therefore not entirely conclusive. Methodism here includes the New Connexion, United, Primitive and Welsh Calvinist.
32. V. Skipp, *The Making of Victorian Birmingham* (Birmingham: Victor Skipp, 1983), p. 116.
33. D. Smith, *Conflict and Compromise: Class Formation in English Society 1830–1914 – A Comparative Study of Birmingham and Sheffield* (London: Routledge & Kegan Paul, 1982), p. 96. The majority of Birmingham's mayors from 1840 to 1900 were Unitarians or Quakers. By 1900, one-quarter of Birmingham's City Councillors was from these two denominations alone.
34. V. Bird, *Portrait of Birmingham* (London: Robert Hale, 1970), p. 93. During the Priestley Riots, a 'Church and King mob' destroyed the New Meeting House (a Unitarian place of worship built in 1732 on Moor Street) at which Joseph Priestley had been appointed pastor in 1780. British loyalists attacked those suspected of being sympathetic to the French Revolution or giving refuge to Jacobeans. The riots broke out following a dinner on 14 July to celebrate the

anniversary of the storming of the Bastille. A good account of the attacks on Priestley is provided in J. Uglow, *The Lunar Men: The Friends Who Made the Future 1730–1810* (London: Faber, 2002), Chapter 37 'Riots'.

35. The British Association, *Handbook of Birmingham* (Birmingham: 1886), p. 78.
36. The Court Leet elected the Parish officers who were assigned to various responsibilities such as Justices of the Peace (Magistrates), who exercised criminal jurisdiction, Church Wardens and Overseers, who administered the affairs of the ecclesiastical parish and managed the poor relief and Surveyors of the Highways, who attended to the building and maintenance of roads and streets. See J. T. Bunce, *History of the Corporation of Birmingham*, Vol. 2 (Birmingham: Cornish, 1885), p. 3.
37. By 1830, the £10 rental qualification that qualified the owner to vote meant that around 7000 of 150,000 inhabitants were given the right to vote in Birmingham.
38. The opportunities presented by the Act were realised in 1838, when a Charter led to the appointment of William Scholefield as the first Mayor of Birmingham. Forty-eight Councillors (the majority of liberal persuasion) as well as 16 Aldermen (chosen by the Councillors from amongst themselves) were sworn into office. See, Gill, *History of Birmingham*, p. 222.
39. Named after Robert Rawlinson, the report attributed the town's bad sanitary conditions to the condition of the sewage disposal system which was under the responsibility of the Town Commissioners. See, Skipp, *Victorian Birmingham*, p. 90.
40. C. Gill, C. G. Robertson, *A Short History of Birmingham from its Origins to the Present Day* (Birmingham: City of Birmingham Information Bureau for the Corporation, 1938), p. 50.
41. The Central Lending Library and Art Gallery and the Central Reference Library followed in 1865 and 1866, respectively.
42. Gill, Robertson, *Short History*, p. 54.
43. In the face of this apparent institutional apathy and ignorance on the part of the Town Council, a number of nonconformist ministers such as John Angell James, George Dawson, Charles Vince and Robert V Dale began to proclaim the new social gospel which many now regard as the platform from which Chamberlain launched his programme of civic improvement. Increasingly supported by local luminaries, particularly Quakers and Unitarians, such as the famous philanthropist Joseph Sturge, the Kenrick and Nettlefold families, and later local politicians such as George Dixon, MP and Mayor for Birmingham in 1866, and Jesse Collings, member of the Town Council since 1868 and Mayor in 1878, these ministers became particularly active in educational reforms. The result of their combined efforts was the formation of the *Birmingham Education Society* in 1867. Pressing educational matters beyond the locality, they founded the *National Education League* in 1868, which famously catapulted Joseph Chamberlain into local and national politics. See, Briggs, *History of Birmingham*, p. 68.
44. Briggs, *History of Birmingham*, p. 35.
45. Gill, Robertson, *Short History*, p. 58.
46. Gill, Robertson, *Short History*, p. 69.
47. M. Handford, *Sounds Unlikely: 600 Years of Music in Birmingham, 1392–1992* (Birmingham: Birmingham Midland Institute, 1992), p. 14.

48. The three-day event was only disrupted by the Seven Year War, but eventually resumed in 1767.
49. E. Edwards, *Some Accounts of the Origins of the Musical Festivals and of James Kempson, the Originator* (Birmingham: Sabin & Stockley, 1882), p. 4.
50. Handford, *Sounds Unlikely*, p. 25. This one-day event was continued at Bartholomew's Chapel until 1838.
51. From 1820, the Festival was extended to 4 days from Tuesdays to Fridays.
52. The greater importance of the morning sessions may be demonstrated by the fact that tickets were more expensive than those for the evening concerts. During the 1820s, tickets cost 10/- and £1 for the morning sessions at St Philips and 7/- and 14/- for the evening sessions at the theatre.
53. Red tickets denoted expensive gallery seats, green for the reserved floor, blue for non-subscribers in the galleries and plain white for non-subscribers on the floor.
54. J. Bunce, *The Birmingham General Hospital and Triennial Festivals* (Birmingham: Benjamin Hall, 1858), p. 107.
55. Bunce, *The Birmingham General Hospital*, p. 91.
56. Handford, *Sounds Unlikely*, p. 68.
57. In 1729, J. S. Bach became its music director. Many of Bach's secular compositions, concerti, for example, were performed.
58. G. & I. Hempel, *Musikstadt Leipzig* (Leipzig: Deutscher Verlag für Musik, 1979), p. 9.
59. Hiller published the *Wöchentliche Nachrichten und Anmerkungen der Musik betreffend* from 1766 until 1770.
60. A. Schering, R. Wustmann, *Musikgeschichte Leipzigs. Band III: Das Zeitalter Johann Sebastian Bachs und Johann Adam Hillers, 1725–1800* (Leipzig: Teubner, 1974 [1941]), p. 427.
61. The *Gewandhaus*, literally translated as 'Cloth Hall', was a traditional trading ground for cloth merchants since the fifteenth century. The building was opened in 1587; the last traders left in 1782.
62. When Polenz was dismissed from his post, he performed Schicht's *Das Ende des Gerechten* ('The End of all Justice') at the University Church whose music director he still was.
63. J. S. Smith, *The Story of Music in Birmingham* (Birmingham: Cornish, 1945), p. 37.
64. Kirk's Popular Guides, *What to See in Birmingham* (Birmingham, 1887), p. 61.
65. Harrison retired in that year.
66. Handford, *Sounds Unlikely*, p. 140–146.
67. Handford, *Sounds Unlikely*, p. 107.
68. Kirk's Popular Guides, *What to See in Birmingham*, p. 61.
69. Notables such as Sullivan, Barnby, Cowen and Stanford were lined up for the post.
70. Handford, *Sounds Unlikely*, p. 183.
71. The series was cut back to four concerts a season with Thomas Beecham, Charles Stanford and Halford himself conducting in turns. This series survived until 1909.

2
The Rise of Cultural Diversity, 1750–1820

Introduction

The basic disparity as to the public role, function and nature of culture in the musical institutions of Leipzig and Birmingham highlights the fact that the concept of middle-class culture is necessarily variable. As the previous chapter explained, on a basic level, this variability was determined by local economic, social and political conditions. This chapter aims to explore further the theme of variability by examining the 'universality' of Enlightenment values, arguing instead for an assimilation of such values according to the need and scope presented by national conditions. This will become particularly evident in the study of religious and aesthetic developments in England and Germany during the late eighteenth century. The latter's importance lies in the fact that each development correlated directly with an extension of the definitions of art, and, consequently, with the cultural practice of the public concerts in the two towns. The chapter ends with an analysis of the press: the nature of music criticism in the journals and newspapers that circulated in Birmingham and Leipzig, to which must also be added a consideration of the role of critics. For the nature of criticism, in particular, clearly reflected dominant philosophical and aesthetic concepts that advanced in accordance with the needs and requirements of local conditions.

The Rise of Cultural Diversity out of the Enlightenment

Classical Enlightenment philosophy was founded upon the firm belief in human progress coupled with the conviction that rational control of nature and society could improve the individual and through him society at large. By availing himself of his eighteenth-century cultural inheritance, the modern individual would assume his rightful place within the world. Reason powered by philosophy was to lead the escape from the tyranny of ossified tradition. By disposing of tradition, Enlightenment man was to become an independent and autonomous individual interacting within a society of like-minded and equally emancipated individuals. Within this society, Enlightenment notions of human perfectibility, educational endeavour and personal achievement rather than the meretricious privileges of birth began to determine the worth of the individual. Education naturally required the individual to reflect upon himself as well as upon his world and time, and this process of individualisation, nourished by reflection, replaced the traditional norms and values of religious dogma with refreshingly new ideas derived from philosophy (moral, religious, practical or natural), literature and aesthetics. These ideas, combined with a revival in evangelicalism (England) and cultural Protestantism (Germany), created a new understanding of the society in which the bourgeoisie lived and which they actively shaped.[1]

The different political and economic contexts of Germany and England, however, created distinct variations on popular Enlightenment themes. In the case of the German territories, the Holy Roman Empire itself was too fractured with its 300 principalities and free imperial towns (*Reichsstädte*), each with different interests in the political and, since the Reformation, in the religious spheres, to be uniformly affected by universal Enlightenment ideas.[2] The lack of political unity meant that the German territories possessed no capital city, no single cultural centre and no national academy which could have aided the formation of a national culture based on the German language. Worse still, culture founded upon the German language was still deemed inferior by the upper and aristocratic echelons of society – the rulers of kingdoms and principalities – where French and Italian languages, cultures and fashions tended to prevail. So long as political absolutism reigned in the German lands (something which was overcome in England with the Glorious Revolution in 1688), the smaller the chance for German language, literature and drama to reach national recognition and cultural status.

Nevertheless, it was paradoxically a small handful of kings and princes within the Holy Roman Empire who introduced long-needed reform and put into practice a number of Enlightenment ideas, albeit by combining the latter with a strict adherence to absolutism. Notable amongst these was Joseph II of Austria with his *Untertanenpatent* (1781) and *Toleranzpatent* (1781) and Friedrich II of Prussia with his *Allgemeines Landsrecht* (the General Legal Code, published after his death in 1794). The persistence of political absolutism as well as the rather underdeveloped, socio-political position of the middle class, however, meant that the latter was given far less scope to translate the Enlightenment ideas that were sweeping across the old territories of the Holy Roman Empire into practical action. As a result, the *Gelehrtenrepublik* remained a cultural factor – it did not merge with the socio-critical protest movements of the time which meant that reforms that could challenge the absolutist nature of German politics remained wanting. Because the middle class remained tied within existing social structures of the territorial absolutism, it could only perform its intended function within the perimeters of literary self-projection.[3] Indicative of this overall impotence is Immanuel Kant's essay *Was ist Aufklärung?* (*What is Enlightenment?*, 1784) which treats Enlightenment primarily as a means of individual emancipation rather than as a concept for political action as propounded by, say, Thomas Paine, or economic freedom as argued by Adam Smith. Nor did Friedrich Karl von Moser call for institutional and political reform in his *Vom Deutschen Nationalgeist* (*On the German National Spirit*, 1765), despite being appalled by the perversion of power in the German states. Instead he argued that progressive change could only be brought about by spiritual transformation and moral renewal. Even Germany's prime Enlightenment representative – Gotthold Ephraim Lessing – did not directly criticise or attack the established Church itself as did, say, Voltaire or Diderot. Rather, he challenged forms of religious knowledge, prejudice and ignorance. In his *Anti-Goeze* (1778; a dispute with Hamburg's chief pastor, Johann Melchior Goeze), for example, he opposed the comfortable assumptions and 'immutable' truths of orthodox theology, arguing that the question of religious truth can never be solved by resorting to biblical or churchly authority since 'religious truth lay in the view of the world that emerged from the gospels, not in the historical record they contained': 'Die Religion ist nicht wahr, weil die Evangelisten und Apostel sie lehrten: sondern sie lehrten sie, weil sie wahr ist'.[4]

Reigning ideas of spiritual transformation and moral education were given a new impetus following the ominous carnage witnessed during and after the French Revolution which led to widespread suspicion of radical transformation of the social and political spheres. Nowhere is this distrust more evident that in the works of one of Germany's most prominent literary luminaries: Friedrich Schiller. In his writings such as *Über die Ästhetische Erziehung des Menschen* (*On the Aesthetic Education of Man*, 1795), Schiller did not articulate a clear concept for a new political order. Rather, it was art and the theatre – the 'moral institution' *par excellence* – which was given the task of accomplishing what revolution so evidently could not. Only the aesthetic education gained through art could usher in the transformational process which could ultimately effect positive changes in the political sphere. Again, the state would retain its traditional physical framework, but would be improved from within.

This emphasis on educational, moral and spiritual development, whilst remaining within existing political structures, spelled the beginning of the notion of the 'apolitical' German, or more specifically, the apolitical *Bürger*. Yet this same emphasis on individual development and education – both being processes which required induction and instruction – became the essence of bourgeois *Kultur*; and in the absence of political influence and economic power, *Kultur* became a vital sphere of action for the German bourgeoisie. It provided the bourgeoisie with a central focus around which a clear class-identity – along with its own values, norms and ethos – could evolve; and it was under the patronage of the *Bürgertum* and within a newly developed art market that a distinct *Kultur* based on the German language and ideas emerged.[5] The inherent aim of *Kultur* – to develop and ameliorate personality, ennoble the mind as well as to cultivate moral and ethical values within the individual – thereby stood in stark contrast to aristocratic values of civility which, as Norbert Elias has pointed out, focused on externalities and results (rather than processes) such as the expression of particular behaviour, polite manners, correct speech and so on.[6]

For the English middle class, on the other hand, the cultural sphere did not develop as a surrogate for political or economic impotence. In Britain, the middle class developed within a state which, since the Glorious Revolution, saw its influence increase steadily. The wars waged between 1739 and 1815 against foreign powers further created a shared set of values, including Protestantism, the sanctity of property, liberty and law, to which should be added the growing economic significance of overseas empire and, of course, the powerful notion of constitutional monarchy. Unlike their German counterparts, the English middle class, already acknowledged as important contributors to the economic prosperity and welfare of the state through their commercial achievements, could voice their demands for political representation within clearly accepted political and national boundaries.

The Enlightenment in England more or less aimed at safeguarding that which had been gained during the seventeenth century. By providing a rational justification for the constitutional monarchy as well as the sanctity of law and property, it stood out by its practicability and viability when compared with its German counterpart.[7] Within this framework, new impetus towards greater parliamentary reform, together with such 'enlightened' movements as the anti-slavery campaign and religious emancipation became prominent in the last two decades of the eighteenth century. In contrast to the German lands, the prime shakers and movers within the reform movements came from nonconformist, non-aristocratic backgrounds, and although a more comprehensive success was only achieved during the 1820s and 1830s, it was during the late eighteenth century that much of the groundwork was prepared. A prime example is the repeal of the *Test and Corporations Acts* in 1827 which allowed nonconformists to partake in public office. The path for its repeal had already been laid in 1779 with the passing of the *Dissenter's Relief Act* by which dissenters in official positions were freed from the obligation to subscribe to the Thirty-Nine Articles. The great number of Protestant missionary and Anti-Slavery societies founded during the last decade of the eighteenth century bear testimony to the dynamism found within the public sphere – a dynamism which was markedly absent within the German lands.

This basic difference between Germany and England was further underlined by the revival of religiosity and rise of aesthetics out of philosophy in the wake of the Enlightenment. Like the concept of culture, religion and aesthetics could only develop within the parameters of what was permissible, and indeed functional, within the national context. This meant that both developments advanced along separate paths in England and Germany.

Religion and Religiosity

The revival of religion and religiosity in its various modes throughout Europe can be seen as a reaction against Enlightenment rationality. Towards the end of the eighteenth century, this revival could cause national cultures to further fragment through their newly asserted values and belief systems.[8] Whilst Leipzig's religious landscape remained relatively homogenous throughout the nineteenth century, with Lutheran Protestantism being the dominant denomination, Birmingham's was marked by religious diversity with the aristocratic and upper middle classes leaning towards Anglicanism, and the middle class towards old Dissent (Presbyterianism, later Unitarianism, Baptism, Congregationalism/Independents and Quakers) and new Dissent (Methodism). Dissent had gathered strength since the *Toleration Act* of 1689 (which outlawed the legal basis for enforced religious uniformity) and continued to grow throughout the eighteenth century by which time it more than challenged the established church as the sole authority on spiritual or ecclesiastical matters. The repeal of the *Blasphemy Acts* in 1797, for example, allowed Unitarians to argue against the doctrine of the Holy Trinity publicly and from the pulpit. With each religious nomination having different attitudes to doctrine, church organisation and liturgical practice, Birmingham's religious sphere was sharply divided indeed. The association of religious denomination with specific historical circumstances (such as those of their origins), created powerful and lasting stereotypes: Anglican as authoritarian persecutors, Roman Catholics as conspiratorial traitors, Methodists as empty-headed enthusiasts, all of which helped to create deeper divisions in the religious sphere of the town.[9] There was, however, one powerful unifying factor, namely, the overwhelming influence of evangelicalism which saturated even Anglicanism from the 1820s onwards.

Evangelicalism reflected a fundamental attitude – a particular way of conducting one's life. It was defined by earnest religiosity which expressed itself in daily bible reading, prayer and a staunch commitment to a life of Christian duty, discipline, high standards of piety and personal morality.[10] Notions such as duty, moral standards and self-improvement provided the bedrock of middle-class morality and conduct, which despite doctrinal differences enabled interdenominational cooperation and promoted solidarity.[11] The rise of philanthropy, which affected all spheres of civic life, was a direct outcome of the evangelical aspiration to do 'good works'. Such unifying influences were, of course, central to Birmingham's Triennial Festival.

As in England, the German bourgeoisie was affected by two religious revivals during early nineteenth century. One was of a more conservative and evangelical nature and corresponded with the general spirit of the post-1815 German Restoration. In an attempt to re-establish the traditional alliance of 'throne and altar', the Church was supposed to act as a pillar of authority legitimising the power of the state whilst the state defended (by use of police and censor) the Church's conservative orthodoxy in the light of modern ideas.[12] By the 1830s, this conservative orthodoxy was supported by a revival of apolitical pietism – a religious trend which had first appeared as a reaction to rigid Lutheran orthodoxy in the seventeenth century. Like Evangelicalism, it stressed feeling, emotion and a personal relationship between the individual and God.

The second revival centred on a more liberal (or enlightened) Protestantism which was most prominently championed by Friedrich Schleiermacher. It argued that religion and philosophy (faith and reason) could co-exist; in this way Protestantism could remain receptive to the central ideas of the age. As Thomas Nipperdey put it:

> ... the world was a revelation of the glory of God, for which mankind was fulfilled in culture and in the progress of culture. [...] People's consciousness of their own time and their own humanity demanded that they constantly reassess the old interpretations of Christianity in the light of their own experience. [...] Liberal Protestantism allowed the middle classes to reconcile the Protestant faith with the new interest in science and philosophy with a clear conscience; and at the same time it allowed them to relate the central tenet of humanity and a civilised society, and all the problems it entailed, to theological reflection and Christian tradition.[13]

Not being as absorbed with feeling and direct religious experience, this liberal Protestantism or *Kulturprotestantismus*, characterised the religious outlook above all of the German urban bourgeoisie. The principal difference from multi-denominational England, where religious affiliation was expressed through church/chapel attendance, charity and public discourse, lay in the belief that 'religion was a matter of faith rather than of good deeds and doctrine'.[14] Rather than reaching outwards to do God's 'good works', the typical German urban bourgeois adhered to Schleiermacher's 'invisible true church' in which religiosity came to denote a private mode of behaviour,[15] with an emphasis on autonomous personality, individual conscience and responsibility and repression of overt emotion.[16] The nature of religiosity in Germany was thus similar to that of *Kultur* in the sense that both were concerned with 'spiritual cultivation, not external form'.[17] Replete with spiritual values and essence, its advocates and defenders based its alleged superior status on the fact that other traditions such as those prevailing in Britain or France were concerned merely with rationally perceptible attributes, for example, outward form, charity or even commerce. In particular, the English middle-class preoccupation with social rather than metaphysical elements prevented their culture from stimulating genuine freedom; the latter, like self-improvement, could only be inspired by the inner self.

Thus, whilst religion in England was deemed to be outward-looking, religiosity in Germany's Protestant territories tended to look into a private, interior world. At the root of this attitude was the pervasive power of idealist philosophy which developed during the eighteenth century and henceforth dominated Germany's philosophical, religious and aesthetic traditions. Here again, the German middle class was sharply differentiated from its English counterpart: German Idealism stood in direct opposition to the English preference for empiricism. These emergent differences in the ways of philosophical inquiry are important because they directly impacted on the assumptions about the role which art was supposed to perform within bourgeois culture.

The Aesthetic Basis of Art in Britain and Germany

New ways of philosophical inquiry began to emerge during the seventeenth century when René Descartes proposed that truth and the world could be discovered through reason, observation and experimentation. Whilst Cartesian rationalism remained provocatively productive in Central Europe, it was rejected by British theorists such as John Locke, George Berkeley and, most decisively, by David Hume. It is here that the schism between British and German ways of philosophical enquiry reached its clearest expression.

Rather than pure reason, the prime intellectual tools in the discovery of 'truth' within the burgeoning British philosophical tradition were, according to John Locke, taken from sensation (outer data) and reflection (upon that data). Both were supposed to fill the empty consciousness (*tabula rasa*). George Berkeley ventured a step further. He questioned the reality of a world existing independently of sensation and reflection; objective reality could only exist when consciously perceived. The decisive step, however, was taken by David Hume, who brought British empiricism to its sharpest definition: no single sentiment/perception could ever fully represent the reality of the object; all impressions were random and all were equally valid. With this insight, the Cartesian system and its derivatives were deemed to have collapsed:

> This once proud edifice, consisting of a rational universe, a world of monads and substances, souls and bodies, working together in pre-established harmony, was torn down [...] and reduced to a chaos of single sensations and impressions, casually occurring as disconnected phenomena and held together only by accidental associations.[18]

The concept of accidental associations was to have a profound impact on British aesthetics, above all in the sphere of music. For they were seen as means through which the nature of aesthetic creations and responses to them were rendered comprehensible in that sensations call to mind corresponding ideas.[19] This encouraged an emphasis on individual and subjective reaction to art as investigations on art 'turned away from the objective conventions governing art to the more subjective conditions of its reception, that is, our sensory perception and emotional responses'.[20] Thus a critic wrote in the *Harmonicon* that music:

> gently touches and agitates the agreeable and sublime passions; [...] it wraps us in melancholy, and elevates us with joy; [...] it dissolves and inflames; [...] it melts us in tenderness, and rouses to rage: but its strokes are so fine and delicate, that, as in a tragedy, even the passions that wound, please. Its sorrows are charming, and its rage heroic and delightful... [Music] awakens some passions which we do not perceive in ordinary life.[21]

Given music's associations with passion, sensuality and feeling, restrictions or limitations had to be imposed. Music should never be used to gratify mere sensual feeling; rather, it was primarily a means to inspire notions of divinity. The aesthetic validity of music could therefore only be judged by the quality of the emotions and ideas they excite within the commonly acceptable parameters of cultivated society.[22] The insistence on individual reception necessitates as much, given that each recipient perceives an object differently: some find it pleasing whilst others may find it displeasing. After all, beauty, according to the tenets of empiricism, does not really exist in the object itself, but in the pleasurable sentiments which it excites: 'it would follow that all pleasure must be essentially beautiful, and consequently that a shameful and criminal pleasure would be essentially beautiful, which theory would destroy every moral principle'.[23] Therefore, only if the pleasure which music arouses is capable of exciting Shaftesburian ideals of 'love of moral conduct and virtue', only if it can 'elevate and ennoble the soul by purifying and strengthening the mind', can it be deemed art.[24]

This view offers some explanation for the relative lack of appreciation of purely instrumental music in England at this time.[25] The continual reliance on the principle of *mimesis* reduced instrumental music to the level of mere entertainment because of its inability to imitate or express anything that could be clearly deemed morally uplifting. Because it was unable to imitate moral precepts, it could not give rise to related virtuous associations and, therefore, could not provide on its own a proper aesthetic experience. Owing to a continual emphasis on music having to mediate to the listener some precisely defined content, only the genres of opera, oratorio and song could acquire true aesthetic status. James Beattie summed up the matter succinctly:

> A fine instrumental symphony [...] is like an oratorio delivered with propriety, but in an unknown tongue; it may affect us to a certain degree, but conveys no determinate feeling; [...] the singer, by taking up the same air, and applying words to it, immediately translates the oration into our own language; then all uncertainties vanishes, the fancy is filled with determinate ideas, and determinate emotions take possession of the heart.[26]

The artistic rules required for the (virtuous) appreciation of instrumental music were simply not provided by British aestheticism. Consequently, a Beethoven symphony would not have been able to contribute to the evocation of virtuous conduct, an elevation of the soul or purification of the mind. Such was only achieved with the rise of German Idealist philosophy and the system of aesthetics it inspired during the early nineteenth century. By this time, of course, it had no bearing on the ways in which the appreciation of music in Britain developed.

Unlike in British philosophical thought, German philosophers of art, and later aestheticians, strove to furnish music with philosophical autonomy, something which was achieved through the idealist philosophy of Immanuel Kant.[27] Before the arrival of Idealism, pure instrumental music was deemed little more than superficial and hedonistic entertainment due to its alleged inability to do more than just touch the senses. As in Britain, instrumental music was not regarded as an 'engaging' art, for it was incapable of involving the entire individual and thus furthering his educational, moral and ethical endeavours.[28] The expression 'Sonate, que me veux tu?' (Sonata, what do you want from me/What are you trying to tell me?) which enjoyed common currency during the late eighteenth century throughout Europe is indicative of this characteristic viewpoint.

New paths, however, were tentatively prepared by Alexander Baumgarten with his *Reflections on Poetry* (1735) and, later, by Immanuel Kant's *Critique of Judgement* (1790). Even though Baumgarten still placed aesthetics (and sense perception) in second place after logic, thus adhering to seventeenth-century rationalist practice, he nevertheless defined aesthetics as a 'faculty that produces a certain type of knowledge in which sensual perception played a valid part'.[29] With Baumgarten's positive evaluation of the senses, art was provided with some philosophical dignity, setting in motion 'a powerful philosophical project that conceived art as a special kind of truth, with deep roots in our cognitive faculties'.[30] Only with Immanuel Kant, however, was aesthetics given independent status within philosophy, which meant that art's potential for cognition, even when compared to that of reason, was finally recognised.

Like David Hume, Kant rejected the notion that knowledge of the external world was beyond doubt. Appearances, he claimed, are all we know, all we can ever know. Beyond Hume, however, Kant claimed that all knowledge is constituted and created by the cognising (and conscious) subject. Our knowledge is thus not a copy of the world but rather, our world is a copy of our consciousness: the external world can only ever be a world as it appears to us – nothing can ever be said about inner reality, the 'thing in itself' (*das Ding an sich*). Aesthetics could now be defined as a realm of experience in which we demonstrate no interest in the actual existence of the object but only in how it appears to us. This guaranteed the independence of aesthetic judgement from any reliance on external validation such as language or images. As experience of an object is accompanied by feelings of either pleasure or displeasure, the aesthetic realm is necessarily subjective – it is our creation. Beauty, similar to knowledge, can be understood only through the subject which means that beauty, independent of external validation and conceptual knowledge, can only lie in the eye of the beholder. With this argument, Kant laid the foundations for a definition of art and beauty which, in theory, is strictly autonomous.[31] As with *Kulturprotestantismus*, the key lies in the individual: the concept of art was deeply rooted within the self.

Although Kant granted art the vital potential for cognition, he was unable to include instrumental music in this equation: to him it remained the lowest of all the arts. The positive re-evaluation and elevation of instrumental music as the greatest of all the arts was only accomplished by his successors during the first decade of the nineteenth century, particularly the Jena Romantics such as Fichte, Friedrich and August Schelling and Friedrich von Hardenberg (Novalis), but also Wackenroder, Tieck and E. T. A. Hoffmann who built on Kantian insights. A few examples will suffice. To Novalis the world was an endless series of changing relationships which were best understood through music because music was not directed towards referentially fixed objects in the world.[32] Wackenroder, in his *Herzensergiessungen eines kunstliebenden Klosterbruders* (1797) and *Phantasien über die Kunst* (1799), argued that musical material is endowed with mysterious expressive potential and that it is only in music, acting as a vehicle to express infinite, insatiable longing and indefinable feelings, that the mystical and the truth which transcends speech are revealed.[33] Jean Paul saw music as a way into the metaphysical dream world, an expression of infinite longing. Kant led German aestheticians and philosophers to the boundaries of the world as it appears to us and invited them and everyone else to look beyond the empirical and purely rational to discover a world hitherto unknown.[34] It was, however, his successors who, by taking this far further than Kant had done, began to recognise this unknown world through the appreciation of instrumental music.

It was the Romantics' celebration, rather than condemnation of the lack of a semantic context within instrumental music that paved the way for its exaltation; it was decreed that music, freed from the mundane strictures of semantics, was superior to all the other arts. As Carl Dahlhaus put it: 'by ridding itself of texts and the expression of definite emotions music does not degenerate into preliterate vagueness, as was believed in the eighteenth century, but rather transcends language to become a prefiguration of the infinite and absolute'.[35] Music was now deemed to grasp a reality of far deeper meanings and senses – the idea itself, infinity, the spirit, even God – everything which was deemed inexpressible in spoken language. Art expressed what cannot be achieved by conceptual thought (providing answers which philosophy could not). Thus, in Germany, music acquired a metaphysical dimension; it became a symbolic key to seemingly impenetrable truths, and, by being taken to the threshold of transcendentalism, the listener was freed from the mundane strictures of materialism and worldliness.

By the early nineteenth century, the aesthetic bedrock of the two countries thus stood at opposite ends of the philosophical spectrum. The only similarity between the two countries was the belief 'that the essential nature of man was not reason [but consisted] of a conglomerate of instincts, habits, feelings or (as German subjectivism illustrated) of an ego which creates and projects its own world...'.[36] The aesthetic norms that were subsequently developed, however, were diametrically opposed to one another. What Germany extolled, Britain avoided: excessive subjectivism and relativism, emotionalism, intuition, speculation and elaborately abstract systems of thought. Whilst German aestheticians speculated on the infinite and indefinable feelings which music, above all, was supposed to express, British aestheticians, insisting on real and tangible concepts, argued that music had to follow the meaning of the words to accentuate the mood they express and thus give music a rational, conceptual basis.[37] As will be seen in subsequent chapters, this simple difference of aesthetic understanding was to have a lasting impact on the formation of each town's music culture – on its content, reception and organisation.

Before that, however, the first phenomenon to be explored is the press. It is studied here because, firstly, the nature of criticism and the role of the critic too were profoundly influenced and shaped by the philosophical and aesthetic values which had developed within national boundaries. Secondly, as the press disseminated these values into the faraway corners of the bourgeois home, it actively participated in the making of bourgeois concert culture, thus forming a crucial part within the corporate institutions of bourgeois culture which constituted the bourgeois public sphere. Given the press' mutually complementary nature to cultural institutions such as the Gewandhaus and the Triennial Festival, the analysis of it in the remainder of this chapter can thus be seen as setting the paradigm for subsequent chapters.

The Public Sphere: the Press as Case Study

Introduction

The press, as a new communicative medium emerging in the late eighteenth century, encouraged an educated discourse amongst the middle classes and helped to create a forum in which new knowledge, ideas and opinions could be expressed and discussed. In theory, these could be readily read and assessed by everyone – beyond regional frontiers – thus creating a level of integration which this rising bourgeois society required.[38] Just as voluntary association provided a common meeting within the public sphere, so the press created a pseudo-congregation within the individual's private sphere. Benedict Anderson's classic formulation in terms of imagined communities is useful is this context:

> Each communicant is well aware that the ceremony he performs [reading a newspaper] is being replicated simultaneously by thousands of others of whose existence he is confident, yet of whose identity he has not the slightest notions. [...] The newspaper reader, observing exact replicas of his own paper being consumed by his residential neighbour, is continually reassured that the imagined world is visibly rooted in everyday life [...] creating that remarkable confidence of community in anonymity which is the hallmark of modern nations.[39]

Thus, readers of newspapers and journals can, each as private individuals, imagine themselves as being part of the wider community constituted by all the other readers. Underlying such developments was the 'reading revolution' resulting from an increase in literacy rates that for the first time allowed for the involvement of large segments of the population in the formation of public opinion.

   With increasing demand for texts, the economic basis of literary production changed too; books, just like any other goods sold on the market, could be replaced if deemed outdated. There emerged a whole new concept of educational advancement as constant progression from antiquated to new, at least as far as progress in the scientific, technological and philosophical spheres was concerned. The journal, and similar printed material, thus acquired a socio-cultural function as a major part of bourgeois culture. As educational credentials had become a significant means by which the bourgeois could identify himself, reading newspapers or specialised journals, particularly in coffee houses and public newsrooms, became themselves status symbols. With respect to his educational and cultural horizons, the reader could demonstrate that he was 'bourgeois' or that he was 'an appointed bearer and guardian of culture that incorporated refinement and public spirit'.[40]

At the same time, socio-economic arrangements regarding publishing proprietorship were undergoing profound changes which subsequently affected the overall organisation of bourgeois culture. With regard to the music journal, for example, the rise of bourgeois printing houses completed the transformation from a courtly to a bourgeois-based music culture. For the first time, it was the publisher – a commercial enterprise – rather than an aristocratic patron who commissioned works of various descriptions.[41] This meant that art and commerce were beginning to merge. In Germany and England, musical journals were produced by its major printing houses. For example, the *Allgemeine Musikalische Zeitschrift* (*AMZ*) was owned by Breitkopf & Härtel; *The Musical Times* and *Musical World* by Novello. Many of these houses also printed and distributed sheet music, teaching manuals as well as books more generally dealing with music. This meant that editors were constrained to align their musical reviews and criticism with other in-house publications. A journal representing a particular cultural ethos was inevitably representative of its publishing house. As the case of Breitkopf & Härtel will show, its owners were as much part of the public sphere as any other. For the *AMZ*, and thus Breitkopf & Härtel, to be successful and commercially viable, the publisher had to lead, form and reinforce cultural norms and values, many of which were identical to the cultural ethos espoused by the Gewandhaus. As a result, more coherent, all-inclusive, assumptions about what constitutes culture emerged which penetrated and informed all the institutions that comprised the cultural sphere.

The press thus became indispensable to the successful maintenance of the corporate institution of bourgeois culture in that it allowed for the formalisation and standardisation of taste and attitudes towards art. Such standardisation was essential, particularly since 'taste' – a private tenet as much as a universal/public concept – helped 'a group to cohere from within and to insulate itself from without. The taste a person had . . . associated him with *his own kind* and separated him from *others*.'[42] It thus mattered what the majority thought. As Heinrich Brockhaus, the owner of one of Leipzig's leading publishing house explained: 'man verschliesse sich auch nicht einseitig gegen das, was das ganze Publikum anerkennt und das eben dadurch seine Berechtigung hat'.[43] As implied by Brockhaus, intrinsic to the successful maintenance of the cultural mission was the creation of a 'universally' valid public consensus ('universal' only in the sense that each middle class granted its cultural, religious and artistic values the status of permanent legitimacy). The inherent plurality of tastes and opinions within the public domain could not, as yet, be accepted by a cultural sphere which had only just emerged; it was the critic, a cultural institution himself, who now assumed an importance which hitherto he had not possessed.

The Enlightenment had taught that there is a reason for everything and that through reason, experience or *a priori* rational deduction, causes could be ascertained. Even the beauties of art were as susceptible to proof as any other, if one but seeks with diligence and discernment. For the press, such notions placed the responsibility of discovering the principles upon which art worked largely in the hands of its critics and editors. The limited benefits gained from private judgement in music as compared with the idea of public judgement lies at the heart of the critic's sometimes inflated claims to authority. For it was principally the critic who ensured that the acquisition of taste – the ability to appreciate and perceive what is perfect and beautiful – was made integral to the middle-class educational ideal; and because natural capacities of discrimination do not exist, taste could, in a typically Enlightenment fashion, be constructed – thus studied and acquired: 'If the vein is there, the precious metal may be purified and polished.'[44] The importance of the undertaking, that of informing and inspiring public opinion, meant that not everyone, and certainly no mere practitioner such as a musician, was deemed appropriate, let alone competent, to take over such important missionary work. The job of the critic presupposed the need for high educational credentials and a firm grip on bourgeois educational ideals. The critic thus arose from amongst their midst.

The differing aesthetic legacies that the Enlightenment bequeathed to England and Germany inevitably affected the manner of criticism by which judgement was passed. Leipzig's preference for instrumental music and tendency towards metaphysical inquiry, for example, necessitated a different approach to criticism than was the case in Birmingham's oratorio and choral culture in which the word served as the predominant yardstick for good taste. A discussion in turn of the journals and the type of criticism prevalent in each town will illustrate how their music cultures developed differently.

The Music Journal in Leipzig's Cultural Sphere

Leipzig, with its numerous publishing houses such as Breitkopf & Härtel (founded in 1719), C.F. Peters (1800), Hofmeister (1807) and Kistner (1823), was already producing pamphlets, journals and books relating to music in large numbers by the early nineteenth century. The symbiotic relationship between the press and Leipzig's music culture was thus present from the start. It was furthered when Leipzig's publishers and book merchants, who had traditionally dominated Leipzig's economic sphere, came to feature prominently within the local cultural and social scene. Leipzig's premier musical journal, the *AMZ*, its editors and publishers, Breitkopf & Härtel, bear ample evidence of this phenomenon.

The *AMZ* was a weekly journal, first published in 1798 and edited by Johann Rochlitz, a former *Thomaner* [45] and theology graduate of Leipzig's University. Christoph Gottlieb Breitkopf (1750–1800), Johann Friedrich Rochlitz (1769–1842), Wilhelm Christoph Härtel (1787–1849) and Hermann Härtel (1803–1875), all participated in the management of the firm and its publications. At the same time, all were members of the Gewandhaus Board of Directors: Breitkopf from 1788 until 1800, Rochlitz from 1805 until 1842, Wilhelm Härtel from 1830 until 1849 and Hermann Härtel from 1834 until 1875. The continuous involvement of publishers and editors in Gewandhaus politics, spanning almost 100 years, highlights the close interaction of press and concert hall. The wider implication of this relationship was that the Gewandhaus concert programme would largely mirror and reinforce the dominant notions present in music criticism of the *AMZ* and *vice versa*. Furthermore, the combination of both helped to define the meaning and importance of music to the educational and cultural endeavours of Leipzig's bourgeoisie. This posed an absolute imperative following the rise of Romantic idealist philosophy that enabled the new instrumental music to be understood and rationalised. Friedrich Rochlitz, the pioneering editor of the *AMZ*, proved invaluable in this respect. Alongside the likes of E. T. A. Hoffmann, Rochlitz proclaimed and introduced a new musical age to the urban bourgeoisie.

Thus, the endless search for details and singularities within a composition, as was common in eighteenth-century listening culture, was superseded by one that valued the opposite: not so much the details and breaches of compositional norms (*Regelverstösse*) but the interplay and correlation between musical details and the stimulating effects derived from them were thought to be of real interest: 'Weniger die Sache selber, als vielmehr deren Wirkung, die es zu erleben gilt, erscheint den modernen Menschen des 19. Jahrhunderts als das Berauschende, das Sensationelle, das Schwindelerregende und Taumelndmachende'.[46] In Rochlitz' subjective musical criticism, the effects emanating from a musical composition are taken as the measure of value, which meant that a whole new range of compositions, especially those of Beethoven, previously thought to lie outside the boundaries of conventional criticism, could now be valued and judged. This opened up a whole new range of opportunities for the critic in that this new music, and how it should be received, had to be made public in a way that could be understood and accepted amongst the concert-going public.

Whereas in the previous listening/reception culture, a composition was likened to a number of separate 'paintings', each having a melody which could be studied and enjoyed separately, more modern compositions – full of ideas, themes, motives, phrases, each leading to the next in quick succession – left the traditional listener in considerable confusion. The listener was barely equipped to experience such novel enjoyment. A note from the diaries of the publisher Heinrich Brockhaus, dated January 1828, demonstrates some of the gaps in understanding typical of the time:

> Abends hörte ich im Concert die siebente Symphonie von Beethoven. Es sind herrliche Stellen darin, aber auch wie in den meisten Beethoven'schen Productionen derart viel seltsame, zu denen mir wenigstens das Verständnis fehlt, und insofern ein Kunstwerk Harmonie aller einzelnen Theile zueinander bedingt, könnte diese Symphonie nicht auf den Namen eines solchen Anspruch machen. Aber doch liegt ein unendlicher Reiz in dieser Symphonie; man fühlt sich gehoben, gerührt, freut sich, und findet sich dann wieder abgestossen.[47]

The amount of effort required to overcome traditional attitudes is highlighted by the fact that throughout the 1810s and 1820s, the new poet-composers/composer-poets (such as Jean Paul and E. T. A. Hoffmann and Robert Schumann) to whom abrupt harmonic changes, tonal mass, flooding of emotions and experience were not an anathema, had published continuously in the *AMZ*. Their main aim was to convey an

understanding of the musical effects emanating from the new compositions. Subjective feelings and impressions, an almost arrogant negation
of all traditional authority, rules and schemes as well as personal identification with the creative powers of the universe, determined the nature
of their music criticism. As Fubini explained:

> Subjektivität in der romantischen Kritik [...] stützt sich auf eine
> Musikauffassung, die in ihr den Ausdruck der Gefühle sieht, und zwar
> in einem Masse, in dem die Gefühle uns gar den Eintritt ins Unend-
> liche ermöglichen und uns den geheimen Pulsschlag des Universums
> fühlen lassen. Das Urteil läuft also nicht Gefahr, sich in den Besonder-
> heiten des Subjekts zu verlieren, denn die Universalität des Gefühls
> verleiht ihm Objektivität und Allgemeingültigkeit.[48]

The Kantian emphasis on the universal validity of feeling would remain
prominent within the cultural ideology of the *AMZ* even throughout the
bitter polemic of the 1840s. The reason for this enduring popularity lies in
the critic's successful attempt to gather, compare and correct individuals'
judgements so that they could be raised to universal validity.[49] Clear perceptions of what was acceptable (right) and unacceptable (wrong) were
turned into universally accepted rules which in turn were later translated
into bourgeois educational principles and cultural norms. These came to
serve as the basis for middle-class music appreciation. As Hans Georg
Nägeli explained in his 'Attempt to Establish Norms for Reviewers in the
Music Journals' (1812):

> Solche Regeln sollen hier aufgestellt werden, wo möglich zugleich mit
> den Belegen und Beweisen, dass sie die rechten und unentbehrlichen
> sind. In wie weit sie dann von den Recensenten dieser Zeitung als
> solche erkannt werden, in so weit können sie ihnen künftighin zur
> Norm dienen.[50]

These rules were to dominate the public perceptions of music for decades
and set the cultural norms for generations of bourgeois concert-goers.
When confronted with the artistic changes which began to make themselves felt during the 1830s and particularly in the months leading up to
the revolution of 1848, these cultural norms proved too unwaveringly
persistent to be affected by change in any significant way. That was despite the fact that the first tide of artistic change was adeptly represented in
a rival journal, the *Neue Zeitschrift für Musik* (*NZfM*), which was founded
in 1834 under the joint editorship of Robert Schumann, Friedrich Wieck

(Schumann's future father-in-law), Ludwig Schunke and Julius Knorr. From that date onwards, both journals regularly provided résumés of Gewandhaus concerts as well as of national and international music festivals. In addition, they announced forthcoming concerts and soloists, published essays on music history, music theory and musical education and advertised newly published sheet music. Obvious differences, however, lay in the type of readership at which they were aimed.

Whilst the *AMZ*, in maintaining its traditionally aesthetic and cultural stance sought cultural legitimacy in the past, Schumann's *NZfM*[51] sought it very much in the present. Rather than supporting tradition, the *NZfM* promoted the cause of artistic progress, most notably in the works of composers like Berlioz, Schubert, Liszt, Chopin and of course Schumann himself, all of whom remained outside the traditional Gewandhaus programme. The *AMZ*, when contrasted with the *NZfM*, was now revealed to stand irrevocably in the service of established public opinion. Previously serving as the guardian of universal public opinion, it had now, since the launch of the *NZfM*, been exposed as representing just *one*, rather than *the*, cultural ethos – and a conservative one at that. The rise of a plurality of opinion, made it apparent that art, like philosophy, politics or science, was no longer sustained by immutable and static laws; in the new age, art was to develop with or without public opinion, with or without bourgeois patronage. This did not mean, however, that the *AMZ* was about to abort its cultural crusade. On the contrary, it remained steadfast in its perceived role as standard-bearer of its particular cultural ethos. If anything, the fronts hardened when the *NZfM* was taken over by Franz Brendel, a staunch Wagnerian, following Schumann's move to Dresden in 1845. Schumann's writings had always been more akin to a satirical attack upon bourgeois dilettantism, taste and concert practice. His efforts, however, appeared positively dilletante-ish and harmless themselves when compared to the new and fierce ideological crusade now led by the revamped *NZfM*. The very nature and identity of bourgeois culture now seemed threatened as the *NZfM* began to undermine its foundations by associating art with the realities posed by the new *Zeitgeist*. Deeply influenced by Hegelian dialectic, Brendel and others thus destabilised the aesthetic foundation of bourgeois culture which had, until then, always been associated with personal categories such as feeling, rather than politics. The political tempest of 1848 raised hopes for a new age; similar expectations were now conferred upon the artistic sphere.

The *AMZ* ceased to exist at the end of 1848 but resurfaced in 1863.[52] During that period, the *NZfM* ruled supreme, although other, less polemical, less politicised and ultimately more popular music journals were founded such as *Die Musik* and the *Musikalische Wochenblatt*. It was left to these publications to continue along the *AMZ* path of traditional, apolitical music criticism and to resume the age-old practice of laying down judgements based on the assumption of universal rules which corresponded to established tastes. This polarisation continued until the end of the nineteenth century, when music journals turned their back on the concerns of public opinion and pursued instead a more scholarly line intended for the use of the practising musician or musicologist. Except for the momentary return to popular rhetoric during the weeks and month around August 1914, they had, on the whole, become of little relevance to the average bourgeois concert-goer.

Music Criticism in Birmingham's Cultural Sphere

Whilst Leipzig's dominant music journal was inextricably linked to the Gewandhaus by way of its ownership and editorial members, such a direct link was absent in Birmingham. Whilst Leipzig's music culture attracted little critical attention from other cultural centres such as Dresden, Weimar or Berlin, Birmingham's concert culture was subjected to criticism from as far afield as London, highlighting the centrality of London as the major cultural centre in England. Until the mid-nineteenth century, Birmingham had no dedicated musical press and consequently could not provide for the same regular and close relationship between its music culture and the press. The music devotee still depended on the London-based journals such as *The Musical Times*, *The Musical World*, *The Fine Arts Journal*, *The Musical Herald*, *The Musical Examiner* and other London publications that were sold at Birmingham's book shops. All of them reported on a number of music festivals throughout England and until the performance of Felix Mendelssohn's *Elijah* in 1846, Birmingham's Triennial Festival was viewed with ill-favour as is demonstrated in an article in the *Musical Examiner* on the 1843 Festival:

> The Birmingham Festival for 1843, is a decided failure. [...] With an orchestra of 400 chosen artists – it only gave one great work. In the evening too – not one symphony – not one concerto – not one concerted piece of any pretensions!! And so much for the Birmingham Festival for 1843 – which, though as a speculation, we believe and hope, for the sake of the noble charity to which its funds are destined, has succeeded – as a matter of art, has been one of the most thoroughly contemptible occurrences on record.[53]

With similar acerbity, *The Musical World* noted on the 1843 Festival:

> On the whole, I consider this Festival the most thoroughly disgraceful, as a matter of art, that ever occurred in Birmingham, if not, indeed, any where else. Except the *Messiah*, not one morning programme was even credible. [...] As for the Evening concerts at the theatre, when it is considered, that with such resources, both vocal and instrumental, not one of the symphonies of the great masters was performed, not one concerto, not one chorus or concerted piece of any magnitude, one cannot but be disgusted as well as disappointed. I am sorry to preach in this vein, but justice demands it. The stupidest thing of all, however, was the performance of bad English versions of bad Italian operas, and this at the grand Musical Festival of a wealthy and populous town like Birmingham – one of the commercial emporiums of the world![54]

Consequently, it was left to the local press, *Aris' Birmingham Gazette* (founded by Thomas Aris in 1741) and the *Birmingham Journal* (1825), to uphold the Festival's reputation within Birmingham's concert-going public. Both these broadsheets provided accounts of each Festival that occupied more space than any other subject, including reports of House of Commons debates and news of the local, national or imperial markets. Despite that, however, Birmingham's concert readers had a comparatively restricted choice between the anti-provincial London-based journals intent on savaging Birmingham's pretensions to cultural achievement and the local press which was equally intent on exaggerating local cultural success:

> ...We are rejoiced from a source that cannot be doubted, that the [1843] celebration excites extraordinary interest not only amongst all circles in the country but also amongst the musical world of France and Germany; and looking to the extraordinary combination of talent announced, this result is certainly not more than might have been very naturally anticipated.[55]

In terms of criticism, there seems to have been no objective and acceptable middle ground between excessive denigration and exaggerated praise. Whether in the more conservative *Aris' Birmingham Gazette* or in the liberal *Birmingham Journal*, the critique of the Festival appeared to mirror the traditional antipathy between a provincial town battling it out against the capital. Only after the triumph of Mendelssohn's *Elijah* in 1846 was Birmingham's contribution to England's music culture acknowledged and positively celebrated. At around the same time, the symbiotic relationship between press and concert culture was intensified in the person of G. A. Macfarren, a composer and critic writing for the *Musical World*, who was also employed by the Festival Committee to write programme notes for the Triennial Festival. With his arrival, and for the first time, Birmingham's Festival audience was provided with professional guidance.

During the 1820s, 1830s and early 1840s, there was no established press authority in Birmingham to provide dominant cultural leadership as was the case in Leipzig. There was furthermore no notion of a 'leading critic' as all reviews were written without a public acknowledgement of the author. This 'lack' of authority was, however, of little consequence because an oratorio and opera culture relies on the word to which music was often deemed subservient. If the word, as is the case in oratorios, was contingent on extra-musical aspects such as virtue and morality, its moral and religious accuracy could be fairly easily determined. For this, a critic was not really required. Every concertgoer in nineteenth century Birmingham would have been aware of Old Testament stories and the messages intrinsic to them. Everyone would have been able to judge whether the oratorio subjects and stories complied with their biblical blueprint. As the music was deemed to exist as an accompaniment to the word, it was judged according to whether it could support the meaning of the liturgy, or the biblical and operatic stories musically, in short, whether it could heighten and intensify the feelings and sentiments emanating from the words alone. The success of soloists was judged according to such principles: whether they could move the soul and stir feelings within the listener. In contrast to Leipzig, where the reader was transported to the metaphysical spheres in which the composition was thought to have had its origins, in Birmingham, music criticism leaned towards the descriptive narrative, often providing a scene-by-scene account in which every detail was laid bare for individual analysis. Criticism was thus descriptive rather than instructive; there was no need for critics to create and institute cultural norms as these were already present in the moral and religious values inherent in the compositions. These values, given their common roots in Holy Writ, were necessarily congruent to the everyday morality of the urban middle class. The prevalence of common notions of religion and morality in music meant that cultural partisanship within the town at least was stifled from the outset – a requirement of Birmingham's public culture. Given the biblical foundations, there could be no equivalent for Leipzig's liberal–conservative divide in Birmingham's music culture where socio-cultural homogeneity was the rule not the exception.

The unifying nature of Birmingham's Festival was further confirmed by the more ephemeral notices in the daily or weekly press. Intrinsic to any critique of the Festival was the emphasis on the evangelical ethos of the event. Given the Festival's association with 'good works', that is, the financing of the General Hospital, newspapers provided detailed accounts of the expenditures, incomes and resultant profits. Often, the amount of profits raised was used as an indicator of the success of the Festival. Reviews would congratulate Birmingham's wealthier inhabitants on the fulfilment of their Christian duty, that is, for having shown compassion to their social inferiors through their financial generosity. By publicly naming local and national dignitaries who attended the Festival, as well as the financial contributions they gave, the perception of the Triennial Festival as Birmingham's premier cultural event was greatly enhanced. Indeed, as the century wore on, published lists comprised Prime Ministers, Members of Parliament, Mayors, the local aristocracy, gentry and manufacturers of local and national repute. The prestige they bestowed upon the Festival was, in turn, conferred back upon Birmingham's local élite. This practice of naming and listing was faithfully maintained throughout the Festival's existence.

Thus in Leipzig and Birmingham, the press developed in accordance with the parameters of each music culture. The content and manner of the criticism voiced reflected the emergent aesthetic and philosophical peculiarities. By way of emphasising particular, often extra-musical, matters, the reader was presented with a definition of what constitutes a public concert with which he could identify. The cultural prestige afforded to newspapers and journals as well as the enormous extent to which they could reach out to the general populace, meant that cultural norms and values were increasingly seen as natural and, therefore, immutable. The results of this will become evident in the following chapter.

Conclusion

Culture, although in entirely different ways, bestowed respectability and status upon the local élites, qualities that previously had been associated solely with property or birth. The new social order which began to take shape at the end of the eighteenth century offered a new range of opportunities which enabled the rising urban élites to make their mark. However, given the absence of any universal cultural standards transcending national borders, each middle class professed very specific assumptions about culture. These assumptions were plainly defined in each town by the wider religious and aesthetic peculiarities as they developed during the late eighteenth century. The discussion on aesthetics has demonstrated how both countries acquired mental attitudes which could support, and indeed inform, emergent cultural representations such as art. In Britain, aesthetics favoured, and indeed necessitated, tangible feelings, moral propriety and social benefit if art was to attain public legitimisation. In Germany, on the other hand, aesthetics were thought to reveal the higher, more ideal, nature of physical (and non-physical) entities. Whereas in England aesthetics were infused with, and indeed contingent on, the concerns of everyday life, in Germany, they were kept in a separate sphere, hermetically sealed off from mundane reality. However, supported by the divergent religious principles that underpinned each country's respective aesthetic ideals, art was equally provided in both towns with clearly delineated foundations. In particular, encouraged and disseminated by the press, such principles and ideas helped to define an emergent middle-class consciousness which was successfully able to impose itself on existing institutional frameworks. The result was a recognisable middle-class culture that was most visibly channelled through the Gewandhaus and the Triennial Festival, for example, in their particular types of repertoires, attitudes to composers as well as the architectural layout of the concert halls. All these phenomena will be discussed in the following chapter.

Notes

1. R. Roth, 'Von Wilhelm Meister zu Hans Castorp' in D. Hein, A. Schulz (eds), *Bürgerkultur im 19. Jahrhundert*, p. 123.
2. The Augsburg Confessional Peace (1555) declared that a monarch or a duke could decide on the religious identity, that is, Catholicism or Lutheranism, of the state including all its subjects. The Peace of Westphalia (1648) extended the choice to include Calvinism. The Westphalian settlement 'froze' the territorial distribution of the three religions which meant that if there were territorial changes after 1648 which transferred territory of one confession to the prince of another confession, the territory retained its original religion. This increased particularism not just by preserving confessional diversity but also by introducing such diversity into single polities. For example, when the Saxon King Friedrich August became King of Poland in 1697, he converted to Catholicism even though Saxony retained its Protestant identity. This

helps to account for Leipzig's pride in its Protestant roots when compared to the Catholic roots of Saxony's ruling house whose seat was in Dresden – Leipzig's main rival. Thus, whilst Protestantism became associated with the national state in England and Catholicism in France, the German territories remained characterised by religious and political particularism until well into the nineteenth century.

3. Z. Batsche, J. Garber (eds), *Von der Ständischen zur Bürgerlichen Gesellschaft. Politisch-soziale Theorien in Deutschland der zweiten Hälfte des 18. Jahrhunderts* (Frankfurt/Main: Suhrkamp, 1981), p. 13.

4. D. Hill (ed.) G. E. Lessing, *Nathan der Weise*, New German Studies Texts & Monographs, 9 (Hull: University of Hull, 1988), p. 21.

5. For a clear example of how a distinctly German literary and dramatic tradition was to be fashioned, see the dispute between Gottsched and Lessing during the 1740s. Here Lessing attempted to argue against the perceived sterility inherent in the French neo-classical tradition which Gottsched continued to praise as a model to German writers.

6. N. Elias, *Über den Prozess der Zivilisation, Soziogenetische und phychogenetische Untersuchungen, Vol 1: Wandlungen des Verhaltens in den weltlichen Oberschichten des Abendlandes* (Amsterdam: Suhrkamp, 1997 [1939]), pp. 98–114.

7. D. Hempton, 'Enlightenment and Faith' in P. Langford, *The Eighteenth Century, 1688–1815* (Oxford: Oxford University Press, 2002), p. 76.

8. There is no exact timeline as to when the Enlightenment came to a close across Europe. Compared to Britain and France, in the German territories it started and ended much later.

9. Hempton, 'Enlightenment and Faith' in Langford, *The Eighteenth Century*, p. 92.

10. L. E. Grugel, *Society and Religion During the Age of Industrialisation: Christianity in Victorian England* (Washington: University Press of America, 1979), p. 27.

11. A. D. Gilbert, *Religion and Society in Industrial England: Church, Chapel and Social Change, 1740–1914* (London: Longman, 1976), p. 58.

12. Sheehan, *German History*, p. 561.

13. Nipperdey, *Deutsche Geschichte 1800–1866*, p. 429. It was out of this liberal Protestantism that a more scientifically radical branch developed which, thoroughly Hegelian, produced the likes of D. F. Strauss *Das Leben Jesu* (1835). Translation taken from T. Nipperdey, *Germany from Napoleon to Bismarck*, translated by D. Nolan, p. 379.

14. M. Eksteins, *Rites of Spring: The Great War and the Birth of the Modern Age* (New York: Doubleday, 1990 [1989]), p. 67.

15. H. McLeod, *Secularisation in Western Europe, 1848–1914* (Basingstoke: Palgrave Macmillan, 2000), p. 157.

16. T. Nipperdey, *Deutsche Geschichte 1866–1918, Bd 1: Arbeitswelt und Bürgergeist* (Munich: Beck, 1992), p. 528.

17. Eksteins, *Rites of Spring*, p. 67.

18. G. N. G. Orsini, *Coleridge and German Idealism: A Study in the History of Philosophy with Unpublished Materials from Coleridge's Manuscripts* (London: Carbondale, 1969), p. 66.

19. M. C. Beardsley, *Aesthetics from Classical Greece to the Present: A Short History* (New York: The Macmillan Company, 1966), pp. 173, 177.

20. N. K. Baker, T. Christensen, *Aesthetics and the Art of Musical Composition in the German Enlightenment. Selected Writings of Johann Georg Sulzer and Heinrich Christoph Koch* (Cambridge: Cambridge University Press, 1995), p. 4.

21. Usher, 'Observations on Music' in *The Harmonicon*, Vol. 5 (1827), p. 45.

22. H. Glover, 'Letters upon Musical Art No 1' in *The Musical World*, No. 18, Vol. 22 (1847), p. 283.

23. Anon., 'On the Just Objects in Music' in the *Quarterly Musical Magazin and Review*, No. 21, Vol. 6 (1824), p. 34–43.

24. The Shaftesburian idea of an 'inner' or 'moral' sense, perpetuated further by the Scottish Common Sense School (Adam Smith, James Beattie), had long been merged with British empiricism. The imagination is capable, through an effort of sympathetic intuition, of identifying itself with its object. By means of this identification, the sympathetic imagination grasps, through a kind of direct experience and feeling, the distinctive nature, identity or 'truth' of the object of its contemplation. See W. J. Bate, *From Classic to Romantic* (New York: Harper & Row, 1961 [1946]), p. 132.

25. Other, more practical reasons for this lack of appreciation in Britain include the lack of professional institutions which could foster instrumental music and the lack of employment opportunities as granted by, for example, aristocratic patronage.

26. J. Beattie, 'On the Power of Association in Music' in *The Harmonicon*, Vol. 3 (1830), p. 107.

27. First attempts were made by rationalists such as Leibniz who believed that the mathematical and rational structure in harmony could provide pleasure because listening to music (that is, following the mathematical calculus) makes us experience enjoyment even before anyone had explained the mathematical relation.

28. E. Fubini, *Geschichte der Musikästhetik* (Stuttgart: J. B. Metzler, 1997), p. 198. Translated from Italian by Sabina Kienlechner.

29. K. Hammermeister, *The German Aesthetic Tradition* (Cambridge: Cambridge University Press, 2002), p. 3. Baumgarten's primary interest was to strengthen the rationalist system by including neglected elements. Rather than breaking with the metaphysics of Leibniz and his populariser Christian Wolff, Baumgarten's aim was to further the cause of rational cognition by arguing that sensual cognition is essential for rational thought.

30. J. J. Sheehan, *Museums in the German Art World: From the End of the Old Regime to the Rise of Modernism* (Oxford: Oxford University Press, 2000), p. 5.

31. Orsini, *Coleridge*, p. 160.

32. S. Sadie (ed.), *New Grove Dictionary of Music and Musicians*, Vol. 19, p. 613.

33. Sheehan, *Museums*, p. 47.

34. L. Pikulik, *Frühromantik: Epoche-Werke-Wirkung* (München: Beck, 1992), p. 34.

35. C. Dahlhaus, *Nineteenth-Century Music* (Berkeley: University of California Press, 1989), p. 31. Translated from the German by J. B. Robinson.

36. Bate, *From Classic to Romantic*, p. 160.

37. K. Ameriks, 'Introduction: Interpreting German Idealism' in K. Ameriks (ed.), *The Cambridge Companion to German Idealism* (Cambridge: Cambridge University Press, 2000), p. 8. In Britain, idealism was treated primarily as negative metaphysical doctrine, as something by which only the 'unreal' could be expressed.

38. W. Faulstich, *Die bürgerliche Mediengesellschaft 1770–1830*, Geschichte der Medien Band 4 (Göttingen: Vandenhoeck & Ruprecht, 2002), p. 21. Faulstich goes as far as to suggest that the new media culture created the identity of the 'Bürger', instilling 'bourgeois' ideals into 'society'.

39. B. Anderson, *Imagined Communities: Reflections on the Origins and Spread of Nationalism* (London: Verso, 1991 [1983]), p. 35.

40. W. Kaschuba, 'German Bürgerlichkeit after 1800: Culture as Symbolic Practice' in J. Kocka, G. Mitchell (eds), *Bourgeois Society in 19th Century Europe* (Oxford: Berg Publishers, 1993 [1988]), p. 392.

41. J. Habermas, *The Structural Transformation of the Public Sphere: An Inquiry into a Category of Bourgeois Society* (Cambridge: Polity, 2000 [1962]), p. 38.

42. Dahlhaus, *Nineteenth-Century Music*, p. 246. Emphasis in the original text.

43. V. Titel (ed.), *Heinrich Brockhaus: Tagebücher Deutschland 1834 bis 1872* (Erlangen: Filos, 2004), p. 406. 'One should not one-sidedly close oneself off to something which the whole public acknowledges and that precisely in this way has acquired its legitimisation' (14 March 1852).

44. Aurelian, 'The Cultivation of Musical Taste and Musical Expression' in *The Musical World*, No. 2, Vol. 31, 8 January 1853.

45. Thomaner are boarding students who perform at religious services at St Thomas Church, Leipzig. To this day, the town is responsible for financing their lodgings and education.

46. U. Schmitt, *Revolution im Konzertsaal: Zur Beethovenrezeption im 19. Jahrhundert* (Mainz, Schott, 1990), p. 22. 'It was less the matter itself but its effect, which had to be experienced, which appeared as intoxicating, sensational, vertiginous and staggering to the modern individual of the nineteenth century.'

47. Titel, *Heinrich Brockhaus*, p. 71. 'In the evening I listened to Beethoven's Seventh Symphony in the Concert. There are wonderful passages but also, like in most of Beethoven's compositions, many strange ones for which, at least, I lack understanding, and in as far as the harmony of all separate parts to one another is required in a work of art, this symphony could not assert its entitlement to the name of such. But still, there is an infinite charm in this symphony; one feels elevated, touched, is pleased, and then finds oneself repelled again.'

48. Fubini, *Geschichte der Musikästhetik*, p. 237. 'Subjectivity in Romantic music criticism ... is based on a conception of music that sees in it the expression of feelings at a level in which feelings enable us to enter infinity and let us feel the secret pulse of the universe. Thus, judgement does not run into danger of losing itself in the peculiarities of the subject because the universality of feeling grants it objectivity and universal validity.'

49. H. G. Nägeli, 'Versuch einer Norm für die Recensenten der musikalischen Zeitung' in *AMZ*, No. 14 (1812), p. 231.

50. Nägeli, 'Versuch einer Norm' in *AMZ*, No. 14 (1812), p. 231. 'Such rules are to be established here, wherever possible with both supporting evidence and proofs that they are right and indispensable. In as far as they are then acknowledged as such by the reviewers of this journal, they can serve them as the norm in the future.'

51. From 1835 Robert Schumann took over as chief editor and Robert Friese published it after 1837.

52. To justify the closure of this journal, the publishers commented that there simply was no need for an 'Allgemeine' (general) journal anymore. It seems, however, that the reason for Breitkopf & Härtel's decision to discontinue the journal was purely financial.
53. 'The Birmingham Festival' in *The Musical Examiner*, 17 November 1843.
54. Anon., 'Birmingham Musical Festival' in *The Musical World*, No. 39, Vol. 18 (1843), pp. 323–326.
55. *Aris' Birmingham Gazette*, 11 September 1843.

3
The Late Eighteenth Century to 1847

Introduction

In the public concert, the assumptions about culture as well as aesthetic developments found their fullest expression. Both influenced every aspect of the public concert: repertoires, perceptions of composers and artists, interior and exterior architecture of the concert halls and the formation of behavioural norms. Again, the starting point from which both music cultures developed was similar: the socio-economic changes taking place in the patterns of public music-making during the middle of the eighteenth century gave the rising middle class the opportunity to transform an older established cultural institution into one representing and promoting its values and ideas. An examination of these initial changes is the basis of this chapter.

The Emergence of the Bourgeois Public Concert

The public concert as a form of communal activity was an imitation of concerts held at aristocratic and royal courts. The important difference, however, was that all members of the bourgeois class had, in theory, equal access and rights which were written down in a formal constitution.[1] In theory, access to the concert was a right to be exercised rather than settled by invitation, unlike the practice at court concerts. In line with the egalitarian principle of individual rights instead of birth right and associated privileges, everyone who was able to pay, either at the evening box office, through annual subscription or the ballot box, could participate in the concert hall's events. A confluence of socio-economic and cultural developments added to the appearance of a distinctly bourgeois phenomenon. These developments are reflected primarily in the progressively institutionalised repertoire as an indicator of the prevailing public taste, secondly, in the role of the conductor and performer as conveyors of artistic ideals, and thirdly, in the concert hall as a meeting space that visually confirmed the new status of the bourgeoisie and its cultural ethos.

First, for much of the eighteenth century composers still wrote for a specific patron and therefore with a specific sense of occasion and type of building in mind: a cantata for the cathedral service, the *Festliche Hymne* for the royal court or opera for the theatre. Once liberated from the restrictions of Church and court, music acquired the status of 'free art', a condition that was necessary for it to enter the world of the bourgeois. There it became swiftly imbued with bourgeois cultural norms and values which ultimately determined what was suitable for cultural consumption. Given the vast spectrum of music available to the Gewandhaus Board of Directors and Birmingham's Festival Committees (of any given period and occasion, ranging from the past to the present), the choice of compositions actually performed and developed for the concert repertoire provides crucial information about the cultural preferences of the bourgeoisie. The type, form and chronological framework of these repertoires thus give a clear indication of the principles and sentiments that guided the middle class, both in Leipzig and Birmingham.

Secondly, the changing status of the practising musician – composer, conductor, soloists – must be considered. Having become part of the commercial world by offering their talents – themselves as much as their work – in the market place, performers strove for success, standing and wealth like any other member of middle-class society. Rather than the preferences of an aristocrat, it was now the norms and values of the concert public that had to be met. The artist who embodied the latter during the first half of the nineteenth century was Felix Mendelssohn. This circumstance is particularly interesting as both Leipzig and Birmingham claimed the privilege of a special relationship with Mendelssohn. They did so, however, for entirely different reasons. The different perceptions of Mendelssohn as artistic authority, in turn, point towards different understandings of his cultural role in both towns.

Thirdly, the new concert halls built during the late eighteenth and early nineteenth centuries demonstrate how the traditional symbiotic relationship between types of music and types of architecture had ceased to exist. It was not so much genres and types of compositions that determined the architectural setting, but the (often extra-musical) cultural preferences of the bourgeoisie. The differing architectural designs of Birmingham's Town Hall and Leipzig's Gewandhaus offer striking evidence for this fundamental change. Each of these phenomena – the repertoire, the artist and the concert hall – developed distinctively in the two towns. Distinctions arose as they were influenced and shaped by the different connotations conferred upon culture, as well as under the impact of a curious fusion of religious, philosophic and aesthetic developments stemming from both the Enlightenment and counter-Enlightenment movements. What remained similar to both, however, was the ways in which both Leipzig's *Bürgertum* and Birmingham's middle class utilised the potential that presented itself in public manifestations (the concert) and artistic institutions (repertoires, artists and concert halls). It was through these phenomena that the emergent middle-class ethos was able to achieve its clearest expression in that the public concert helped Birmingham's and Leipzig's middle class to further define and propagate their respective values regarding education, moral propriety and public status. In doing so, it allowed them to make more definite assumptions about their socio-cultural identity and distinctive roles within the societies they lived. This proved particularly important during times when political representation, for example, still eluded them.

The Repertoires

The repertoires projected an image of how the body of concert-goers liked to perceive itself and how it liked to be perceived by others. The concert programmes of Leipzig's Gewandhaus and Birmingham's Triennial Festival provide ample evidence for this, as each highlight patterns in musical preferences that can be used to identify the cultural ethos present within each concert hall and its public. Set in a socio-political context, the correlation between historical circumstances and resultant distinctiveness of ideas and institutions can be amply demonstrated.

Leipzig

The great crusades for national independence encapsulated by such dates as 1775 (Poland) and 1776 (America) made a great impact on the German territories, particularly during the years of French occupation since the late eighteenth century. Feelings of national unity focused on Gutenberg and Lutheran Protestantism, Germanic mythology, legends and language intensified; 'foreign', that is, French language and artistic styles, still a point of reference for cultural and social standing within aristocratic and royal circles, was shunned in the light of an emerging nationalistic consciousness.[2] During the late eighteenth and early nineteenth centuries, however, this nationalistic consciousness was carried mainly by the literary sphere. Until the inception, dissemination and acceptance of transcendental idealism during the 1810s, music was still deemed to be an entertainment, rather than an art committed to higher purposes and thus unable to convey intellectual, moral or nationalistic stimulus. The Gewandhaus repertoire[3] provides evidence for this: although instrumental music came to the fore from the 1780s onwards – particularly with Haydn, Friedrich Schneider, later with Andreas and Bernhard Romberg, Dussek, Anton Eberl and Rudolph Kreuzer – operatic excerpts, sung in Italian, retained their popularity unchanged. Thus, the duets and arias by foreign composers such as Pasquale Anfossi, Dominico Cimarosa, Gazzaniga, Pietro Guglielmi, Vinzenzo Martini, Paisiello, Piccini, Antonio Sacchini, Antonio Salieri, Guiseppe Sarti, Storace and Tarchi as well as those of German origins such as Carl Heinrich Graun, Johann Adolph Hasse, Franz Seidelmann and Joseph Weigel remained immensely popular during the last two decades of the eighteenth century. Certainly, the majority of these were no longer performed after the turn of the century. But neither were composers professing a penchant towards instrumental music. Thus, the popularity of Carl Ditters von Dittersdorf, Adalbert Gyrowetz, Franz Anton Hoffmeister, Leopold Kozeluch, Johann Amadeus Naumann, Franz Pichl, Ignanz Pleyel, Anton Rosetti, Robert Schuster, Stamitz, Giovanni Vauhall, Anton Wranitzky and Anton Zimmermann did not extend into the 1800s.

Whilst some were forgotten over time, others achieved considerable prominence in the Gewandhaus repertoire. Again, there were instrumental as well as composers of operatic works with no discernible distinction made either between a composer's origins or the language chosen for the libretto. Thus the works of such varied composers as Johann Friedrich Reichardt, Christoph Willibald Ritter von Gluck, Friedrich Heinrich Himmel, Gasparo Spontini, Zingarelli Ferdinand Paer, Vincenzo Righini, Peter von Winter and Simon Mayr were equally well received and performed during a time when German art, literature and philosophy were dominating the culture sphere of the *Bürgertum*. The Gewandhaus would have appeared uninterested in the wider political and social developments, had it not been for the supreme and unconditional reverence for Haydn, Mozart, Spohr and, in particular, Beethoven since the 1810s. Whilst Haydn and Mozart had already dominated the symphonic and instrumental part of the Gewandhaus repertoire since the 1780s (alongside, of course, their religious and operatic works), it was Beethoven who rose to cultural supremacy during the 1810s. The table below (Table 3.1)

Table 3.1 Premières of Beethoven's Symphonies and their First Performance in the Gewandhaus

Beethoven symphonies	Premieres in Vienna	First performance in Leipzig
1	April 1800	November 1801
2	April 1803	April 1804
3	April 1805	January 1807
4	March 1807	March 1811
5	December 1808	February 1809[101]
6	December 1808	March 1809
7	December 1813	December 1816
8	February 1814	January 1818
9	May 1824	March 1826

demonstrates the short time spans between the Viennese premieres of Beethoven's symphonies and their first performances in Leipzig.[4] In stark contrast to other public concerts, in the Gewandhaus, Beethoven's symphonies were performed 137 times between 1801 and 1827; by 1820, performances of his works outnumbered those of Haydn and Mozart combined.[5] Leipzig's reverence for the classical trinity, particularly Beethoven, resulted in the town being commonly perceived as one of the major centres of contemporary music throughout the German territories.

This veneration for their instrumental works, however, had very little to do with an increase of a nationalistic consciousness and resultant penchant for all things German. Rather, this reverence for Haydn, Mozart and Beethoven was directly related to the rise of idealism during the 1810s which led to the acceptance of instrumental music as the most supreme of all the arts, as this extract from an essay published in 1815 by Amadeus Wendt, a regular contributor to the *AMZ*, demonstrates:

Wenn allen übrigen Künsten etwas vorliegt, was erst durch den Wunderblick des Genius verklärt aus dem Boden der Wirklichkeit erhoben und in das Elysium der Ideen versetzt zu seyn scheint, so scheint die Tonkunst gleichsam in diesem Lande selbst erzeugt, und redet, gleich dem Weltgeist, durch Sturm und Donner, durch das sanfte Wehen des Frühlings, ... eine Wundersprache, die nur dem verständlich ist, dem das Gehör nicht eine Fülle äussere Klänge, sondern das Innere der Welt und die geheimsten Tiefen des Herzens ausschliesst, in die kein sterbliches Auge schaut.[6]

Similarly, E. T. A. Hoffmann whose essay *Beethovens Instrumentalmusik* (1813) has become the archetypal expression of this aesthetic attitude, declared:

> [Musik] sucht das tiefe Gemüt für die Ahnungen der Freudigkeit, die herrlicher und schöner als hier in der beengten Welt, aus einem unbekannten Lande herüber, ein inneres, wonnesvolles Leben in der Brust entzündet, einen höheren Ausdruck, als ihn geringe Worte, die nur der begangenen irdischen Lust eigen, gewähren können.[7]

This is vintage German transcendentalism. In this view, music represents an unknown world which has nothing in common with the prosaic confines of the external one. Within this unknown world, all definite expressions are left behind the veil of a transcendent longing within the individual's inner world. This in itself might explain the reluctance of the *AMZ* and the Gewandhaus, both fully supportive of Romantic idealism, to engage with the nationalistic agenda which flooded the cultural sphere of the day. (Who would have been oblivious to, for example, J. G. Fichte's *Reden an die deutsche Nation* and Ernst Moritz Arndt's *Was ist des Deutschen Vaterland?*) Similarly, whilst Friedrich Rochlitz, the *AMZ*'s first editor, might have been actively promoting music's importance to national culture during the late 1790s,[8] no such things can be observed in his capacity as a member of the Gewandhaus Board of Directors – a post he held between 1805 and 1842. Here, his primary role was to ensure that the new ideals concerning the propriety of art were maintained. As in the political sphere, the gulf between literary treatment and institutional reality, so typical of the German public sphere, remained potent; even during the 'wars of liberation', the idea of 'Germany' very much existed merely within the romantic imagination.

The fact that Leipzig's Gewandhaus did not respond to these nationalist trends is indicative of the general impotence of Germany's public sphere. After all, during French occupation and subsequent military battles, Leipzig was hit where the town was most vulnerable: in its economic sphere. The trade blockade against Britain imposed by the French until 1813, as well as tariff policies favouring France, naturally reduced the possibility of any real economic upturn. Following liberation, the Russian authorities levied punitive taxes because of Leipzig's commercial ties with the French, thus further suppressing economic growth. At the Vienna Congress of 1815, Leipzig lost out on internal markets, as 58 per cent of Saxony's land mass was distributed to the victors.[9] Furthermore, the destruction of Leipzig's infrastructure during the final stages of the war was considerable: the villages outside the town became one massive battlefield and the inner town one gigantic infirmary with most public buildings, including the Gewandhaus, serving as military hospitals. Whilst these were clearly local grievances, they did not by themselves foster any pro-national allegiances. Neither did it presage that Leipzig's *Bürgertum* saw themselves as martyrs of the German nation. Rather, they saw themselves at the receiving end of Saxony's (or rather its royal family – the Wettiner's) diplomatic inanity perceived through its alliance with the French against Prussia. Compared to Dresden, the seat of the royal house, Leipzig and its bourgeois élites were, after all, shouldering the costs of the Wettiner's alliance with Napoleon. As anti-aristocratic sentiments do not by themselves promote pro-German reactions, the Gewandhaus did not constitute a means – public or clandestine – through which the ideal of the 'German nation' and its cultural foundations could be defined or promoted. Rather, it was primarily designed to endorse the ideals of Leipzig's middle class. Despite local hostilities towards French occupation, Leipzig's local institutions were not reformed to serve nationalist ends. Just as the 'national' institutions such as the Holy Roman Empire, the Confederation of the Rhine, the German Confederation[10] and the North German Confederation meant little to 'Germans' until the 1870s,[11] so too was the Gewandhaus never part of the greater nationalistic crusade.

Two reasons stand out. First, in the wake of the Congress of Vienna which inaugurated the German Restoration period and led to the formation of the *Deutscher Bund* – a loose organisation of individual states and principalities which had little impact on the autonomy of each so far as economy, trade or justice was concerned – liberal aspirations to national unity were indefinitely obscured. Indeed, according to bourgeois–liberal views, the *Deutscher Bund* became an instrument of the reactionary forces against the unity of the nation both by constitutional constraints and by means of fierce political repression.[12] In such an atmosphere, culture, particularly when enjoyed in public, could not be used to channel political aspirations to national unity. Secondly, as the previous chapter explained, aesthetics in Germany favoured non-referential qualities in music. The elusive character of transcendental idealism precludes any involvement with political reality. Aesthetics and thus music were deemed a realm far removed from an actual, public and time-related existence. During the German Restoration period, which began in the same year that Wendt published his essay in the *AMZ*, this flight into private isolation was little short of a blessing in disguise. Especially since the *Karlsbader Beschlüsse* (Carlsbad Degrees) of 1819, the political sphere was consolidated in its authoritarian and repressive disposition, giving further incentive to the withdrawal either into the complacent world of the inner self, defined by passivity and resignation, or the world of art, science, history, characterised by its staunchly apolitical and ethereal overtones. Just as the modern and progressive spirit, once thought to have been encapsulated in Beethoven's heroic period, had become largely irrelevant by the 1820s, so too was instrumental music increasingly reduced to serve the apolitical cultural ambitions of the bourgeoisie.[13] As the 1830s, a decade of insurgent uprisings throughout Europe, opened, the artistic standing of the Gewandhaus was purely determined by aesthetic qualities. Yet this same period also witnessed wholesale prosecution of professors and students (especially at Leipzig's University that had suffered continuous political oppression since the Congress of Vienna) with departments such as History and *Germanistik*, which had actively and directly contributed to liberal thinking, being targeted in particular.

Similarly, the literary sphere became increasingly politicised highlighting a continually growing schism between music and its sister arts. The July Revolution of 1830, for example, led to the formation of a loosely connected literary movement, named Young Germany (*Junges Deutschland*) with Karl Gutzkow, Heinrich Laube, Ludwig Börne, Georg Büchner and Heinrich Heine as its principal advocates. Their highly politicised literature caused Metternich to call for the prohibition of the movement, citing primarily its dangerous contribution to the abandonment of morality and moral worth of the nation.[14] The closest musical equivalent to the ideas of *Junges Deutschland* was Robert Schumann and other contributors to the *NZfM*, but even his most satirical assaults refrained from overt political discourse. Given that there was no institutional support, such as musicology pursued at universities, no high-profile witch-hunts (such as those of the *Göttinger Sieben*, Robert Prutz and Heinrich Hoffmann von Fallersleben[15] who were dismissed from their university employment following another wave of state-organised repression) were ever associated with music. Removed from any non-aesthetic concerns, concert music became the exclusive domain of a bourgeois culture divorced from everyday political issues.

This process was helped by the perceived intricacy and equivocation of instrumental music, first celebrated by the Romantic Idealists. By emphasising the elusive, thus exalted, nature of instrumental music, Kant's successors inadvertently contributed to the then commonly held assumption that music was accessible only to those who were open to this mysterious musical language. Not everyone, it turned out, could subscribe to Beethoven's realm of ideas. After all:

> Seine Gefühlsmannigfaltigkeit ist unermesslich, seine Töne verkünden immer eine nie empfundne, nie genossene Wonne, das Ueberidische oder Unterirdische wird an den irdischen Klang geknüpft, und stets erscheint er neu und unerschöpflich. [...] ... dass es ihm eben so wohl möglich ist, den tiefsten Abgrund des kämpfenden Herzens, wie den süssen Liebeszauber des unschuldigsten Gemüths, den herbsten, tiefsten Schmerz, ..., das Erhabenste, wie das Lieblichste in Tönen zu schildern und auszusprechen, so neigt doch sein Geist zu den Darstellungen tiefsinnigen Ernstes, feuriger Schwärmerey und erhabner Pracht mit vorzüglicher Liebe hin, und setzt die höchsten Affecte in harmonische Bewegung.[16]

By means of such rhetoric, the bourgeois – educated, sensitive and persuaded of the existence of deeper emotional and mystical spheres – was thus provided with an excellent means of cultural distinction. It was cultural distinction in the sense that any understanding of Beethoven's music required a thorough comprehension of the aesthetic norms which nourished it. Compared with the perceived superficiality of an opera culture which was, after all, still dependent on 'mundane' representational and textual references, the understanding of instrumental music was deemed to require a higher quality of sensitivity and education. This education could only be provided by way of partaking in cultural institutions such as attending concerts and reading music journals.

The Making of a Canon

The greater the advancement of the awareness of essentially bourgeois musical understanding in Germany, the more this needed to be provided with cultural and historical legitimacy. This was achieved, via the press, in two ways: firstly by proposing a correlation between the rise of the middle class and the rise of the symphony as the apotheosis of instrumental music; and secondly, by associating the ancient classical ideal (which was refashioned during the eighteenth century) with the instrumental music of the early nineteenth century. Consequently, during the late 1810s, the *AMZ* embarked on a series of essays designed to stress and legitimise the specifically bourgeois character of instrumental music, with the rise of the symphony as its epitome. The ascent of bourgeois music culture thus coincided with the arrival of Joseph Haydn with whom the new age of the symphony was thought to have commenced. The comparison with opera which dominated the musical culture of aristocratic courts symbolically echoed the disparity between the established, hierarchical and rigid social order and the modern, bourgeois-dominated mobile society; between the traditionally frivolous entertainment of aristocratic court culture (particularly in Dresden) and contemporary, progressive and enlightened culture as could be found in the Gewandhaus; and finally between excessively lavish Catholic baroque traditions and ascetic Protestant neo-classicism. The latter already points to the second path to cultural legitimisation: 'classicism'. Indeed, the term began to acquire currency within the music journal during the early 1820s.

Previously, Romantic Idealism had helped instrumental music to be celebrated as a legitimate and respectable art. Now, classicism helped to provide many of the norms and values which subsequently determined the ethos of *Kultur* in the Gewandhaus. The culture of antiquity, seen through contemporary eyes as a time of prosperity that had nourished unparalleled levels of artistic creation, was revived (or reinvented) as an ideal in eighteenth-century Germany, indeed in Europe as a whole. The key figure in this process was Johann Joachim Winckelmann (1717–1768) with his highly influential *Gedanken über die Nachahmung der griechischen Werke in der Malerei und der Bildhauerkunst* (Reflections on the Imitation of Greek Works in Painting and Sculpture, 1755) and his *Geschichte der Kunst des Alterthums* (History of Ancient Art, 1764). Since Winckelmann, it was believed that the study of classical antiquity would develop not only the aesthetic sensibility of modern man, but also sharpen his intellectual and moral faculties, for the act of contemplating Greek art, Winckelmann argued, informed the mind as much as it touched the senses. Underlying this assumption is Winckelmann's association of the beauty of Greek plastic art with ethical standards: the 'noble simplicity' (lack of frivolous ornaments) and 'serene grandeur' (avoidance of emotional excess) of plastic objects reflected similar properties of the soul. This meant that (timeless) qualities such as nobility, composure, beauty and moral grandeur could all be cultivated within individuals through the pursuit of art, thus helping humanity to regain its ideal of perfection. If the elitist connotations of the concert hall were not already achieved through the valorisation of aesthetics since the early 1810s, the noble aspirations now conferred upon music by way of its classical properties irrevocably spelled out the difference between the frenchified aristocracy with its penchant for mere 'civilisation' – the superficial display of decorous manners, customs and rarified language – and the middle class with its affinity for what it believed to be the profound authenticity of *Kultur*.

Following Winckelmann, classicism's positive impact on the modern individual was reinforced and advanced by other leading minds of the late eighteenth and early nineteenth centuries: Lessing, Kant, Herder, Schiller, Wilhelm von Humboldt, and, of course, Goethe. For all their differences of temperament, these men were united in the conviction that the aesthetic and moral education of the individual would necessarily lead to the improvement of society as a whole. Indeed, the September massacres of 1792 in France had thoroughly undermined the belief among the literary and intellectual élite at large that a new social order could ever be advanced by radicalism and revolution. Rather, by the late eighteenth century, it was thought that only the enduring search for the timeless values of beauty and truth would procure the refinement of humanity and thus lay the foundations of a just society.

Hence, the trajectory of German history did and would always directly impact on the definition of the classical ideal. Whereas during the 1770s and 1780s, classicism, in plays and literature, developed as a direct counteraction against the moral distortion and corruption of the German courts with their values rooted in the *ancien régime*, during the mid-1820s, classicism had been relieved of such noble obligations.[17] In this form, during the 1820s, classicism entered into the realm of instrumental music which, in turn, entered the timeless and unchanging world of bourgeois *Kultur*. Music was the last of the arts to undergo this transformation. Whilst formal classical characteristics, such as symmetry, balance, proportion, are obviously reflected in the structure of, say, the sonata or the four-movement symphony, it was through the values attributed to German classicism that art and aesthetics were thought to exert a beneficial influence on the moral health of the modern citizen. As with the literary classicism of the Weimar period (from the 1790s), classicism in music distanced itself from political interests and, during the 1820s, was removed from socio-political criticism. Instead, the classical ideal of ennobled humanity (which dominated literary production since the late eighteenth century) came to the foreground, complete with the values of nobility, beauty, composure and so on.

Under such circumstances, instrumental music became less susceptible to new ideas produced by the forward thrust of time; indeed, it was no longer deemed part of time at all. The decline of progressive sentiments clearly manifested itself in a repertoire pattern which, from the 1830s, showed little signs of change even though all Leipzig's musical heroes had been dead for a decade or two.[18] Mozart and Beethoven retained their prime position in the Gewandhaus repertoire; no one believed that their achievements could be superseded by contemporary endeavours. Accordingly, journal critics never ceased to deplore the void they believed was left after Beethoven's death. A Biedermeier mentality of gentle nostalgia had taken hold; its peculiar pathos spawned the age of *Epigonentum*, the evocative term which denotes derivative writers forced to work in the shadow of greater predecessors.

However, the elimination of 'progress' from this increasingly docile cultural sphere provided fertile ground for the institutionalisation of the classical canon as an indispensable vehicle of bourgeois respectability. The classical ideal, taken out of its historical context, was made universally valid, and a discernment and knowledge of what was 'classic' (of whatever historical period) became part of a humanist education essential to bourgeois notions of *Kultur*. Any value judgements made of classicism depended on reception; and the prestigious accolade now automatically accorded to classicism depended, in turn, on the willingness of the concert-goer to acknowledge the classical status of a composition. In return, such acknowledgement demonstrated the educational and cultural refinement of the audience. The underlying basis of this development was the contention that no single historic epoch could claim a monopoly on classicism. Rather, 'any historical epoch in which mental improvement and education were striven for, and borne fruits to it as a result, has necessarily produced truly classical works'.[19] In an attempt to legitimise its pervasive influence, the early nineteenth century was now deemed such an epoch with Leipzig's bourgeoisie as its vanguard. Under middle-class patronage, the culmination of all artistic and educational advances to date had been achieved with Beethoven via Haydn and Mozart. Such a powerful socio-cultural construct as classicism was not something the *AMZ*, as the mouthpiece of Leipzig's music culture, would lightly jettison. Instead, by the mid-1830s, all the critical forces in the *AMZ* coalesced to form a united front against the new generation of composers whose output was considered as little more than artistic mediocrity, a manifestation, even, of decline. This was the beginning of a cultural schism between the traditionalists and the 'modernisers' which was to last for the best part of the nineteenth century. A comparison of the literary output of the two journals highlights their contrary perspectives.

The main object of contention between the *AMZ* and the *NZfM* during the mid-1830s was Hector Berlioz. Whereas to the *AMZ*, Beethoven posed the absolute apotheosis of instrumental music, to Schumann and the *NZfM*, Berlioz was celebrated as his worthy successor: with his

Symphonie Fantastique, Berlioz brought to a conclusion what Beethoven had striven to do in his Ninth Symphony – namely to liberate instrumental music from its formal constraints.[20] With Berlioz's *Symphonie Fantastique*, the genre of instrumental music was deemed finally and irrevocably exhausted: 'Seine Instrumente ringen nach dem Worte, wie nach der Erlösung, ebenso wie die Bässe im letzten Satz der Beethoven'schen 9ten Symphonie.'[21] The *AMZ*, by contrast, saw in the *Symphonie Fantastique* little more than artistic degeneration. First, Berlioz's choice of subject matter – his intense depiction of love, including dark premonitions, jealousies, opium overdose and ensuing visions of murder and execution – was hardly congruent with the noble aspirations of *Kultur*, let alone idealism's claim to non-referential qualities of instrumental music. Secondly, the way in which Berlioz musically portrayed these ideas was contrary to contemporary artistic beliefs. With Beethoven serving as artistic benchmark, the need for formal restraint and noble composure was still a prerequisite for all musical productions. In that respect, according to the *AMZ*, Berlioz duly failed:

> Wenn solche maasslos passionierte Kunstproducte oft eine augenblicklich das Gemüth in Beschlag nehmende Wirkung hervorbringen, so finden wir doch in Allem was sich dauernd als schön in der Kunst bewährt hat, noch etwas Anderes als diese stürmende Leidenschaftlichkeit. [...] in der Kunst überhaupt aber [ist] das ruhig Formale, im weitesten Sinn, an welchem das leidenschaftlich Bewegte und Veränderliche als bewegt und veränderlich sich zu erkennen gibt. [...] Auch wo die Anmuth hervortreten will, wo eine Melodie auftaucht und sich ergeben möchte, wird ihr alsbald mit harmonischer und rhythmischer Quälerei so arg zugesetzt, bis sie sich aus Verzweiflung selbst wieder in den Höllenpfuhl stürzt und sich die glühenden Wellen über den Kopf zusammenschlagen lässt, zu endloser Peinigung.[22]

Compositions created during a post-Beethoven age had evidently removed themselves from the objective logic of classicism. In its subjectivity, 'stormy passion' and its highly stylised and expressive lyricism it was too 'obscure' and wild to appeal to the judgement of the listener and the critic, still accustomed to the ideals of classical serenity and objective notions of beauty. The *Symphonie Fantastique*, defined by its excessive, intoxicating, stirring, draining melody and tone colours, immediately affecting the listener, could not be reconciled with traditional ideas of the 'eternally beautiful'. Thus, along with Schumann, Liszt and later Wagner, Berlioz remained outside the increasingly rigid

Gewandhaus canon. Although their works could be enjoyed as orchestral performances in the theatre, it would have been impossible to see them as part of the concept of *Kultur* as embodied by the Gewandhaus. If anything, it was by way of comparing the achievements of the new generation of composers with the artistic norms inherent in the Gewandhaus canon that audiences could, paradoxically, further their understanding of the pivotal role of classicism in bourgeois *Kultur*: 'Berlioz bildet ja das Publikum dadurch, dass die Massengewalt Berlioz ignorierte', the *NZfM* remarked somewhat scornfully.[23]

The continual endorsement of the Viennese School at the expense of the new generation of composers heralded the end of Leipzig's enviable reputation as a centre of contemporary music. At the same time, it presaged Leipzig's cultural conservatism in which the ideals of the classical canon, re-fashioned and re-coded, came to signify the essence of bourgeois music culture. By way of its supposed potential to reveal divine truth, it was venerated, almost consecrated. Its moral and artistic integrity unquestioned, classicism became a defining characteristic of Leipzig's 'cultural experience'. Shielded and protected, it proved cogent and lasting, remaining unaffected by major social and political upheavals. It even remained undiminished when 'war broke loose in the kingdom of harmony'.[24]

Leipzig in 1848

For almost 20 years, the Gewandhaus and Leipzig's main music journal, the *AMZ*, had endorsed the classical canon as the foremost cultural ideal. Held up as the epitome of learned and enlightened culture, Leipzig's music scene did little to encourage the performance of works of an entire new generation of composers active during the 1830s and 1840s, such as Berlioz, Liszt, Chopin and Schumann. Over time, this policy of exclusion created firm views on cultural propriety which also served as the cultural foundations of the Gewandhaus. By the early 1840s, however, this increasingly comfortable routine of ideology (and resultant cultural complacency) was disturbed by the advent of the *avant-garde Neudeutsche Schule*. Similar to the Young Hegelians (a movement criticising society and religion), the *Neudeutschen* represented an uprising against tradition and the mummification of life and nature. Driven by notions of modernity, progress and an unshakeable belief in the future, the movement rose against what they thought to be the increasing trivialisation of traditional concert life brought about by the commonly perceived permanence of classical values. For its protagonists – Liszt, Wagner, Franz Brendel and the writer's collective at the *NZfM* – art was necessarily the expression of its time and thus had to progress with time. As the movement was defined by Hegelian dialectic the continual development of art was thought to lead inevitably to its constant improvement. As the movement was also influenced by notions of worldliness, heathenism and political activism, suspicion of the *Neudeutschen* was not wanting.

Given the Gewandhaus' cultural stance, Leipzig provided fertile ground for a clash of ideologies, particularly during the turbulent months of 1848/1849. In many ways, 1848 demonstrates just how insular and removed from worldly reality bourgeois concert culture had become; the latter can be seen to represent the natural conclusion to the developments which had taken place since the 1810s – the early days of the aesthetic valorisation of music. The cultural conflict can be ascertained by contrasting contributions of the *AMZ* with those of the *NZfM* which, since Schumann's move to Dresden, was edited by Franz Brendel. Subjects of disagreements ranged from aesthetics to individual compositions, but it is through the concept of time, more precisely the arrival of a new *Zeitgeist* and its supposed impact on contemporary music and concert cultures, that the clash between conservatives and progressives becomes particularly clear.

The notion of a *Zeitgeist*, a force which acts through historical epochs defining and shaping each and expressing its spiritual/mental (*geistig*) and moral convictions, was certainly a well-known concept in educated circles as well as amongst the general reading public. From Voltaire, Herder, Kant, Schiller, Goethe to Hegel, the notion of identifiable qualities and values within separate epochs had been widely discussed and disseminated in journals and newspapers. Hegel's philosophical tenets, in particular, penetrated deeply into all artistic and intellectual disciplines: literature, the fine arts, music, history and philosophy. The effect on each was that they became purpose-oriented (*zweckorientiert*) in that each was supposed to affect and improve (in accordance with dialectical logic) the social, political and cultural condition of the day.[25] To the *Neudeutschen*, art had precisely this function.

The weeks and months before 1848 certainly raised hopes that a new *Zeitgeist* had arrived. After all, for the first time in history, Germany seemed as if it was about to be unified under a democratically elected parliament, ending over 30 years of political repression and censorship. The granting of the freedom of the press, in particular, meant that politics became the subject of free debate leading to unprecedented political discourse amongst all strata of German society. As will become evident, however, the Gewandhaus remained unaffected by this new *Zeitgeist*, and the concert free from all political contamination. The reasons for this can in part be found in the precarious political developments surrounding 1848/1849.

The dominance of traditional political forces, supported by a conservatively oriented bourgeois faction in Leipzig's first municipal council, was a decisive factor in the defeat of the bourgeois–liberal revolution in 1848/1849.[26] Unlike in Prussia, where the accession of the devoutly Christian King Friedrich Wilhelm IV in 1840 heralded an age of stubborn conservatism, the accession of the Saxon King Friedrich August II in 1836 led to attempts at liberal reform. During the early 1840s, however, continued liberal pressure tested his level of tolerance beyond breaking-point and these reforms were reversed. Further restrictions to existing civil rights were forced through when the conservative Traugott von Könneritz was elected First Minister in 1843 in place of the reform-enthusiast Bernhard von Lindenau. Some sporadic worker uprisings followed in 1845 in Leipzig which were further intensified due to worsening living conditions brought about by harvest failures and economic recession between 1845 and 1847. A final and decisive incentive was news arriving from France chronicling the successful announcement of the Republic. In March 1848, street barricades were erected and popular unrest followed in Munich, Vienna and Berlin, even though Saxony itself remained calm. Reforms extending to the freedom of the press, male voting rights and freedom of assembly and associations (creating an army of new organisations, the most important being a network of *Vaterlandsvereine* which resembled a political party) were carried through. However, these were repealed when renewed violent protest broke out in 1849 after King Friedrich Wilhelm IV of Prussia refused to accept the Imperial crown offered by the all-German Frankfurt Assembly. All hopes were thus directed towards the implementation of the Frankfurt constitution in the various kingdoms and principalities. Although the Saxon *Landtag*, dominated by liberals and democrats, willingly accepted the constitution, the Saxon King dissolved the *Landtag* after it passed new fiscal legislation without royal consultation. When the Prussian army threatened to enter the state in order to disperse a demonstration of the national guard, bloody uprisings followed in Dresden. Its unexpected escalation (the baroque Zwinger and the opera house built by Gottfried Semper – himself on the barricades – were burned down on the instruction of the 'professional revolutionary' Bakunin) led to many reconsidering their position and retreating; the overpowering military force finally led to the cessation of violence.

Following the end of political turmoil in 1849, the Saxon state minister denied the legitimacy of the liberal constitution as set out at the German

National Assembly in Frankfurt and re-introduced the old *Ständeverfas-sung*. Further repression of civil liberties as well as renewed censorship followed everywhere, and Leipzig's political life succumbed to it. The student fraternities and the entire German Worker's movement were disbanded and declared illegal. Well-known liberals, mainly academics and leaders of the *Leipziger Deutschen Verein*, which had supported the national constitution, were persecuted and expelled from Saxony; the best known examples were the Germanist Moritz Haupt, the historians Theodor Mommsen and Karl Biedermann, as well as the art historian Otto Jahn. Artists such as Semper and Wagner were also forced to leave.

Whilst a bourgeois minority, a large part of the *petite* bourgeoisie, students, peasants and the majority of Leipzig's workforce participated in the uprising, the majority of Leipzig's bourgeoisie, manufacturers, bankers and some academics, by contrast, remained passive. Instead, they pressed for a compromise with the crown and aristocracy in exchange for political power. This was despite the staggering rise of the Democratic movement, particularly since the mass protest of 1845, and despite the towering presence of Robert Blum in Leipzig's town politics.[27] Given the conservative stance of Leipzig's *Bürgertum* on the political stage during that time, it is hardly surprising that its cultural sphere remained equally hostile to the radical philosophies of the time. Add to it the peculiar nature of German aesthetics, and it is easy to see why Leipzig's music culture could retain its hallowed independence from even the most turbulent worldly affairs. The *AMZ*, as always, provides the necessary clue – a clue which also points to the culmination of more than 30 years' effort in constructing the necessary aesthetic framework for the maintenance and furtherance of such an attitude.

Because music, according to contemporary notions and the *AMZ*, is rooted in the *Gemüt* (disposition[28]) rather than reason, it remains necessarily non-conceptual (unlike philosophy or literature). Being non-conceptual, music could not be formulated in terms of the *Zeitgeist* and thus could not and should not ever be brought into conjunction with time or its transient socio-political ideas:

> Ist das Wesen des politischen Seins stets an die herrschende Idee eines gegebenen Zeitmomentes gebunden und eine gewisse Unfreiheit des Individuums darin nimmer zu verbannen, so soll das Gemüth in seinen Kunstgenüssen frei sein; es soll die besten Gaben der Vergangenheit, so wie der Gegenwart empfinden können.... Je weniger der Geschmack sich einer bestimmten Richtung nur ergibt, je allgemeiner, allumfassender er alles Aechte und Schöne aller Zeiten zu

empfinden und zu geniessen vermag, je freier er sich demnach von aller Parteinahme, desto kunstwürdiger ist er.[29]

Art transcends time and thus the *Zeitgeist*. In the same way that Sophocles, Euripides, Dante, Tasso, Shakespeare and Goethe can never be declared antiquated, neither can Bach, Handel, Haydn, Mozart, Beethoven and Spohr. For the *AMZ*, the value of art cannot be judged by its mere relevance to any particular age, but only by its inherent and timeless aesthetic qualities:

> ... die Sprache des Herzens, die unaussprechbaren Gefühle der Seele, Eifersucht, und Rache, Liebe, Lust und Schmerz, werden gefühlt in ihren tausendfachen Modifikationen, so lange noch Menschenherzen schlagen. Und die Darstellung dieser Seelenzustände ist die Hauptaufgabe der Tonkunst [...] die uns zu schildern vermag, und da am mächtigsten ist, wo Worte nicht mehr ausreichen, um all' die unendlichen Regungen und Gefühle wieder zu geben die eine Menschenbrust in diesem Erdenleben bewegen.[30]

Similar to the early days of the Jena Romantics, music was still deemed the symbolic key to the metaphysical kingdom. The *NZfM*, by contrast, argued along typically Hegelian lines:

> Die Entwicklung der Geschichte ist ein ununterbrochener Strom; sei der Inhalt, welcher eine Epoche bewegt, der grösste und mächtigste: dieser Inhalt hat seine Zeit, mit welcher er steht und fällt. Es treten andere Epochen ein mit anderem Inhalt; jener frühere wird herabgesetzt zum Moment, er ist ein [...] überwundener Standpunkt und es wird der Beruf für die Träger jedes geistigen Gebietes, dem Strome der allgemeinen Bewegung zu folgen, und dem geistigen Inhalte jedes Zeitabschnittes willig als Organ zu dienen. Auch die Kunst ist berufen, den jedesmaligen Inhalt ihrer Zeit in ihren Werken zur Erscheinung zu bringen.[31]

As far as the *NZfM* was concerned, because all art is always a copy (*Abbild*) of its time, art can only be judged in conjunction with its time. 'The important thing' declared the Hegelian Robert Prutz, 'is always in how far a man and his work has managed to present himself as mouthpiece of his time and how little or how much the spirit of his century has revealed itself within him'.[32] The first to have successfully done so was, of course,

Beethoven who had raged with the storms of the time. He had, according to the *NZfM*, inscribed in his music the democratic–republican spirit of the French Revolution, allowing its aims and ideals – *liberté, egalité, fraternité* – to be expressed musically. Beethoven's daring declarations in favour of republicanism and democracy were reconstructed so as to be congenial to the political agitation of the 1848 generation. His example was raised to be a glaring reminder to the artist that, once again, he was supposed to carry the flag for liberal reform. A programme of action was drawn up by Brendel at the first meeting of the *Deutscher Musikerverein* which took place in Weimar in 1846.[33] In this document, the artist was supposed to subsume the spirit of the time – the first step in the acquisition of political consciousness.[34] To ensure the artist's release from a profession dependent on class, Brendel sent petitions to the provisional *Nationalversammlung* as well as the Prussian Minister for Education and Culture.[35] Given that centralised ministries were already affecting the political as well as economic spheres, Brendel saw no reason why the state – a ministry for culture headed by suitably qualified artists – could not do the same for the arts. After all, in the same way that trade and industry enhance material well-being, so art increases the moral and spiritual well-being of the nation. An art parliament (*Kunstparliament*), *Kunsttag* as well as a *Kunsthof* were to guarantee free artistic progress. As all artistic appointments, for example *Kapellmeister* in theatres, concert halls and operas, were determined by the *Kunstparliament*, all control of artistic matters would thus have been transferred from middle-class cultural authorities to state ministries. Not surprisingly, neither the state nor the cultural authorities were in any way inclined to pay much attention to Brendel's proposals. To Selmar Bagge, then the editor of the *AMZ*, it was inconceivable that reigning ministers and aristocrats could decide on the beautiful and the sublime, domains previously monopolised by the bourgeois critic and traditional cultural institutions.[36] Rather than the artist acquiring independence from previous artistic epochs, it was precisely the study of previous masters that produced the contemporary artist. In contrast to the *NZfM*, the *AMZ* insisted that:

> Ein kritisches Genie kann sich nicht anders herausbilden, als durch Studium vorhandener Werke der bezüglichen Kunst, durch Abstrahieren der Kunstregeln und Kunstmaximen [...] es bildet daran seinen Geschmack, sein Urtheil, nur mit dem Unterschiede, [...] dass es nicht blos über Anderer Kunstwerke reden, sondern selbst welche gestalten lernt. [...] Die wahre, praktisch befähigende höhere Schaffenslehre liegt allein in den Musterwerken selbst. Aus diesen weht dem

Schüler der belebende, kräftigende, begeisternde Athem des schaf-
fenden Kunstgenius entgegen, der Frühlingsrausch, der die Knospen
seines Talentes hervorlockt. An diese Muster muss der Schüler mit
aller Fülle und Ehrfurcht, mit Glauben und Vertrauen in ihre Grösse
als Enthüller der ächten Kunstgeheimnisse treten.[37]

As much as Liszt, Brendel and Wagner would have liked to have deemed
themselves the rightful successors to Beethoven, thus appearing as the
natural conclusion to Germany's recent, eminent cultural past, the *AMZ*,
as well as the Gewandhaus, remained staunchly opposed to any associations with contemporary developments. Beethoven was not the greatest
artist because his music expressed this or that revolutionary feeling, but
because he best portrayed the sentiments of the soul and the heart; sentiments which were valid 'so long as hearts shall beat'. The very concepts of
time, progression and artistic succession were plainly deemed irrelevant.
Such predilection is also mirrored in the repertoire which demonstrates
how the classical canon had retained its pre-eminent positions within
the Gewandhaus during the 1848/1849 season (Graph 3.1).[38]

All of the composers whose work was most performed (up to Cherubini) belonged to the classical period. They were concert rather than
Church composers and, apart from Spohr, were all dead. To stress the
point, in a concert heralding the second half of the nineteenth century
(held on 1 January 1850), only the works of those who had died before
1850 – Haydn, Beethoven, Weber, Cherubini, Schubert and Mendelssohn – were performed. The *Neudeutschen* were, of course, making an

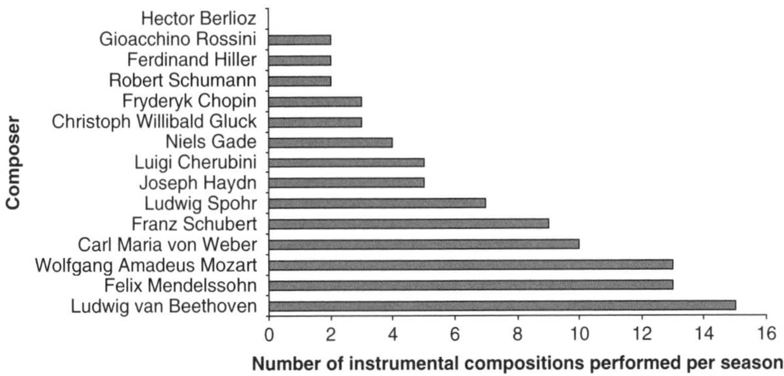

Graph 3.1   Repertoire Breakdown Gewandhaus 1848/1849

impact in other concert halls, even in Leipzig's theatre, and as such belonged to the cultural sphere of the *Bürgertum*. However, as mentioned before, the cultural ideology of the Gewandhaus was dominated by the concept of *Kultur* and its associated values, and as such, clashed with the artistic philosophy of the *Neudeutschen*. As such, the Gewandhaus was, as yet, unable to accept a plurality of artistic and cultural perspectives.

Birmingham

Just as Germany's philosophical tradition provided the aesthetic framework for Leipzig's music culture, so too did Birmingham's Triennial Festival take its incentive from the British philosophical tradition. As mentioned earlier, this tradition was characterised by *mimesis* and, linked to it, was a process of associations by which an aesthetic experience could be rendered comprehensible. A sensation (sound, visual image) could call to mind an association with an idea which corresponds to that sensation. An example, taken from *The Musical World* demonstrates the process: 'We go to an oratorio of Handel as we go to a view of the Alps, or St Peter's at Rome, or to the Falls of Niagara ... to be raised to a mood of real sublimity, to have our nature brought out, to feel a succession of grand ideas passing through the mind, which hardly recognised itself in such lofty company....[39] Music, in touching the senses, arouses intense joy or sorrow. Administered in correct doses, these were then thought to contribute to the ennoblement of the mind and spirit. As G. A. Macfarren remarked on the beauty of oratorios:

> ...oratorios elevate the minds of those who hear it [sic] to a more refined, a nobler, a sublimer appreciation of those mysteries ... and by a universal sympathy are made in speaking of all to speak to all; in this, the highest province of the art, the truly sublime work before us can never be exceeded. It portrays in succession every shade of devotional sentiment, hope, faith, piety, resignation, repentance, exultation; and all with as much truth as effect – with as much effect as the capacity of the audience, whatever may be their degree of musical intelligence, from the wholly uninitiated to the most highly cultivated, can appreciate.[40]

From the outset, therefore, art had to fulfil a definite purpose in that moral and ethical stipulations had to be met. This requirement was fulfilled by vocal music and, specifically, by vocal music of a sacred content. Most instrumental music, on the other hand, was deemed to be devoid of social and moral values. As such it was, perhaps, in danger of provoking too much criticism, thus compromising the success of the Festival. An obvious exception is Beethoven's Pastoral Symphony. Although difficult to describe (the effect it produces varies too widely), 'it requires but little exertion of the imagination to transport yourself to the green fields of the country, to fancy you see the herds of cattle and hear the various pastoral sounds which animate a beautiful landscape, with the sun bursting forth in all its splendour; in short to have excited in your breast those feelings which country scenes continually produce'.[41] But even though such music could procure such pleasant images, it was not thought to raise the listener to a level of sublimity. Yet it was precisely this function that real art was supposed to perform. The three instrumental movements of Mendelssohn's *Lobgesang* fared better, but only because they 'are intended to suggest by musical expression an endeavour to acquire the state of mind necessary to enter with faith and zeal into the solemn task of praise'.[42]

The only musical genre deemed worthy of the name of 'high' art was the oratorio – the one genre able to utter 'truth to the heart in tones at once of simple grandeur and angelic sweetness'.[43] Originating in the eighteenth century, oratorios differed from the Italian operas in that they brought in elements that were 'indebted to the English masque, the choral anthem, French classical drama, ancient Greek drama, and the German historia'.[44] They were also written in the English language which 'meant that at least some of the absurdities and conceits that were part of the tissue of the usual opera libretto had to be renounced, since they could no longer be decently concealed under the cloak of a foreign language'.[45] Their inextricable link with the Bible meant that oratorios could fulfil most adequately the requirements posed upon culture by British national philosophy. Combined with its association with public charity, elevation of the public spirit and ennoblement of the mind, oratorios ensured that Birmingham's urban élite, steeped in the evangelical tradition, was safe to partake in cultural enterprise. Given their biblical content, oratorios did not provoke the fear of losing grace before God, thus compromising chances of eternal salvation. Everyone in nineteenth-century England would have known the biblical stories and the sonorous message they advocated. And, indeed, the G. A. Macfarren quotation shows no reference to its specific religious content – it was taken as a matter of course. Some oratorio libretti, such as that of Samson, only begin the story line half way through their biblical counterparts: the concert-goer was assumed to have known why Samson was blind and held captive by the Philistines. The concert programme did not provide any background information. Closer study of the content of the oratorios performed at the Festivals further explains their attraction.

As mentioned above, Georg Friedrich Handel's oratorios constituted the most important ingredient of Birmingham's oratorio culture, as indeed they did throughout England. The most privileged place in Birmingham was held by Handel's *Messiah*. '…We know nothing', the *Birmingham Journal* declared in 1837, 'that does more credit to the universal musical taste of England than the crowding to listen, year after year, with still craving and unsatiated delight, to the great master piece of George Frederick Handel'.[46] Whilst most of the other stories portray the lives and vicissitudes of one or another Jewish leader, *Messiah* tells the story of Christ. Given its cultural proximity to the Christian tradition, therefore, it held a theological importance beyond that of any other oratorio. As a series of contemplations on the Christian idea of redemption (including Old Testament prophecies of Christ's coming and New Testament passages on his life and death, along with themes of resurrection and redemption), *Messiah* does not express esoteric mysticism nor does it play upon intellectual, denominational or theological concerns. Rather, Handel's librettist, Charles Jennens, used the emotive and poetic language of biblical excerpts. What is noticeable is that particularly offensive passages of the biblical blueprint are omitted by Jennens, such as Herod's order to have all children of Jesus' age slaughtered. The crucifixion, too, is not mentioned. What the listener was left with were purely spiritual notions of Christ's inspirational nature and redeeming power. The zenith of the work would always be the Hallelujah chorus, exclaiming that most faithful of all biblical expressions: 'For the Lord God omnipotent reigneth' inspiring the audience with a kind of religious awe. As the *Quarterly Review* noted:

> …The spirit of faith and of praise found expression so sublime that it would seem as if no form of ascription could be worthier of the Divine Object. [...] To the great utterance of praise he has added the sentiment of love in its most exquisite forms, and to faith he has given a character of touching confidence. In his harmony the human and divine seem to be harmonised; the aspiration of man is attuned to the nature of precept of Christ.[47]

Whereas in other oratorio libretti, reported speech was transformed into active dialogues, in *Messiah*, all biblical excerpts were left unchanged. Being sacrosanct and incontestable, the scriptural texts of *Messiah* remained immune to passing tastes and fashion. As the *Birmingham*

Journal noted: 'However slowly and reluctantly people may come forth to call for other musical entertainment, there is no slackness in respect to Messiah.'[48] As far as Birmingham was concerned, *Messiah* became the staple diet of the Festival and, bar one or two exceptions, was performed without fail on every third Festival morning until the Festival's demise in 1912. Its importance and popularity is demonstrated by the fact that it alone was responsible for raising one-third of all profits.

Similarly emotive, but far more didactic, were Handel's other biblical oratorios which were based on stories from either the New or the Old Testament, with the more popular ones such as *Samson, Saul, Deborah, Joshua* or *Solomon* drawn from the latter. Apart from *Judas Maccabeus*, the story of which is found in the first book of Maccabees in the Apocrypha, and *Israel in Egypt*, the story of which is taken from the book of Exodus and supplemented by the psalms, all the other popular oratorio subjects – Joshua, Deborah, Jephtah, Samson, Saul, Solomon, found their biblical counterparts within the deuteronomic history books – Deuteronomy, Joshua, Judges, Samuel and Kings. All these tell the story of the tribes of Israel from their arrival in the Promised Land to their exile in Babylon. In each, there is a sense of God's purpose for his people so long as they remain obedient. Canaan could not be conquered by military might – it could only be captured through a venture of faith. The book of Judges especially, whilst telling the tale of a fragmented society, moral decline, worship of other idols and gods and lack of leadership, still conveys the idea of forgiveness if people repent and turn to God. Everyone – though mainly kings – are judged by one criterion: namely, whether or not the individual is faithful to God. Art here is strongly didactic in that each character's life espouses a particular moral lesson: Saul's life is a stern reminder that disobeying God's commands will cost the nation dearly, whilst Solomon who, despite God's initial favour, has that favour taken away for having lost his faith in God by introducing Baal worship. The temple he built means nothing unless it is maintained by obedience and faith. A particularly interesting case is Samson, the story of which is taken from the Bible via Milton's *Samson Agonistes*. Here, Samson's life is a warning against taking God for granted – against abusing a holy calling. Accepting his sorrowful state of blindness and incarceration as God's judgement for his earlier wrongdoing, Samson continues steadfastly to believe in God. This belief takes him so far as to challenge the Philistine giant Harapha who is obeying his own gods. The contest between the two is a contest between Samson and God against Harapha and the Philistine gods. Samson's words, when asked to attend the Philistine festival where the contest took place, highlight his resurgence of strength owing to his continuing faith in God: 'I am a Hebrew, and our laws forbid my presence at their vain religious rites...Am I so broke with servitude to yield to such absurd commands? To be their fool, and play before their god? I will not come.' It was a prologue to Samson's ultimate sacrifice: to pull down the Philistine temple which buried Israel's enemies but also, tragically, himself.

Beyond their inherent moral lessons, oratorios could also be appreciated for their patriotic sentiments as England's middle class was transformed into God's chosen people. The tradition originated during the eighteenth-century when patriotic identity became closely allied with religion.[49] Handel, again, supplied the goods by playing upon the comparison between England and Israel. Prime examples are the *Te Deum*, composed to honour the English military victory at Dettingen, and *Judas Maccabeus* (only second to Messiah in popularity in Birmingham), which glorified the successful English military campaign under the Duke of Cumberland against the Jacobite rebels, culminating at Culloden, and 'freeing this new Britannic entity from the Catholic continental entanglements of the Stuarts'.[50] The biblical parallel is the Maccabean rebellion. At the time, Judah was dominated by the Selucid Empire; its emperor Antiochus Epiphanes tried to compel the Jews to forsake the laws of their ancestors and to reconsecrate the temple of Jerusalem in the name of Zeus. The Maccabean rebellion was therefore a revolt against attempts to erase Jewish culture, laws, customs and nationhood. The eighteenth-century version was against the invasion, both military and cultural, of Catholicism. As its biblical counterpart Israel, England succeeded and defended its Protestant laws and culture – the foundation stones of the nation. Conversely, if the references to the nation of Israel were too obvious – thus making its transposition into an English context a more difficult undertaking – they could always be omitted. In *Israel in Egypt*, for example, the Passover – the root of Jewish religion, culture and nationhood – is not mentioned. What remains is a God who rescues his people, however desperate their plight, and who is in control of history and the whole world.

Each in its own way, oratorios were symbolic of the bourgeois élites themselves, as their own philosophy, perceptions and values were thought to be reflected in the ideas found in the epics of Handel's major choral works. Time and time again, similar notions of obedience and ultimate sacrifice even in times of Job-like desolation and despair could be aired. All of these resonated perfectly with the religious sentiments of England's provincial middle class. This was particularly so as oratorios did not concentrate on liturgical practices and theological concerns, but on human experiences, failings, trepidations and stern faith in God. The biblical stories demonstrate the omnipotence of God and the fact that their situation, success or misfortune, depended on faith and trust in God alone. The immediacy to personal life was ensured by Handel's librettists, Charles Jennens and Thomas Morrell, who transformed reported speech within a biblical narrative into active dialogues, engaging a number of soloists and a choir. Moreover, Handel 'preferred his heroes stricken with misfortune, his soldiers defeated, his lovers jilted, his wives widowed or abandoned, his young women frail ...'[51] which meant that the characters were allowed to develop, either positively or negatively. Combined with a monumental display of choirs, orchestras and soloists, oratorios were able to encourage the listener to engage in emotional empathy with the subject concerned – the essence of English aesthetics.

Nothing in Handel's oratorios is abstract, metaphysical or theoretical.[52] Thus, the experiences of Job, Saul, Samson or any other character were likely to have found strong echoes particularly at a time when a sense of God was still commonly intrinsic to everybody's life. Sacred music and moral concepts, therefore, could be appreciated by a middle class of whatever denomination (except, of course, for the more puritanical-minded denominations such as the Quakers who fervently opposed such performances on the grounds that sacred music performed in secular venues such as town halls and theatres was little short of blasphemy[53]). As William Weber noted:

> The Oratorios stood above England's religious divisions. Since the librettos had a moral as opposed to a metaphysical focus, they established a common ground for expressing certain basic religious beliefs that reunited the English as no other area of the nation's culture had done....[54]

As Birmingham's pattern of religious observance was characterised by a plurality of denominations – established and dissenting – oratorios were thus able to unite rather than divide audiences. Indeed, as the list of benefactors, published in the *Birmingham Journal* and *Aris' Birmingham Gazette*, reveals, a number of denominations was represented with no single one standing out either in size or donations made. The Festival acted as a unifying force with no denomination being in any way favoured or disadvantaged by the performance of oratorios because human experiences and their moral implications possess universal qualities. The religious stories and characters portrayed in oratorios were thought to aid character-formation through spiritual elevation and moral instruction. Irrespective of religious denomination, oratorios provided virtuous entertainment which could be commonly appreciated by all. This was, of course, integral to the assumptions about what constituted culture in Birmingham.

As in Leipzig, the canonisation of particular kinds of music and the cultural institutionalisation of taste were necessary despite the self-explanatory nature of oratorios, given their reliance on well-known texts. Handel's consecration as the principal leader of English music culture, as well as the centrality of the Handelian oratorio in Birmingham's bourgeois music culture, meant that the parameters for all future choral and oratorio writing were established in line with Handel's popular oratorios, much to the detriment of English music culture. 'When we look back over the century and a half that followed Handel's death', writes Winton Dean, 'we are confronted by a lunar landscape of extinct oratorios thrown up in what passed for the Handelian image, with only Mendelssohn's *Elijah* ejecting an occasional and modest shower of sparks'.[55] Like classicism in Leipzig, Handel's oratorios became the standard-bearer of oratorio production in which content and function and an insistence on the authenticity of biblical precedents and religious sentiments were of paramount importance if social respectability was to be maintained. A mere digression from the perceived model could result in critics launching highly subjective attacks. The German composer Georg Häser and his oratorio *The Triumph of Faith* was received with ill-favour for precisely that reason:

Of the composer little appears to be known; his reputation, even in his own country, is certainly not high, and yet, to judge from the quality of this work, it is as high as he deserves. The subject is rather a strange one for an oratorio; the hero is Peter the Hermit, a fierce fanatic, whose insane scheme of obtaining, by means of the sword, possession of the Holy Sepulchre, almost depopulated the fairest countries of Europe, and deluged Asia with blood. The unholy triumph of this mischievous madman and his deluded followers, forms the subject of Häser's piece, and is celebrated by songs of praise and thanksgiving to the Almighty! This might have suited a theatrical Opera; but the subject and sentiments of an oratorio ought to be in accordance with the religious opinions and feelings of the audience. Its treatment as well as subject, is theatrical. It contains a love-story, a pair of lovers are introduced, each of which endeavours to save the other by self-accusation of an offence about to be punished with instant death – a white lie, which might be very pretty in a play, but is somewhat out of place in an Oratorio.[56]

This oratorio exhibited nothing of what the Birmingham audience expected from a national epic, and Peter the Hermit was an unlikely candidate to equal Samson or Judas Maccabeus, let alone serve as a national hero. In no way did Häser's oratorio resemble the definitive attributes of a Handelian oratorio, either in content or in form. To the 'skilled picture readers with a keen appetite for character and episode',[57] it demonstrated no concern for faith nor allowed any arousal for religiously inspired sentiments. It offered nothing with which the bourgeois could identify, either as an individual or as a collective body. Owing to Häser's digression from the standard oratorio form, The *Triumph of Faith* was, in some eyes, little more than sacrilegious. The intrinsic value of music was ignored in favour of an attack on the offending content. Neither the critic nor the listener would have encountered much difficulty in appreciating the blasphemous blunder Häser had committed.

By contrast, the evening sessions offered within the framework of Triennial Festival were not expected to do more than just entertain. Although well attended, they did not carry the same cultural importance that was bestowed upon the morning performances. The conglomerate of numerous operatic arias, recitatives and duets, interspersed by songs, glees, a movement from a symphony or concerto, did not allow any artistic coherence to emerge. As the *Birmingham Post* remarked rather sniffily: 'In the modern history of the Festival, the evenings have been set apart to the production of the lighter class of music, by way of relief to the graver studies of the mornings, or to suit the taste of those to whom oratorio, with its necessity for sustained thought, was unsuited.'[58] Until the 1860s, no composition was performed in its entirety; quite often the name of the composer was not even mentioned which meant that his private and public virtues could not be ascertained. As far as the morally more serious morning concerts were concerned, however, these were essential. An artist with a dubious private life could hardly be expected to create art of any spiritual or moral value, nor partake in bourgeois culture.

The demand to dispense with political and religious sentiments within public culture effectively pre-empted the use of the evening sessions from any non-entertainment purposes. The anti-aristocratic sentiments inherent in Mozart's *Marriage of Figaro*, for example, were discarded. Excerpts were not chosen for their revolutionary sentiment but for their potential to provide opportunities for virtuosity. Nonetheless, like the morning sessions, the evening repertoire was also required at least to follow the dictates of English aesthetics: the glees, songs and operatic excerpts had to stir emotions, arouse passion and even encourage an empathetic engagement with the subject. The press rarely dealt with the inherent message of the opera from which the excerpt was taken. Rather it described in detail whether the soloist was able to convey the essence of pathos, joy or sorrow in his or her performance.

Both the morning and evening performances offered potential for outward monumental display. On the one hand, this was conducive to the required level of effectiveness by which oratorios as well as operatic excerpts were to be rendered. On the other, this allowed for the Festival to gain widespread, even national, attention. The first step towards this was the opening of the Town Hall in 1834 which allowed for the majesty of the oratorio culture, in particular, to be complemented and indeed visually enhanced. With the new building, a far greater amount of space was available, spurring an increase of choral and instrumental musicians who could partake in Birmingham's premier cultural event. The underlying assumption was that the bigger the choir, the greater the attraction. This preoccupation with size was visually confirmed by the posters attached to the walls of the Town Hall and other public buildings. Whilst conductors and organists were given a relatively small font size and were announced at the bottom of the page, the size of the choir and orchestra as well as the cast of soloists would feature prominently, being easily discernible to the passing eye.

The trend towards increasing monumentalism was necessarily accompanied by an exaggerated importance attached to the quality (or the reputed quality) of performing vocalists. Vocalists were hired from the ranks of the fashionable and the famous with a reputation throughout England and especially London, their names brightly advertised on the walls of the Town Hall. The appointments of John Braham, Clara Novello, Madame Stockhausen or Mrs Knyvett – the most sought after vocalists of the day – all aided the transformation of the Triennial Festival from a provincial phenomenon to a national or even international event. Despite eating further into the cash surpluses available for the General Hospital, the increasing level of expenditure necessary to afford the glamorous artists of the day highlights the importance of, and the need for, constant improvement – material and musical – to maintain Birmingham's cultural reputation and image. The ideal of progress at any cost was coming to prevail within the musical culture of the city, demonstrating that 'Birmingham [...] aimed beyond brass, claiming the cultural leadership of the West Midlands'.[59]

So far, this chapter has demonstrated how the music cultures of Birmingham and Leipzig advanced in accordance with the requirements imposed upon culture. From their modest beginnings during the late eighteenth century, both concert cultures developed to become the dominant cultural institutions within their local confines. The rise of both was accompanied by the infiltration of bourgeois values – be these educational or religious – leading to the *embourgeoisement* of the public concerts. This process was largely accomplished in both towns by the mid-nineteenth century; the cultural parameters had been irrevocably set. Given that both concert cultures were inextricably linked to their respective cultural norms, very little scope for revision was left. Too much cultural capital had been invested – indeed, cultural norms had become too internalised – for anything to be allowed to destabilise this cultural construct. What followed during the second half of the nineteenth century, therefore, was more a matter of proliferation of common themes, rather than cultural reorientation.

The Role of the Artist

In both music cultures, the artist was supposed to represent and convey the cultural ethos to the wider public in a manner deemed congruent with the latter's aspirations. The differing definitions of culture presage a difference in the expectations placed upon the artist. Mendelssohn's appointment in both towns during the 1830s and 1840s provides an especially good comparative opportunity both to discern this difference and to explore the meaning of culture within each bourgeois culture even further.

Felix Mendelssohn in Leipzig

In the same way that the ideals and values of classicism determined the qualitative judgements made of instrumental music, so too did they determine the role and expectations of the *Kapellmeister*. The personification of Leipzig's cultural conscience was Felix Mendelssohn who took over as *Gewandhauskapellmeister* in 1835. In him and through him, cultural respectability found its most celebrated physical manifestation. This was due to his persona – his upbringing and personal traits – which was congruent with that of the bourgeoisie he served. His continuing reliance on the classical heritage (a further 92 performances of Beethoven symphonies were given between 1835 and 1847) allowed for traditional classical qualities and middle-class virtues to be publicly recognised as being dependent on one another. He was the physical manifestation of Leipzig's cultural ethos as it had been defined during the 1810s, a time when music, as we have seen, was aesthetically valorised. An excerpt from E. T. A. Hoffmann's seminal essay *Beethovens Instrumentalmusik* suggests what was expected from the artist:

> Der echte Künstler lebt nur in dem Werke, das er in dem Sinne des Meisters aufgefasst hat und nun vorträgt. Er verschmäht es, auf irgendeine Weise seine Persönlichkeit geltend zu machen, und all sein Dichten und Trachten geht nur dahin, alle die herrlichen, holdseligen Bilder und Erscheinungen, die der Meister mit magischer Gewalt in sein Werk verschloss, tausend-farbig glänzend ins rege Leben zu rufen, dass sie den Menschen in lichten, funkelnden Kreisen umfangen und, seine Phantasie, sein innerstes Gemüt entzünden, ihn raschen Fluges in das ferne Geisterreich der Töne tragen.[60]

This quasi-religious attitude inherent in transcendental idealism, informed by a moral sensitivity and noble dignity, was a precondition for the performance of music in the Gewandhaus of the early nineteenth century. It was a means of ensuring that music remained within the confines of artistic respectability and avoided the loss of cultural value through individualistic or subjective conceptions of the composition. It was a means, too, of ensuring that music remained within the confines of bourgeois classical values and was not performed to merely fill idle moments or merely to titillate the ear. The role of the composer, inextricably linked to the same values of classicism – nobility, composure, timelessness, moral grandeur – was therefore to protect and enhance the status of bourgeois culture in all its manifestations.

Through Mendelssohn, bourgeois values were not only assured of survival but also positively celebrated. This was important, especially at a time when the classical tradition of 'noble simplicity and serene greatness' was being challenged on two fronts. The one front was represented by the likes of Schumann; the other principally by Paganini. Whilst the first could be treated with a kind of benign indifference, the latter was more difficult to counter as Paganini's astonishing virtuosity posed the threat of a magnetic attraction which allowed him to command radically different aesthetic responses, rather than meet the conventional requirements of the bourgeois concert-goer.

Firstly, the difference between Mendelssohn and Romantics like Schumann was one of composure versus tension: Mendelssohn had never been regarded as the 'tortured genius' commonly associated with the Romantic artist. What the bourgeois public saw in Mendelssohn was not the 'Seelenqualen der Romantiker mit Mondnächten and Sturmgewölk, nicht die Sehnsüchte nach etwas Verlorenem, nach der blauen Blume, nicht die Einsamkeit und Ich-Verlassenheit – nein: Hier wirken die Kräfte der Klassik, Klarheit der Gedanken, Ordnung der Gefühle, hier wird der Spuk inszeniert aus Lust am phantastischen Spiel'.[61] Particularly, under the editorial guidance of the Wagnerian Franz Brendel, Schumann's *NZfM* further polarised the tensions between classicism and romanticism. The clash was clear: whilst the Romantic Schumann was consumed by details at the expense of order, Mendelssohn presented his thoughts in a clear and formal manner; whereas Schumann never concealed his distaste for theoretical rules, in Mendelssohn's works, 'nothing is dared unless it is certain to work';[62] whilst Mendelssohn was portrayed as complying with the laws and requirements of his art, Schumann came across as the nonconformist individual wasting his creative energies in a constant defiance of musical proprieties.

Secondly, as far as cultural respectability is concerned, Mendelssohn stood out as he never suffered from any of the ailments commonly associated with the spiritual agony of the misunderstood Romantic artist: unrequited love (Schubert, Berlioz), long delay before he could marry due to the father's intervention (Schumann), depression and insanity (Schumann, Hölderlin, Lenau, Grabbe, Lenz) and syphilis (the majority). In short, Mendelssohn was the physical manifestation of Goethe's axiom: 'What is Classical I call healthy, what is Romantic sick…Most modern work is Romantic not because it is modern but because it is weak, sickly and ill, and old work is not Classical because it is old but because it is strong, fresh, joyful and healthy'.[63] What Goethe had in mind, of course, was that for art to remain healthy, it had to maintain an intimate link with the acquisition of aesthetic knowledge rooted in morality.[64] As such, Mendelssohn's artistic role could never be compared with that of the *mere* virtuoso artist whose performance practice was usually associated with a circus-like display of individualistic novelties. The most extreme manifestation of the *mere* virtuoso during the 1830s was Nicollo Paganini.

Whilst Mendelssohn served to uphold respectable norms in art and thus his association with Leipzig's socio-cultural norms made him indispensable to the town's *Bürgertum*, Paganini's less lofty purpose was to entertain and to enchant/bewitch the concert-going bourgeoisie. The origins of this distinction can be traced back to the 1770s, to the literary movement of the *Sturm und Drang* and the belief of its young proponents in the sanctity of Nature. Such a belief was formed during the Enlightenment, when Baroque and neo-classical forms of art were deemed unnatural and were thus abandoned. Instead, the natural alliance to nature and the true organic form as artistic ideal gained currency.[65] As part of this, the Romantic imagination began to enrich natural feelings with the demonic, the ominous and the unconscious, thus producing the model of the artistic magician (*Hexenkünstler*). By evoking an ever more mysterious world, the latter appeared to introduce the seductive power of the irrational into the public sphere of performance. This correlation between art, irrationalism and sorcery found its literal embodiment in Paganini who thus posed a sharp contrast to classicism with its ascetic, ethical sedateness. As he performed the 'unperformable' with consummate ease to the astonishment of the public, Paganini seemed to have indeed descended in direct line from the ancient *Hexenkünstler.*

On Paganini's stage, technical proficiency alone no longer sufficed: personality, the ego, body language and novel effects were just as important as the performance itself. In stark opposition to E. T. A. Hoffmann's ideal of the self-effacing and noble artist, the attraction of Paganini began with his facial expression, general eccentricity and ended with his performance style. Such phenomena underlined a perceived irrationality that his physical appearance did nothing to refute: his clothes were old-fashioned and seemed rather neglected, and his physical appearance (already showing signs of deformation caused by the mercury poisoning administered to cure his syphilis) was that of a skeleton from the grave. Heinrich Heine, already in self-exile in Paris, and writing for the *Augsburger Allgemeine Musikzeitung*, recalls one of Paganini's concerts:

> Paganini dressed from head to foot in black. His body, racked with pain, was slowly wasting away from syphilis. He glided rather than walked across the stage like a menacing vulture gently floating into position to consume its prey. His eyes had receded deep into their sockets, and this, together with his waxen complexion, gave him a spectral appearance which was enhanced by the dark-blue glasses he sometimes wore. The mercury prescribed for his morbo gallico had attacked his stomach and rotted his jawbone, causing his teeth to decay and fall out and his mouth to disappear into his chin.[66]

Not only was Paganini of breathtaking, even demonic, ugliness, thus full of sexual allure in a nineteenth-century sense, he also had a reputation which suited his histrionics. This reputation was nourished to a considerable degree by association with the well-known Faust myth, which witnessed a Europe-wide resurgence in popularity in the literary, dramatic and musical spheres after Goethe published his *Faust: Der*

Tragödie erster Teil in 1808, and especially after the astonishing completion of the vast Second Part, published shortly after his death in 1832.[67] Nikolaus Lenau's *Faust* (1836), in particular, took up the theme of musical virtuosity and the magnetic power of mesmerism.[68] When Lenau's Mephistopheles seizes the violin to play a waltz (later to be set to music by Liszt), Faust and everyone else can do nothing but surrender to the delirium in the music. Thus, music's potential to seduce and mesmerise the listener had already become a common topos of popular literature and the theatre. Once the idea had gripped the imagination of the reading and listening public, it was only a short step to believing that Paganini actually possessed the demonic gifts that his stage appearance already intimated. Indeed, speculation that Paganini had himself struck a bargain with Mephistopheles was widespread during the 1830s. As Paganini, himself wryly noted: 'How easy it is to play with the reputation of an artist merely because men, inclined to indulge in idleness themselves, cannot conceive it possible that he may have studied as closely in his own chamber and in full possession of his liberty, as he would if he had been chained up in a dungeon.'[69] According to popular stories, it was while in prison (following the murder of his wife and rival) that he was visited by Satan who taught him the art of playing the violin in exchange for his body and soul.

Such lurid rumours and accusations merely added to Paganini's seemingly infinite attraction. In no way did they diminish his success. Although every serious music journal deplored Paganini's public histrionics, people flocked to hear and see him, paid well above usual prices and naturally wanted in return to be entertained in an unusual manner. In the eyes of some, however, entertainment was all that Paganini would ever be able to provide. As Heinrich Brockhaus, one of Leipzig's most successful publishers, noted in his diary following a typical Paganini performance at Leipzig's theatre:

> Mir kommt es vor, als foppe Paganini das Publikum mit seiner Kunstfertigkeit und mache sich selbst lustig, wenn ein rasender Beifall die Folge davon ist. [...] Wenn ich auf die Beurtheilung Paganinis für die Nachwelt Einfluss hätte, so würde er als Künstler einen sehr untergeordneten Rang, als Virtuos einen sehr hohen einnehmen.[70]

Paganini's alleged debauchery and corrupt tendencies were greatly amplified when contrasted with the respectable citizen, Mendelssohn, whose commitment to classical purity was matched by his pious, serious and sensitive nature. Mendelssohn came from a privileged family background and received his musical training as part of a higher, more comprehensive, classical education. Grandson of the renowned philosopher, Moses Mendelssohn, and son of the affluent merchant banker, Abraham, Felix was taught by private tutors. Further study at university produced a well-rounded and educated adult who was familiar with Baroque counterpoint, fugue, choral harmonisation and classical orchestration. Proficient in ancient and modern languages, his education was completed by 'grand tours' throughout Europe, as was customary for the offspring of the wealthy bourgeoisie. In short, Mendelssohn was the public representative of the enlightened and cultured *Weltbürger* – a citizen of the world – who exemplified the bourgeois *Bildungsideal*.

Similarly, because the purity of Mendelssohn's art was deemed integral to the *Bildungsideal*, the lure of financial gain was supposedly anathema to his artistic ideology. He thus inevitably appeared as the antipode to Paganini's shallow and commercial virtuosity that shamelessly exploited the paying public, attracted by what they saw as much as by what they heard. As one of Mendelssohn's obituarists succinctly put it:

> ...seine Gaben [wurden] nur zum edelsten Zwecke der Kunst verwendet....Er hätte seine Glücksgüter verwenden können zum Genusse des Lebens im gewöhnlichen Sinne. Statt dessen arbeitete er unablässig und vergalt der Gottheit ihre Geschenke durch redliche Erfüllung ihrer Aufträge, wahrscheinlich auf Kosten eines längeren Lebens.[71]

Public recognition and admiration for Mendelssohn were widespread. During his lifetime, for example, he received an honorary doctorate from the University of Leipzig, honorary citizenship of the town, as well as the title of Saxon Director of Music (*Sächsischer Kapellmeister*) from the Saxon King. His funeral procession was attended by 2000 people. Paganini, on the other hand, after refusing the last sacraments, was denied a Christian burial (further perpetuating the myth of a demonic fiddler possessed by Beelzebub).

Apart from protecting the image of the ideal artist in the classical sense, Mendelssohn also protected the cultural tradition of the Gewandhaus. Showing judicious appreciation of historicism, a movement which had also captured other cultural and intellectual realms during that time, Mendelssohn instituted the 'Historic Concerts'. At these events only composers of similar historic periods were performed in any one concert. During the 1837/1838 season, for example, secular pieces of Bach's music were followed by compositions of Handel, Gluck and Viotti. (The influence of Mendelssohn in the choice of Bach is noticeable.) The next concert celebrated Haydn, Cimarosa, Naumann and Righini. In the third of the series, works by Mozart, Salieri, Méhul and Andreas Romberg were performed, and the fourth concluded with Abt Vogler, Beethoven and Weber. During the 1840/1841 season, concerts were dedicated exclusively to Bach and Handel in the first, Haydn in the second, Mozart and Beethoven in the third and fourth, respectively. Thus, not only was Leipzig provided with a dependable classical cultural heritage, his historical programme (beginning with the bourgeois age) also served to emphasise the importance of the *Bürgertum* in the development of enlightened culture and the fine arts. The deliberate emphasis on developments in the history of music (itself grounded in sound academic notions) undoubtedly helped further to inculcate an awareness of the correspondence between the classical and the bourgeois age. Both appeared as the acme of development in their respective spheres.

In sum, Mendelssohn was the epitome of the post-Enlightenment bourgeois artist. Closely resembling the bourgeois in education, taste and social background, he functioned both as servant to true art and sobriety and as the representative of the classical ideal in the present. It was through him that the respectability of bourgeois culture was assured, that indeed the respectable could be held up against the merely entertaining – embodied by Paganini, Herz, Thalberg, Carl Tausig with their seemingly inexhaustible repertoire of Fantasias and Variations on popular operatic themes. Indeed, it was their very distance from the musical ideals cherished by the Gewandhaus that paradoxically allowed their performances to be tolerated as the meretricious, if exciting, product of ephemeral showmanship.

Mendelssohn: the 'foster-child' of Birmingham

Mendelssohn was to Birmingham what Michelangelo was to the merchant princes of Florence during the Renaissance. He was the first artist of international repute that Birmingham could claim for itself. His *Elijah*, which made its triumphant appearance in Birmingham in 1846, was a milestone in Birmingham's claim to cultural status. For it was in their concert hall, built and maintained with their subscriptions, that *Elijah*, 'hailed as the younger brother of Handel's great oratorios ... [and] immediately acclaimed as a masterpiece second only in greatness to Messiah', had been performed before its première in London or Vienna, where the revised version was only performed the following year.[72] With this performance, Birmingham's reputation as the site for the grandest of all provincial music festivals was well and truly established. As the *Birmingham Journal* noted:

> None who were present on that memorable occasion can ever forget it. The proudest day in the life of one of the most brilliant and original geniuses that ever enriched the art of music with imperishable bequests was also the most glorious epoch in the musical annals of this great and flourishing emporium of commerce and industry, where the production of such a work as Elijah, and the enthusiastic appreciation it encountered, showed that the heart of the manufacturer, the merchant was not dead to a sense of the beautiful, but alive to all those pleasurable and edifying impressions which the most refined and elevated manifestation of art are formed to create. Mendelssohn was indeed the foster-child of Birmingham....[73]

If there was ever any doubt that 'high' art and commerce could exist in unison, then *Elijah* had finally dispelled it. The success of *Elijah*, supported by the bourgeois industrial élite of Birmingham, had demonstrated that art indeed depended on the prosaic world of commerce and industry as much it enriched it. With his oratorio, Mendelssohn gave Birmingham's middle class what it required most: an equilibrium between the mundane sphere of business and the spiritually uplifting world of art. The proclamation of Mendelssohn as a second Elijah by Prince Albert further enhanced his reputation as *the* Victorian artist and *Elijah* as *the* Victorian masterpiece.[74] Thus, in contrast to Leipzig, where music culture was already enshrined in its past by the middle of the nineteenth century, Birmingham had to wait until this moment to experience the climax of its cultural enterprise.

Elijah was thought to be the modern culmination of oratorio compositions. It tells the story of the Old Testament prophet Elijah, who was sent by God to counter the reign of King Ahab and Queen Jezebel who were intent on eliminating the worship of God throughout Israel. Elijah was accused of killing the priests of their god Baal and blamed for the consequent drought and famine. Despised and fearing for his life, Elijah stuck to his task, and, despite ensuing hardship, he continued to believe that 'he that shall endure to the end, shall be saved'. Elijah, the individual hero, is rewarded for his unfailing belief in God after earlier calls for proof of God's existence had remained unanswered. Like most of Handel's oratorios, *Elijah* thus played upon the concerns of faith, as it emphatically stressed the existence and truth of God. Thus, Mendelssohn understood what Birmingham desired of its culture; he knew, unlike Häser, that the merit of any great work lay 'first in the subject which besides that it excites the universal sympathy of every Christian, and especially of every Protestant public, [must] afford many and great opportunities of musical expression of the highest order'.[75]

Using excerpts from Old Testament books – mainly 1 and 2 Kings but also Lamentations, Jeremiah, Deuteronomy, Exodus, Hosea, Chronicles, Isaiah, Samuel, Malachi and Psalms – Mendelssohn's *Elijah* offered no coherent plot but, rather, concentrated on a number of loosely arranged situations/scenes such as Elijah prophesising 30 years of drought; the fulfilment of this prophesy followed by the lamentations of the people of Israel; the widow's cries over the death of her son and Elijah's returning him to life; the murder of the priests of Baal on Elijah's orders and Jezebel's subsequent edict to have Elijah killed; Elijah's retreat to the desert; his encounter with God, followed by his ascension to heaven. In each of these scenes, Mendelssohn put an enormous emphasis on the presentation of identifiable human feelings such as anger, fear, despair and doubt, emotions that would have resonated within every mid-century concert-goer. A good example is the scene describing Elijah's escape to the desert in desperation over the apparent failure of his life's work. Concentrating on the presentation of Elijah's inner disposition, his desire to resign himself in the desert, his complete physical and emotional exhaustion, Mendelssohn shows how Elijah's enduring faith is rewarded when he is re-awakened at the sight of God appearing before him. In order to aid Elijah's translation to a nineteenth-century setting, that is, to allow the 'superimposition of their [middle-class] evangelical temper'[76] onto the biblical subject, Elijah is not portrayed as the iron-fisted man who proceeds with undaunted courage against the people, king and the supercilious individual who turned away from God, a God who was thought to avenge the transgressions not of the fathers but of their children. Rather, Mendelssohn's Elijah is a pious and praying man, soft and compassionate, easily moved by sorrow, 'strong in sincerity of intention, great in aspiration of sound, meek in kindliness of heart, beautiful in purity of manners, and god-like in patient endurance'.[77] Like the conventional Victorian Christian, Elijah was portrayed as a man of undying faith in God's giving and grace.

To support the efficacy of the scenes, Mendelssohn applied an unprecedented level of drama to the composition which, enhanced by a monumental display of choirs, orchestras and soloists, was meant to promote the listener to exceptional heights of empathy. In fact, the concentration on the drama was done paradoxically at the expense of the moral lesson inherent to the story, for neither the role of the prophet to the Jewish nation nor his theological–political significance was given overriding importance. Mendelssohn's choice of collaborator hints at his intentions. Unlike *Paulus*, his previous oratorio, the libretto for *Elijah* was not written by Julius Schubring, a Lutheran minister, but by Karl Klingemann, a Legationsrat [ambassador] to the Hanoverian Court in London, and friend of the Mendelssohn family. The libretto which the two worked on was conceptualised as follows:

> Nicht die Gestaltung eines im christlichen Sinne exemplarischen Lebenslaufs sollte diesmal im Vordergrund stehen, sondern die Darstellung dramatisch bewegter Situationen, nicht die allgemeine geistliche Bedeutung des Stoffes war dem Komponisten diesmal wichtig, sondern die Möglichkeiten, die sich durch ihn für die Komposition packender, lebendiger Charaktere und Szenen ergaben.[78]

For such an undertaking, Klingemann, who had already collaborated with Mendelssohn on an opera libretto, appeared to be a far more suitable candidate than Schubring, who even though possessing an incomparable knowledge of the Bible, was deemed too dry, devoid of dramatic eloquence and rhetorical skills, to make his contribution count.

The outcome of this collaboration was, as far as Birmingham's middle class was concerned, an advance on Handel's *Messiah* where the story gradually grows in intensity from the prophecy and advent of the son of God to death, culminating in Christ's resurrection. The stories of Elijah, by contrast, afford a number of dramatic climaxes. One of the most effective scenes concerns the cries of the widow for the salvation of her son, followed by the overflowing gratitude and devoted submission to God's will. This scene, in particular, struck a deep sympathetic vein in the concert-goer as it involved the tormented soul and its eventual salvation/release – a favourite topos in middle-class evangelicalism. But whereas a contributor of the *AMZ* wrote of embarrassment at the endless droning and whinging of the mother that was thought to result in a display of nervous passion rather than depth and warmth,[79] a critic in *The Musical World* held a strongly contrary view:

> The high soprano tones of the voices, the shrill piercing notes of the oboe … seem like sudden darts and throbs of pain, all combine to make a wonderfully graphic picture of anguish and despair. The

solemn strains that accompany the prophet's words contrast most beautifully with the murmurs of distressed humanity.[80]

In line with English aesthetic requirements, Mendelssohn had succeeded in creating a scene of enormous emotional impact that could appeal directly to the religious sentiments of Birmingham's middle class despite the loss of the customary moralising didacticism. By encouraging the listener to engage in emotional empathy with the subject concerned, Mendelssohn penetrated deeply into the religious vein of Victorian England. The English aesthetic tradition with its emphasis on evangelical fervour naturally lent itself to dramatic expression, and it was Mendelssohn who became its apotheosis.

For the middle-class citizens of Birmingham, the first performance of *Elijah* epitomised notions of progress and musical innovation which were not only vital to the town's cultural reputation but also congruent with its political and economic accomplishments. Through the sensational impact of Mendelssohn's *Elijah*, Birmingham's middle class was able to dispel age-old accusations of philistinism which their concentration on business and commerce had brought upon them. Thus, whilst in Leipzig, Mendelssohn served primarily to enshrine a cultural ideal which was increasingly criticised for encouraging cultural complacency resulting from a retrospective orientation, in Birmingham, Mendelssohn was thought to have revitalised its music culture. Birmingham had finally got its Michelangelo, and for the time being at least, the town was nationally recognised for being in the vanguard of artistic innovation. The Town Hall was the centre of the musical universe.

The Town Hall and the Gewandhaus

The Importance of the Concert Hall

The concert halls provided the largest congregational space outside the theatre and the church, and provided a platform upon which collective activities were pursued and collective cultural identities formed. They allowed for cultural conventions to be made public and, in turn, to receive their public confirmation. The reason for this is that concert halls were built and maintained with public subscriptions thus reflecting the cultural conventions of the time. The influence of aesthetics and national philosophies upon musical preferences and artistic expectations has been discussed earlier. What follows is an attempt to demonstrate how these also had an effect on the architectural layout of the concert halls themselves. The aesthetic foundations of each music culture were ubiquitously pervasive; combined with the musical preferences, they reached as far as to affect the behavioural norms of the audience. Unlike in previous chapters, where I dealt with each town in turn, I will now explore this comparison by taking up specific themes in relation to both towns at once.

Purpose, Layout and Design of the Concert Halls

As Leipzig's music culture was based on weekly subscription concerts, the Gewandhaus concerts lacked any sense of dramatic occasion. Owing to the frequency of the events, the concerts did not therefore engage the attention of the populace as a whole. Situated on the periphery of Leipzig's town centre, the Gewandhaus did not impinge on the general populace in the same way as Birmingham's centrally placed Town Hall which was 'the pride and the boast of Birmingham ... the most conspicuous building as well as the finest specimen of architecture in the town'.[81] Apart from the Music Festivals, it was utilised for public meetings of both celebratory and political nature; until the building and opening of the Council House in 1886, it was the social, cultural and political focal point of Birmingham. Reminiscent of other original Grecian temples, the Town Hall represented the *polis* of Birmingham, irrespective of political or religious creed. Its importance to the collective body of Birmingham's inhabitants was visually confirmed by the Town Hall's location: it stood on a hill towering above any building in the vicinity (Figure 3.1).

As a place for social events and public occasions, above all the Festival, the Town Hall attracted the attention of the wider population, wealthy and poor alike. Throughout the nineteenth century, the press would always begin its Festival accounts by describing the scene outside the Town Hall, giving the impression that the Festival was an event, open to all the classes, in which everyone played his or her part according to station. Thus, whilst the prosperous members of society would process into the Town Hall, the less fortunate ones would gather outside and watch the proceedings which began with the audience's arrival in horse-drawn carriages and ended with their imposing entry into the building. Such ceremony enabled Birmingham's middle class to display publicly middle-class status and authority, enhancing the social constitution of mid-Victorian society. The overall function of both public concerts also shaped the interior appearance of the respective concert halls. By adding to it the amalgam of aesthetic tradition, musical preferences and behavioural norms, the intrinsic character of cultural space was fashioned accordingly.

Leipzig first acquired a concert hall in 1781 when the medieval 'draper hall' ('Gewandhaus') was redesigned and refurbished by the architect

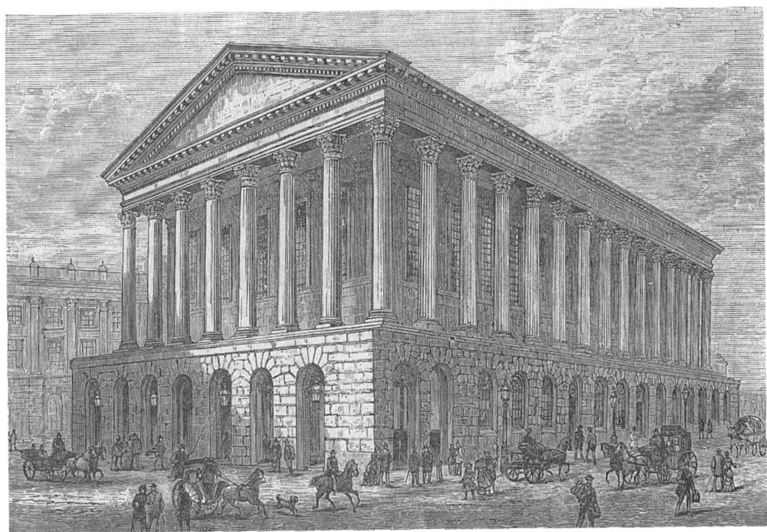

Figure 3.1   Birmingham's Town Hall (Town Hall 16, printed with kind permission of *Birmingham Central Library*)

Johann Friedrich Carl Dauthe to accommodate the so-called *Leipziger Konzerte*, which from then on were named after the Gewandhaus. At that time, the theatre and the church were the only two public meeting spaces in the town, and it was the latter on which the spatial layout of the concert hall was modelled. The first picture below shows Leipzig's St Thomas's Church (Figure 3.2) and the second Leipzig's Gewandhaus (Figure 3.3).

As far as spatial layout is concerned, the Gewandhaus closely resembled the seating order of St Thomas's Church. The similar décor of both is demonstrated by the fact that within a particular seating order, women were exclusively confined 'to the centre of the room, sitting in two vis-à-vis divisions – that is, sideways to the orchestra whilst the gentlemen crowded behind them'.[82] One reason for this spatial imitation of ecclesiastical space may be that the Protestant Church, having provided an acceptable moral framework for gatherings for centuries, could act as a substitute for the absence of codes and ethics appropriate to this new secular environment. This should not, however, be taken to indicate that the Gewandhaus sought direct association with religion; it merely sought to ensure that existing notions of decency within this secular congregational space could be more readily maintained (notwithstanding the obvious physical discomfort produced by such a seating order).

Figure 3.2   Leipzig's St Thomas's Church, around 1930 (BA 1984/19117, printed with kind permission of *Stadtarchiv Leipzig*)

As far as the interior designs are concerned, the Gewandhaus added a uniquely visual confirmation of classical values because architecture, too, incorporated the ideals of Winckelmann's Greece. The 'noble simplicity and serene greatness' is here represented by architectural simplicity, clarity, balance, logic and sobriety. The reasons for this are twofold. Firstly, the lack of festive space was meant to emphasise the difference of

Figure 3.3   Gottlieb Theuerkauf's 'Altes Gewandhaus' (1781, printed with kind permission of *Stadtgeschichtliches Museum* Leipzig)

bourgeois culture from its aristocratic baroque-inspired counterpart and its associated frivolities and hedonistic leanings, a contrast indicative of the denominational divide: the 'internalised world of Protestantism versus the external and representational world of Catholic Baroque'.[83] Whilst to the aristocrat, culture was a means of entertainment, to the bourgeoisie it was a means of spiritual elevation; bourgeois public space was thus designed accordingly: 'to reinforce the role of art as a source of virtue as well as enlightenment, of morality and delight, civic improvement and individual cultivation'.[84]

Secondly, the 'noble simplicity' associated with classical architecture was in harmony with the characteristics intrinsic to Leipzig's aesthetic tradition and concert repertoire. The sobriety was congruent with the way instrumental music was, according to transcendental idealism, supposed to be perceived. In turn, the infinite possibilities, as far as music's ability to express the inner or outer world is concerned, are mirrored in the lack of representational, that is visual, decorations. Scrolls and other decorative features of non-classical architecture (such as Baroque or Rococo) were thought to distract the audience from proper artistic contemplation. Art could thus be inwardly received and appropriated with the solemn respect it was thought to deserve. The only representational feature in the refurbished hall was its elaborate three-part ceiling painting based on classical imagery. A work of art in itself, it depicted the expulsion of the old art by the new, led by Apollo and three of the nine muses – Terpsichore, Polyhymnia and Thalia.[85] All the ceiling paintings were designed by Adam Friedrich Oeser (1717–1799), the director of the Leipzig *Kunstakademie*, founded in 1764, and painted by Johann Ludwig Giesel, an artist from Dresden. The intended messages of the paintings could not be misread. In fact, the meanings were so obvious that Friedrich Rochlitz deemed it necessary to explain the details only once the picture quality grew so poor that the paintings were barely recognisable. In 1814, he describes the painting on the ceiling of the ante-room as follows:

> Auf einer, nur zum Theil erhellten Wolke ruhet ein ernstes, würdevolles, doch schönes und mildes Weib, tief im Nachdenken verloren: ein Buch ist vor ihr aufgeschlagen, ein brennendes Licht steht neben diesem. Ein frischer, kräftiger, unbefangenen heiterer Knabe... putzt ihr das Licht. [...] Man kann wohl nicht treffender andeuten, was für Zuhörer man in den Saal treten zu sehen wünscht! Das Weib ist nämlich die forschende Beurtheilung, die würdige Kunstkritik; der Knabe, der sorglose, herzige Kunstgenuss. [...] Der Hauptgedanke des Bildes heisst...: Hier gehe ein, wer ernstes, aber mildes Urtheil, oder, wer lebendigen, unbefangenen Sinn für Genuss, beydes in Beziehung auf die Tonkunst, mit sich bringt.[86]

The ceiling painting in the main concert hall represents a celebration of the muses in which Apollo presides on his throne observing the spectacle unfolding before him. The half-sisters of music – lyrical and dramatic poetry – the goddess of love, Amor, and others are present; each character is engaged in his/her own activity eventually leading to the notion of silent contemplation. Finally, the demonic Marsyas, attempting to take over Apollo's throne, is thrown out in the direction of the actual exit doors. The overtly classical subject matter could only but reinforce the cultural precepts and musical preferences of the Gewandhaus' patrons; the references to such muses in the paintings paid homage to the noble art of music and demonstrated a stylistic coherence between the arts – architecture, art and music –

embodied in the concert hall itself. The combination of these phenomena left no room for ambiguity as far as the cultural ethos of the concert hall were concerned. The classically humanistic ideals ruled supreme.

Secular pretensions were further demonstrated in the Gewandhaus by the lack of an organ, a powerful symbol of Church music, or choir stalls. The predominance of instrumental music deemed such accessories obsolete. Birmingham's choral culture, by contrast, required a magnificent Town Hall organ which became instantly an object of great pride:

> On the present occasion, the public interest was increased from the unusual novelty attending the celebration of the festival... In the orchestra has been erected a new organ, which, excepting the one in York Minster, is the largest instrument that has yet been built, either in this country or on the Continent. It stands about 52 feet high and has five towers in front, extending nearly forty feet. In the middle tower is placed the thirty two feet pipes, the effect of which must be heard before imagination can conceive their sublime and solemn tones.[87]

Despite the Town Hall's impressive organ and full chorus seating, its layout was indubitably based on the more secular form of entertainment – the theatre (Figure 3.4). The surrounding décor of the Town Hall and its organ was opulent and highly decorated and was in itself a monument to bourgeois industry and achievement. The combined effect bestowed cultural respectability upon Birmingham and its inhabitants; with such manifest opulence, the reputation of Birmingham as a major seat of oratorio culture was greatly and visibly enhanced. The very nature of oratorios espousing sublimity, grandeur and majesty naturally necessitated concert halls which could do them justice. In an age when religiosity was still intrinsic to everyday life and public culture, such aggrandisement of public space for the visual glorification of sacred music was indeed an act of genuine piety in a Victorian sense. As such, accusations of an incipient rise in secularisation (and subsequent protests) particularly by the Quaker contingent of the town, could easily be countered.

The size of chorus and orchestra had always been indicative of the appeal and success of oratorio festivals, whether in London, Norwich or Liverpool. With the opening of the Town Hall in 1834, an orchestra of around 400 musicians could be accommodated, many more than

Figure 3.4   Interior of Birmingham's Town Hall (Town Hall 52, printed with kind permission of *Birmingham Central Library*)

was possible in St Philip's Church, the original venue for oratorio performances. Owing to the dependence of Birmingham's music culture on display and commercial success, the Town Hall quickly became a vital component in it, underpinning Birmingham's claims to cultural eminence, as these excerpts from the *Birmingham Journal* demonstrate:

> The band was exceedingly strong and effective, and numerically inferior only to the host collected at the grand performance at Westminster Abbey in June last. So admirably, however, is the room adapted for sound that we are assured four hundred performers produce much more effect than double that number would in Westminster Abbey. It is said, indeed, to be by far the best music-hall in Great Britain, if not in Europe.[88]

> The doors of the new Town Hall opened at 7 o'clock, but long before the hour arrived they were besieged by a company, and when opened, the vast area and large galleries of this spacious building were rapidly occupied and so completely filled that numbers were compelled to stand during the whole of the performance. When the hall was lighted

up and the company seated, the scene was grand beyond description, and one which, we think, has never been surpassed in Great Britain.[89]

Birmingham's middle-class cultural ethos always depended on outer sensation – audible or visual – to authenticate its aesthetic experience. The combination of architectural splendour, vast organ as well as seating space which could accommodate a chorus and orchestra of gigantic proportions allowed for the intrinsic majesty of oratorios to be visually matched and, indeed, amplified. Add to that the representational display outside the Town Hall, and one can see how the civic and cultural authority of Birmingham's bourgeois élite was emphatically and publicly asserted.

Both Leipzig's and Birmingham's public spaces were designed in line with the cultural ideology of their urban élites. The visual features of the concert halls thus reinforced the kind of music performed, which led to a more comprehensive understanding of each. The formation of specific behavioural norms followed a similar pattern.

Behavioural Norms

The concert hall not only visually publicised cultural conventions with regard to particular music styles but also promoted certain modes of behaviour, fashions and social etiquette. Recent research has dealt with the change in listening etiquette, as traditional ways of listening to music were replaced by new sets of behavioural norms. Richard Sennett, in his *Fall of the Public Man*, has argued that bourgeois concert-goers increasingly began to control their feelings and emotions during a performance, displacing the old spontaneity experienced during the eighteenth century, now regarded as somewhat primitive emotionalism. Silence became a symbol of respectability. Sennett sees this as the result of increasing anonymity and the rising number of *nouveaux riches* within bourgeois society: the more towns expanded, the more the population became an unknown entity.[90] As private individuals, 'faced with a society of equals where the individual felt slight and insignificant',[91] the middle class could only acquire confirmation of their bourgeois credentials by reference to the other, largely unknown, group of concert-goers. This translated into a need for a clear set of norms to which one could conform, and silence was one of these.

James Johnson, in his *Listening in Paris*, has also drawn attention to the emergence of silence within the concert hall. In addition to conformist anxiety, Johnson argued that impoliteness, perceived to be expressed through personal conversation, whistling or stamping one's foot in time to the music, was increasingly regarded as a sign of disrespect for the musical experience available in the concert hall. Listening to music required emotional depth and could only be properly appreciated by adopting an intense, silent and inward manner. Thus,

> ... gone were the days when you could mill about the parterre if the singing got monotonous, or visit the next box when you heard a good conversation, or continue with your parlour sketches as the musicians played from over in the corner... now they made you listen.[92]

Going beyond Johnson, given the difference in the social, cultural and artistic constitution of the two towns, there were necessarily differences in the timing and manner in which the transformation of the concert etiquette of silence took place. An analysis of Leipzig's and Birmingham's concert halls reveals that notions of silence during a public concert were very much conditioned by particular musical styles and the cultural milieu or social ambience provided by the architectural layout and interior design of the concert halls themselves.

In Leipzig, a transformation in the way people listened to music is already noticeable with the opening of the Gewandhaus in 1781. Previous to the *Gewandhauskonzerte*, the Grand (merchant) Concerts were held at Leipzig's coffee houses where the public concert was as much a social as it was a cultural occasion, providing opportunities for frivolous and light-hearted entertainment and amusement. With regard to the Grand Concerts, Johann Friedrich Reichardt noted in 1771, that is, prior to the new Kantian and romantic aesthetic:

> Übrigens ist dieses Concert wie alle öffentliche Concerte beschaffen... als einen hellen Saal voll galanter Gesellschaft, die vielleicht ein wenig mehr gepudert ist, ein wenig steifer sitzt und ein wenig unverschämter über die Musik raisonniert, als in andern grossen Concerten geschieht, übrigens aber die schöne Gabe des Plauderns und Geräusches mit allen übrigen Concertgesellschaften gemein hat. Zwar steht dafür ein Kaufmann, der die Besorgung des Concerts auf sich hat, zur Wache und klopft, wenn jemand gar zu laut spricht, mit einem grossen Ladenschlüssel ans Clavier, welches er zugleich verstimmt, indem er jenen das Stillschweigen anbefiehlt, die es dennoch nicht halten.[93]

Although Reichardt as Kapellmeister to the Prussian king was certainly more accustomed to grand and lavish concert halls, his comments were not unusual. Detlef Prasch, a satirist and critic, reviewed the Grand Concerts along similar lines:

> Ich bin mehrmals dagewesen, habe die Musik allezeit so gewählt und so aufgeführt gefunden, dass sie wohl jedermanns Aufmerksamkeit verdiente, und gleichwohl hab ich gesehen, dass nur der geringste Theil des Auditoriums diese Aufmerksamkeit schenkte. Dieser lorginiert die Frauenzimmer, jene mustert den Putz ihrer Nachbarinnen, und bey den rührendsten Stellen sogar flüstert man dass ich meine, die Herren und Damen abonnieren blos, damit sie sagen können, dass sie Stützen des Grossen Konzertes sind.[94]

With the opening of the Gewandhaus, however, perceptions and styles of reception changed. The aesthetic precepts of classical architecture, further underlined by the interior designs and paintings, already indicated the kind of comportment and conduct deemed appropriate within the concert hall. This was despite the fact that the aesthetic precepts of instrumental music were yet to be developed and the association of instrumental music and classicism still to be established. A visual 'signpost' dispelled any remaining doubts: what was already intrinsically implied by the muse Polyhymnia – a serious woman of a pensive and meditative disposition – was further demonstrated by the axiom *Res Serva est Verum Gaudium*[95] which was affixed above the orchestra platform – clear for all to see. The axiom was taken from Seneca's 23rd letter ('On the True Joy which Comes from Philosophy') of his *Epistulae Morales*.

> Real joy, believe me, is a serious matter. [...] The yield of poor mines is on the surface; those are really rich whose veins lurk deep, and they will make more bountiful returns to him who delves unceasingly. So too those baubles which delight the common crowd afford but a thin pleasure, laid on as a coating, and every joy that is only plated lacks a real basis. But the joy of which I speak, that to which I am endeavouring to lead you, is something solid, disclosing itself the more fully as you penetrate into it. Therefore I pray to you ... [...]; look toward the true good, and rejoice only in that which comes ... from your very self. [...] Do you ask me what this real good is, and whence it derives?

> I will tell you: it comes from a good conscience, from honourable pur-
> poses, from right actions, from contempt of the gifts of chance, from
> an even and calm way of living which treads but one path.[96]

It is interesting that a representative of stoicism, the ancient philosophy
which advocated the mastering of passions and emotions in order to
overcome the outside world and to find peace within oneself, was
chosen to provide a suitable motto. The association of stoic reflection
and introspection was naturally conducive to music's solemn purpose
which demanded, for any genuine appreciation, the mental disposition
appropriate for its reception. This pre-empted the use of music as mere
entertainment, and instead, promoted its use as a way to ennoble and
refine the individual. The visible motto above the orchestra platform
thus acted as a constant reminder to the good burghers of Leipzig what
was expected of them in their new concert hall.

The change in attitude was noticed. Lowell Mason, a regular American
visitor to European music festivals and concert halls, described Leipzig's
Gewandhaus concerts as 'a kind of high school, where taste is formed in
the young, and perfected in the old, and where the knowledge of musical
science, the appreciation and love of musical art are made manifest'.[97]
As to the behaviour of the audience he noted that:

> There was a silence during the performance of music. The moment
> the music ceased, then indeed there was a perfect buzzing of voices,
> and very loud talking all over the room, but at the signal for the com-
> mencement of the music, all was still, and we were not prevented
> from hearing the music by those whisperings so annoying in some
> places.[98]

On the whole, the Gewandhaus and its audience scored highly for
civilised behaviour, giving the impression of a cultivated and refined
civic culture. The solemnity created during the concert was no doubt
influenced by the rapidly increasing perception of classicism as a serious and sober experience. With the rise of idealist philosophy during
the early nineteenth century, the need for sobriety became an absolute
necessity for the essence of the hereafter, eternity, the spirit, even God
Himself, were thought to be directly comprehensible through music.
Listening became an individualised and inwardly oriented act which,
to achieve its proper ends, required silence, tranquillity and equanim-
ity. At the same time, the silence observed by the collective body of
concert-goers reinforced the dominant cultural ideology and practice

within the Gewandhaus and subsequently served as another point of reference within the bourgeois cultural experience.

The behavioural norms in Birmingham's concert culture were similarly prompted by the constitution of its music culture. Given the Festival's duality – a theatre culture, as demonstrated in the evening concert, and an oratorio culture, as highlighted by the morning concerts – concert etiquette was determined according to the distinction between the 'sublime' oratorio and the merely 'entertaining' opera. As in Leipzig, the audience responded to a performance in line with the precepts of the composition. There were no universally applicable codes of conduct in responding to musical compositions. The following newspaper excerpt describes an audience reaction following the performance of *Messiah*.

> The shouts of hundreds, the blast of trumpets, the deep, dire parsons of the organ, the thunder of the drums, conspire to fill the mind with such overwhelming, indescribable sensation that most trembled while many wept as children, so uncontrollable were their feelings. During the performances of the concluding choruses 'Worthy is the Lamb', 'Blessing in Honour' and the 'Amen', so totally absorbed and lost for understanding in the majesty of the music and so deep and universal was this feeling, that when the band had ceased, a death-like silence prevailed and it was not after some minutes, that a foot was moved or a word was spoken.[99]

Listening to oratorios was accompanied by a sense of reverence, similarly to the ways in which religious services were conducted in churches and chapels. As England's aesthetic tradition encouraged the listener to engage with, to emphasise with, the subject – its fortunes, calamities and trepidations – the concert-goer naturally responded in accordance with his or her own disposition which was, presumably, not dissimilar to any other concert-goer. It was thus a communal experience as well as an intensely personal one. Either way, as in Leipzig, audiences had to listen attentively in order to be moved, and for this, silence was required.

The response to operatic performances, by contrast, appeared akin to the way culture was appropriated in the theatre, thus demonstrating a different set of behavioural codes. The following excerpt describes an interaction between the performer and the audience during a glee performance:

> Horncastle's round 'What laughing faces here are met', excited universal shouts of laughter. On the entrance of Mr Terrail, dressed as

Miss Wagtall, the audience broke through all restraint, and greeted him with every demonstration of their mirth, which he took apparently with equal good humour. To increase the ridiculous situation of the parties, Mr Terrail, in making his exit, from being unaccustomed to appear in female attire, missed his footing, and again set the house in an uproar by falling.[100]

In a similar way to Leipzig, the behavioural norms in Birmingham's Town Hall correlated with, and indeed complemented, the musical styles pursued and the analogous reception it required. A performance of an operatic character promised little in the way of spiritual elevation and moral instruction and thus could be approached with a more light-hearted and facetious attitude. (Sure enough, operas could also reduce the listener to tears – the aria sung by Norma in Bellini's eponymous opera, during which she contemplates killing her children, being perhaps the most obvious one.) As audiences continued to respond to a musical performance according to its perceived genre, Birmingham's audience did not have a universal behavioural protocol to follow. This only changed during the early twentieth century, when respectable art was no longer ultimately defined by a particular musical style but solely by virtue of its association with the concert hall itself.

Conclusion

This chapter has aimed to demonstrate how the public concert, once freed from its aristocratic ethos and practice, could develop in accordance with bourgeois ideals and norms. These emergent cultural norms were shaped by, and were thus conducive to, bourgeois notions of equality, morality, aesthetics, education and religion. From the outset, therefore, Leipzig and Birmingham's concert cultures could not be the same. The absence of any universally valid assumptions about the legitimate role and meaning of music prevented any such similarities.

The combination of the phenomena discussed in this chapter – the repertoires, expectations demanded of cultural leaders and artists, the concert halls – generated cultural ideals which suited, and indeed complemented, the respective town élites. In reinforcing each other they created powerful assumptions about culture and art which came to represent an important part of these élites' class-identity. As the following chapters will demonstrate, this proved powerful enough to withstand pressures for change during the second half of the nineteenth century.

The cultural pattern remained potent so long as the underlying precepts –
religion and aesthetics – retained their validity and importance within
the bourgeois sphere. Only once they faltered could the cultural matrix
change too.

Notes

1. H.-U. Glogau, *Der Konzertsaal: Zur Struktur Alter und Neuer Konzerthäuser*
   (Hildesheim: Georg Olms Verlag, 1989), p. 72.
2. For example, Frederick the Great immensely disliked the German language,
   declaring that it was fit for use only by his servants. His penchant for all
   things French included his admiration for Voltaire whom he tried to attract
   to San Souci in Potsdam.
3. The following names are derived from the *Statistik der Concerte im Saale des
   Gewandhauses zu Leipzig* (a list of composers in alphabetical order) in Dörffel,
   Geschichte der Gewandhausconcerte, Appendix pp. 1–79.
4. Data derived from J. Forner, *Die Gewandhauskonzerte zu Leipzig*, Vol. 2
   (Leipzig: VEB Deutscher Verlag für Musik, 1981), p. 61.
5. Doerffel, *Die Geschichte der Gewandhausconcerte*, p. 163.
6. A. Wendt, 'Höhere Tonkunst' in *AMZ*, No. 21, 24 May 1815, p. 345. 'If all the
   other arts possess something that can only apparently be transfigured from
   earthly reality and translated into the Elysium of ideas by the miraculous
   vision of genius, music seems as it were to have been born in this very
   realm and speaks, like the world spirit, through storm and thunder, through
   the gentle birth pangs of spring, . . . a miraculous language that can only
   be understood by those whose ears exclude not an abundance of external
   sounds but the inner world as the most secret depths of the hearts, depths
   into which no mortal eye can peer.'
7. E. T. A. Hoffmann, *Beethovens Instrumentalmusik*. 'Music seeks a feeling for
   the premonitions of joyfulness that is more splendidly and more beautifully than is possible here in this limited world and ignites in the heart an
   inner blissful life coming from an unknown land, a higher expression than
   mere words that are attached to earthly pleasures, can convey.' The essay
   was first published anonymously in the *AMZ* in 1810. In 1814, it was published in his *Kreislerianer*. The text can be accessed via the Projekt Gutenberg:
   http://gutenberg.spiegel.de/etahoff/essays/beethove.htm.
8. C. Applegate, P. Potter, 'Germans as the People of Music' in C. Applegate,
   P. Potter (ed), *Music and German National Identity* (Chicago: University of
   Chicago Press, 2002), p. 5.
9. That Saxony was allowed to exist at all (Friedrich Wilhelm II wanted the
   whole of Saxony) was due to the Austrians and British who were alarmed at
   the prospect of an even stronger Prussia.
10. The Holy Roman Empire was demolished in 1806. It was known as the *Rhein-
    bund* [Rhenish Confederation] until the Congress of Vienna of 1815 which
    established the *Deutscher Bund* [German Confederation].
11. J. Breuilly, 'Introduction' in J. Breuilly, *19th Century Germany: Politics, Culture
    and Society 1780–1918* (London: Arnold, 2001), p. 2.

12. J. Whaley, 'The German lands before 1815' in Breuilly, *19ᵗʰ Century Germany*, pp. 17, 19. Princes and kings were not sovereign but subordinated, however loosely, to the *Reich* which, in turn, guaranteed the status quo.

13. This period spanned 1803–1814. During that period he produced the third and fifth Symphonies, the Waldstein Sonata and Fidelio. All of these were thought to capture the heroism of a revolutionary age.

14. F. Sengle, *Biedermeierzeit: Deutsche Literatur im Spannungsfeld zwischen Restauration und Revolution 1815–1848*, Vol. 1 (Stuttgart: Metzler, 1971), p. 178. The movement was banned in 1835.

15. J. Hermand, *Geschichte der Germanistik* (Reinbek: Rowohlt, 1994), p. 43.

16. Wendt, 'Höhere Tonkunst' in *AMZ*, No. 21, 24 May 1815, p. 351. 'His diversity of feeling is immeasurable, his notes always pronounce a never-before felt, never-before enjoyed, bliss, the celestial and subterranean is tied to the earthly sound and he constantly appears to be new and inexhaustible. [...] ...that he is also able to describe and express the deepest abyss of the struggling heart, as well as the sweetly erotic magic of the innocent soul, the harshest, deepest pain, ...the epitome of what is sublime and lovely whilst his spirit is inclined towards the portrayal of profound sincerity, fiery rapture and sublime splendour with excellent love, and sets the highest affects into harmonious movement.'

17. S. L. Marchand, *Down from Olympus: Archaeology and Philhellenism in Germany, 1750–1970* (Princeton: Princeton University Press, 2003), p. xx.

18. Doerffel, *Die Gewandhauskonzerte*, p. 183. Carl Maria von Weber, principal director at Dresden Court Opera House died in 1826, Beethoven in 1827, Schubert in 1828, Haydn and Mozart had been dead since 1809 and 1791, respectively.

19. C. B. von Miltitz, 'Was heisst klassisch in der Musik?' in *AMZ*, No. 50, 16 December 1835, p. 840.

20. Hoplit [Richard Pohl], 'Hektor Berlioz III' in *NZfM*, Nr 25, 16 December 1853, p. 262.

21. Hoplit, 'Hektor Berlioz I' in *NZfM*, Nr 23, 2 December 1853, p. 240. 'His instruments wrestle with the word as much as with redemption like the basses in the last movement of Beethoven's Ninth Symphony.' According to Richard Wagner's *Kunstwerk der Zukunft*, Beethoven's Ninth Symphony was the last representation of the symphony. Within its confines progress was no longer possible. He considered Franz Liszt and himself to stand at the beginning of a new artistic age, an age which was, above all, defined by the symphonic poem and the music drama. Beethoven's true successor is therefore not Berlioz but Liszt and above all Wagner himself.

22. Anon., 'Nachrichten' in *AMZ*, Nr 11, 15 March 1843, p. 218. 'Whenever such extreme passionate art products generate an immediate effect upon one's disposition, in everything that has been proven to be eternally beautiful we find something other than this burning passion. [...] in art, in general, it is the calm form in the widest sense against which passionate turbulence and variation can be revealed as turbulent and variable. [...] Where grace wants to emerge, where a melody appears and wants to submit itself, it will immediately be plagued with harmonic and rhythmic torment to an extent that it will throw itself back into hellfire out of sheer desperation and be beaten by scorching waves breaking upon its head, to eternal torment.' This passage

in particular echoes Winckelmann's *Gedanken über die Nachahmung*, p. 21. 'Kenntlicher und bezeichnender wird die Seele in heftigen Leidenschaften; gross aber und edel ist sie in dem Stande der Einheit, in dem Stande der Ruhe.' [The soul becomes more pronounced in burning passions; yet it is grand and noble in the state of unity, in the state of calm.]

23. Hoplit, 'Hektor Berlioz I' in *NZfM*, Nr 23, 2 December 1853, p. 238. 'Because the force of mass public opinion ignored Berlioz, Berlioz actually educates the public.'

24. G. W. Fink, 'Abschied des Redakteurs' in *AMZ*, No. 52, 30 December 1841, p. 1135. 'Da ist jetzt Krieg im Reiche der Harmonie.' Fink refers to the emerging schism between the progressives and conservatives.

25. P. U. Hohendahl, *Literarische Kultur im Zeitalter des Liberalismus 1830–1870* (Munich: Beck, 1985), p. 124.

26. The bibliography for the 1848 revolutions is extensive. Good introductions are provided by W. Siemann, 'The Revolutions of 1848–49 and the Old Regime' in M. Fulbrook, *German History Since 1800* (London: Arnold, 1997) and his *The German Revolution of 1848–49* (London: Macmillan, 1998 [1985]). See also Sheehan, *German History*, W. Hardtwig, *Revolution in Deutschland und Europa 1848–49* (Göttingen: Vandenhoeck & Ruprecht, 1998), F. L. Müller, *Die Revolution von 1848/49* (Darmstadt: Wissenschaftliche Buchgesellschaft, 2002) and J. Sperber, *The European Revolutions, 1848–1851* (Cambridge: Cambridge University Press), 1994.

27. Robert Blum rose to political prominence with the liberal–republican movement of the early 1840s. He became a town councillor in Leipzig in 1846 and was later elected to represent Zwickau in the Frankfurt parliament. There, he led the radical–liberal faction which insisted on the principle of popular sovereignty. When non-German ethnic groups within the Habsburg Empire attempted to gain sovereignty, Blum and others travelled to Vienna in support. He was swiftly arrested and tried by the authorities despite the fact that membership of the Frankfurt assembly should have granted him immunity. His execution was often used to highlight the powerlessness of the Frankfurt assembly and his death to portray the failure of the revolution itself. Future labour and socialist movements would greatly utilise his persona and death for their own ends.

28. *Gemüt* defies straightforward translation. It could variously mean 'soul', 'temperament', 'mind' or 'disposition'.

29. S. Friedrich, 'Parteiung auf dem Gebiete der Tonkunst' in *AMZ*, No. 41, 11 October 1848, p. 659. 'If the nature of all political being is always tied to the dominant Idea of any given moment in time and a certain unfreedom of the individual can never be banished, the soul should be free in its artistic appreciation; it should feel the best gifts of the past as well as the present.... The less one's taste is bound to a particular direction, the more general, more encompassing one's ability to appreciate and enjoy the genuine and beautiful of all times, the freer from all partisanship, the more worthy of art it becomes.'

30. J. Schucht, 'Der überwundene Standpunkt in der Musik' in *AMZ*, No. 33, 16 August 1848, p. 537f. 'The language of the heart, the inexpressible feelings of the soul, jealousy, and revenge, love, lust and pain, are felt in their thousandfold modifications so long as mortal hearts shall beat. And the

representation of these states of the soul is the main task of the music [. . .] which is able to depict and is most potent when words are no longer able to reproduce the infinite movements and feelings which stir a human breast in this earthly life.'

31. F. Brendel, 'Fragen der Zeit' in *NZfM*, No. 37, 4 November 1848, p. 213f. 'The development of history is an incessant stream; whether the idea which moves one epoch be the greatest and mightiest: this idea has its time with which it stands and falls. Other epochs will enter with a different idea; the previous one will be reduced to the moment, it has become a [. . .] conquered point of view and it is the professional responsibility of those bearers of all spiritual/intellectual spheres to follow the flow of general movement, and to serve willingly the idea prevalent in any given period of time. Art too is obliged to reveal the prevalent idea in its creations.'

32. Prutz quoted in Sengle, *Biedermeierzeit*, p. 218.

33. A similar movement was taking place within the field of *Germanistik*. Leading scholars and writers – for example, J. Grimm, E. M. Arndt, L. Uhland, M. Haupt, G. G. Gervinus – organised the first *Deutschen Germanistentag* in 1846. It provided a platform to propagate their opposition to censorship, ultramontanism, even Denmark's claims to Schleswig-Holstein. Musicians were, of course, not yet established in public bodies such as universities. See Hermand, *Geschichte der Germanistik*, p. 46.

34. F. Brendel, 'Fragen der Zeit II' in *NZfM*, No. 33, 22 April 1848, p. 193f.

35. F. Brendel, 'Eingabe an das königlich preussische Ministerium der geistlichen-, Unterrichts- und Medicinal-Angelegenheiten' in *NZfM*, No. 16, 22 August 1848, p. 85. The petition was also signed by C. F. Becker, C. Hentschel, A. F. Riccius and A. G. Ritter – all contributors to the *NZfM*.

36. S. Bagge, 'Der Künstler und das heutige Publikum in ihren gegenseitigen Anforderungen' in *AMZ*, No. 17, 24 April 1867, p. 135.

37. J. C. Lobe, 'Fortschritt III' in *AMZ*, No. 11, 15 March 1848, p. 169. 'A critical genius can only be formed by way of studying existing works of the art concerned, by way of abstracting artistic rules and artistic maxims [. . .] from these, it forms taste, his judgement, differing only in that he does not just talk about other works of art but learns to create some of his own. [. . .] The true, practically enabling higher study of creation lies alone in the exemplary works themselves. From these alone there streams the invigorating, nourishing, rousing breath of the creative artistic genius, the exhilaration of spring which entices forth the buds of his talent. The student must approach these examples with all the wealth and reverence, with faith and conviction in their pre-eminence as revealers of the true artistic secrets.'

38. Graph based on data derived from Doerffel, *Geschichte der Gewandhauskonzerte*, Appendix pp. 1–79.

39. The Times, 'Popularity of the Oratorio' in *The Musical World*, No. 36, Vol. 37, 3 September 1859, p. 573.

40. G. A. Macfarren, 'Handel and his Messiah' in *The Musical World*, No. 14, Vol. 24, 7 April 1849, p. 216.

41. B. 'Beethoven's Pastoral Symphony' in *The Musical World*, No. 40, Vol. 17, 6 October 1842, p. 320.

42. Anon., 'Mendelssohn's Lobgesang' in *The Musical Times*, No. 58, Vol. 3, 1 March 1849, p. 125.

43. Anon., 'The Progress and Influence of Music' in *The Musical World*, No. 3, Vol. 25, 19 January 1850, p. 39.

44. D. J. Grout, C. V. Palisca, *A History of Western Music*, 4th ed (London: J. M. Dent & Sons, 1988 [1960]), p. 531.

45. Grout, Palisca, *A History of Western Music*, p. 532.

46. *Birmingham Journal*, 23 September 1837.

47. *British Quarterly Review*, 'Mendelssohn' in *The Musical World*, No. 24, Vol. 35, 13 June 1857, p. 374.

48. *Birmingham Journal*, 23 September 1837.

49. L. Colley, *Britons: Forging the Nation 1707–1838* (New Haven, London: Yale University Press, 1992), p. 44.

50. D. Martin, *Christian Language and its Mutations: Essays in Sociological Understanding* (Aldershot: Ashgate, 2002), p. 9.

51. W. Dean, *Handel's Dramatic Oratorios and Masques* (Oxford: Oxford University Press, 1959), p. 43.

52. Dean, *Handel's Dramatic Oratorios*, p. 39.

53. H. Richard, *Memoirs of Joseph Sturge* (London: S. W. Partridge, 1864), p. 61. Sturge, a prominent local Quaker, refused to pay the rate on the grounds that oratorios performed in secular establishments (i.e. the Town Hall) were contrary to his religious conviction.

54. W. Weber, *The Rise of Musical Classics in 18th Century England: A Study in Canon, Ritual and Ideology* (Oxford: Oxford University Press, 1996 [1992]), p. 121. Handel wrote music for Roman Catholics, Lutherans and Anglicans alike.

55. Dean, *Handel's Dramatic Oratorios*, p. 129.

56. *Birmingham Journal*, 23 September 1837.

57. J. H. Buckley, *The Victorian Temper: A Study in Literary Culture* (Cambridge: Cambridge University Press, 1969 [1951]), p. 138.

58. *Birmingham Post*, 29 August 1861.

59. Davidoff, Hall, *Family Fortunes*, p. 441.

60. Hoffmann, *Beethovens Instrumentalmusik*. 'The real artist only lives in the work which he appropriates and now executes in exactly the way it was conceived by the master. The artist disdains to assert his own personality in any way, and all his thoughts and efforts are designed to recall the magnificent, sweet visions and appearances which the master enclosed with miraculous power in his composition, and bring them back to bustling life shining in a thousand colours so that they surround the human being in light, twinkling circles, and whilst arousing his fantasy, his inner soul, carry him in rapid flight into the distant spiritual sphere of sounds.'

61. J. Forner, 'Felix Mendelssohn Bartholdy: Es flogen ihm hundert Herzen zu im ersten Augenblicke', in V. Hauschild, *Die Grossen Leipziger: 26 Annäherungen* (Leipzig: Insel-Verlag, 1996), p. 238. . . . not the 'torments of the soul of the Romantics with moon-lit nights and stormy clouds, not the longing for something long lost, the blue flower, not the loneliness and self-desolation – no, here the powers of classicism, clarity of thought, order of feelings are at work, here the supernatural manifestations are staged out of desire for the fantastic play'.

62. F. Brendel, 'Robert Schumann mit Rücksicht auf Mendelssohn-Bartholdy' in *NZfM*, No. 35, 30 April 1845, p. 147.

63. J. P. Eckermann, *Gespräche mit Goethe in den letzten Jahren seines Lebens*. The text can be found via the Project Gutenberg: www.gutenberg.spiegel.de/ eckerman/gesprche/gesprche.htm. (Volumes one and two published in 1837, Volume 3 in 1848) 'Das Klassische nenne ich das Gesunde und das Romantische das Kranke. Und sind die Nibelungen' klassisch wie der Homer, denn beide sind gesund und tüchtig. Das meiste Neuere ist nicht romantisch, weil es neu, sondern weil es schwach, kränklich und krank ist, und das Alte ist nicht klassisch, weil es alt, sondern weil es stark, frisch, froh und gesund ist' (2 April 1829).

64. P. Bishop, R. H. Stephenson, *Friedrich Nietzsche and Weimar Classicism* (New York: Boydell & Brewer [Camdon House], 2004), p. 10.

65. W. Muschg, *Studien zur tragischen Literaturgeschichte* (Bern: Francke, 1965), p. 10.

66. H. Heine, *Florentine Nights* (London: Methuen & Co. Ltd., 1927). Translated by Charles Godfrey Leland.

67. E. M. Butler, *The Fortunes of Faust* (Cambridge: Cambridge University Press, 1952), pp. 352–356. Butler provides a comprehensive list of Faust plays and novels. Around 58 plays and novels dealing with the Faust legend were written between Lessing's Faust fragment of 1759 and the revolution of 1848. A total of 95 were written by 1947 (Thomas Mann's *Dr Faustus*). The heyday for Faust stories since 1800 seems to have been the 1810s and 1830s. Also, by the mid-nineteenth century, secondary sources began to appear, such as F. Peter's *Die Literatur der Faustsage bis Ende des Jahres 1848* (Leipzig, 1849).

68. The word 'mesmerise' has its origins in the person of Franz Anton Mesmer. A physician, by trade, he believed that all physical phenomena are interconnected and evolved a theory that living creatures influence each other by an omnipresent tenuous substance which he termed 'animal magnetism'. During the cures he effected (supported by semi-darkness, soft music, mysterious gestures), Mesmer frequently induced hypnotic states in his patients. Mesmerism is employed as a literary motif by some Romantic writers. See H. and M. Garland, *The Oxford Companion to German Literature* (Oxford: Oxford University Press, 1976), p. 589.

69. Paganini himself, when accusations circulated at an unprecedented velocity, published a letter in the *Revue Musicale* (1831), in which he refuted, with good humour, all the speculations. He emphasised the absurdity of the story according to which he must have had a mistress, a rival and committed murder at the tender age of seven.

70. Titel, *Heinrich Brockhaus*, p. 91. 'It appears to me as if Paganini with his artistic skillfulness is making fun of the audience and is secretly laughing to himself when a rousing applause follows. [...] If I had any influence on the judgement for future generations of Paganini, he would occupy a very subordinate rank as an artist but a very high one as a virtuoso.'

71. 'Nekrolog: Dr Felix Mendelssohn Bartholdy' in *AMZ*, Nr 52, 29 December 1847, p. 913. ...his gifts were used only for the noblest purposes of art.... He could have used his riches to enjoy the common pleasures of life. Instead he worked incessantly and repaid the gifts he received from God through

the honest fulfilment of His commands, probably at the cost of a longer life'.

72. J. Werner, *Mendelssohn's Elijah: A Historical and Analytical Guide to the Oratorio* (London: Lowe and Brydone, 1965), p. xii.

73. *Birmingham Journal*, 'The Birmingham Festival, Mendelssohn, etc' in *The Musical World*, No. 29, Vol. 36, 17 July 1858, p. 453.

74. R. L. Todd, *Mendelssohn: A Life in Music* (Oxford: Oxford University Press, 2002), p. 547.

75. Anon., 'Mendelssohn's St Paul' in *The Musical World*, No. 31, Vol. 31, 30 July 1853, p. 483.

76. Dean, *Handel's Dramatic Oratorios*, p. 136.

77. Anon., 'Mendelssohn's Characteristics' in *The Musical World*, No. 22, Vol. 31, 3 June 1854, p. 372.

78. A. Forchert, 'Textanlage und Darstellungsprinzipien in Mendelssohn's Elias' in C. Dahlhaus, *Das Problem Mendelssohn* (Regensburg: Gustav Bosse Verlag, 1974), p. 63. 'Not the creation of an exemplary narrative in the Christian sense was primarily envisaged here but the representation of dramatic situations, not the general religious significance of the content was important here to the composer but the potential it provided him with the captivating, lively characters and scenes inherent to the composition.'

79. O. Jahn, 'Ueber F Mendelssohn Bartholdy's Oratorium Elias' in *AMZ*, No. 8, 23 February 1848, p. 120.

80. D, 'Mendelssohn's Elijah' in *The Musical World*, No. 18, Vol. 22, 1 May 1847, p. 278.

81. W. Showell, *Dictionary of Birmingham – A History and Guide* (Oldbury: Walter Showell & Sons, 1887 [1885]), p. 261.

82. H. F. Chorley, *Music and Manners in Germany: A Series of Travelling Sketches of Art and Society* (London, 1841), p. 105. It is unclear from the sources whether the practice of separating men and women during the concerts continued during the nineteenth century.

83. M. Steinberg, *Listening to Reason: Culture, Subjectivity, and Nineteenth-Century Music* (Princeton: Princeton University Press, 2004), p. 69.

84. Sheehan, *German Museums*, p. 78.

85. In ancient mythology, Apollo, the god of music, was the leader of the nine muses. Terpsichore is the muse of dance and dramatic chorus, Polyhymnia the muse of sacred hymn and Thalia the muse of comedy and pastoral poetry.

86. F. Rochlitz, 'Oesers Deckengemälde im Leipziger Concertsaale' in *AMZ*, No. 27, 7 July 1813, p. 452. 'On a partly illuminated cloud rests a serious, dignified, yet beautiful and mild woman, lost in deep thoughts: a book lies open before her, a burning light stands beside it. A fresh, strong, naturally cheerful boy polishes the lamp for her. [...] One cannot intimate more adequately what kind of audience one wishes to enter in this hall! The woman, in fact, represents the investigative judgement, dignified art criticism; the boy the carefree enjoyment of art. [...] The central thought of the picture is this: Let anyone enter who brings with him a serious, but mild judgement, or, a lively, natural sense of enjoyment, both in relation to music.'

87. *Birmingham Journal*, 11 October 1834.

88. *Birmingham Journal*, 11 October 1834.

89. *Birmingham Journal*, 11 October 1834.
90. R. Sennett, *The Fall of Public Man* (London: Faber and Faber, 1986 [1976]), p. 263.
91. J. Johnson, *Listening in Paris: A Cultural History* (Berkeley: University of California Press, 1995), p. 234.
92. Johnson, *Listening in Paris*, p. 236.
93. In his *Briefe eines aufmerksamen Reisenden*, Reichardt gives an account of his experiences during an extra concert in *Drey Schwanen*. Quoted in Schering, Wustmann, *Musikgeschichte Leipzigs,* p. 418. 'Incidentally, [Leipzig's grand] concert is arranged like all public concerts...a bright hall filled with gallant society, perhaps a little more powdered, a little stiffer and a little more impertinent in its judgements on music than is observed in other grand concerts even though it shares the beautiful gift of chat and noise with all other concert societies. Indeed, a merchant guards the concert proceedings and insists on silence, even from those who refuse to be quiet, by banging his shop key against the piano if anyone speaks too loudly, thereby putting it out of tune.'
94. D. Prasch, *Vertraute Briefe über den Politischen and Moralischen Zustand von Leipzig* (London, 1787), p. 125. 'I have attended the Grand Concert several times and have always regarded the choice and performance of music worthy of everyone's attention. However, I saw that only the tiniest part of the audience paid attention. A man peers at the young ladies, a woman inspects the finery of her female neighbours and even during the most touching pieces, people are whispering and I began to wonder whether these ladies and gentlemen were subscribing merely in order to appear to be pillars of the grand concerts.'
95. The translation allows both 'True Joy is a Serious Matter' and 'It is a Serious Matter to Bring Joy.'
96. Seneca, *Ad Lucilium Epistulae Morales*. Translated by R. M. Gummere (London: Heinemann, 1925).
97. L. W. Mason, *Musical Letters from Abroad: Including Detailed Accounts of the Birmingham, Norwich, and Dusseldorf Musical Festivals of 1852* (New York: Mason Brothers, 1853), p. 32.
98. Mason, *Musical Letters*, p. 26.
99. *Aris' Birmingham Gazette*, 11 October 1834.
100. *Birmingham Journal*, 11 October 1834.
101. This was by no means the norm: Berlin, for example, waited another 15 years for symphoney No. 5 to be performed.

4
Post-Mendelssohn to *Fin-de-Siècle*

Introduction

As the first half of the nineteenth century drew to a close, the respective musical canons of Leipzig and Birmingham as part of the middle-class cultural experience had been firmly institutionalised. The Gewandhaus and its audience could be identified by a preference for classical values which, in turn, led to a rejection of strictly non-classical compositions such as Wagner's music drama or Liszt's symphonic poems as part of its cultural experience. In Birmingham, by contrast, where the doctrinal adherence to musical styles (e.g. classicism, romanticism) was, on the whole, absent, musical and artistic developments could be more readily accepted so long as, of course, they stayed within the parameters of artistic propriety. Similar to the Gewandhaus Board of Directors, the Festival organisers continued to insist on the by now traditional patterns of cultural respectability.

This chapter aims to establish how both concert ventures responded to the immense economic, social, cultural and political changes taking place during the second half of the nineteenth century. These changes will be examined through a study of their repertoires, the role of cultural leaders and the public space from the death of Mendelssohn in 1847 to the onset of the *fin-de-siècle*. (So far as Leipzig is concerned, the opening of the second Gewandhaus in 1884 will be dealt with.) In particular, attention will be focused on how the direct attachment (Birmingham) or lack of attachment (Leipzig) of their music culture to more ubiquitous, yet ephemeral, socio-cultural phenomena was affected by the inevitable progress of time – often regarded as a pernicious challenge to all kinds of tradition. Before dealing with these issues, however, an account of the philosophical developments in Britain and Germany during the second half of the nineteenth century is provided.

Mid-nineteenth-century Philosophy and its Impact on Culture

Advances made in the aesthetic sphere during the second half of the nineteenth century had a decidedly smaller impact on the public sphere than it had during the formative years of bourgeois culture. During the 1810s and 1820s, aesthetics (or religiously informed aesthetics in England) had become inextricably woven into the cultural matrix of bourgeois culture which meant that they began to inform the boundaries of cultural respectability as well as cultural practices. The close linkage of these earlier ideas in bourgeois culture meant that advances in the aesthetic and philosophical spheres since the 1850s would have to wrestle with firmly established cultural conventions. Even though some aesthetic discoveries might have profoundly affected the individual, they could not alter significantly bourgeois culture as a whole as the case of Arthur Schopenhauer in Germany might demonstrate.

Although Schopenhauer became a favourite with the educated bourgeois (*Bildungsbürger*) during the second half of the nineteenth century, as well as with the artistic élite, his posthumous work had little influence upon the wider public sphere as an institutionalised body. This is, firstly, related to the philosophy he advocated in his *Die Welt als Wille und Vorstellung* ('The World as Will and Representation', 1817).[1] His insistence that only art makes life tolerable because the concentration on the object, loss of self-consciousness, detachment and disinterestedness 'relieves the restless craving of the will, and for a short time at least, can get us over the pains of being', may have fascinated the individual but it could not possibly serve as a basis for a respectable middle-class culture, particularly in Leipzig, whose cultural identity had been founded on solidly classical attributes such as serenity, nobility and restraint.[2] Secondly, his aesthetic theory attributed an importance to the artist and art which required a level of autonomy which the public concert was unwilling or unable to provide. The demands made on subjectivity and the irrational will in the individual would have rendered the entire bourgeois cultural matrix obsolete. Finally, the sombre pessimism regarding human existence and the persistent emphasis on human suffering might have struck a chord during Germany's Restoration period (during which *Die Welt als Wille und Vorstellung* was conceived), but it could not do so during the 1860s and 1870s – a time of unprecedented economic prosperity, militaristic and national euphoria. In sum, one of the most widely read aesthetic treatises could only ever really affect the singular artist or the *avant-garde*-minded individual – it was of no relevance to the broader institution of bourgeois culture.

Highly significant was the rise of formalism, a system which was influenced by mid-century positivism – the enthusiasm for and confidence in scientific methodology. It held that music must be judged in accordance with its intrinsic qualities alone. Thus, Eduard Hanslick in his *Vom Musikalisch-Schönen* ('The Beautiful in Music', 1854) insisted that music does not possess some special relationship with feeling or emotions, requiring neither words, thoughts nor action to achieve its perfection.[3] Following Hanslick, musical aesthetics witnessed a comprehensive redefinition and expansion in subject coverage in that this new scientific pursuit encouraged efforts to establish laws concerning physio-somatology of tones, musical theory, the nature of harmony, melody and rhythm and to discover and rediscover older music. The intricacy inherent in this kind of enquiry (which provided for an academic method of enquiry which was suitable for entering on a university career[4]), combined with the lack of interest in the aesthetic and cultural values of music, rendered it incompatible with the needs of *Kultur*. However, even though Hanslick refrained from endorsing the metaphysical kingdom, his scientific approach did nothing to weaken or undermine either classicism or the Gewandhaus canon. If anything, his appointment as the Viennese correspondent of the *AMZ*, in which he took a determined stand against the *Neudeutschen* whilst championing Brahms, endeared him greatly to the traditional-minded concert-goer.

Thus whilst there was no shortage of new and important aesthetic developments, until Nietzsche, these no longer necessarily advanced either in support of or in opposition to bourgeois culture but existed independently and alongside it. The reason for this is that the philosophical, literary and musical achievements of its classical period – Herder, Kant, Humboldt, Goethe, Schiller, Beethoven – had long since taken their privileged place within the ubiquitous ideal of bourgeois *Kultur*. Having become cultural institutions themselves, their cultural status was indomitably and irrefutably part of the definition of what constitutes *Kultur*. Given that it was with and through them that the bourgeois was able to conceptualise the world and his place within it, no new aesthetic or philosophy which succeeded them was to have such a powerful and all-embracing effect on the wider public sphere. Nothing would shape the common understanding of the bourgeois world, art and education as Kant, Schiller, Humboldt and Goethe had done in their time. As in the early nineteenth century, (by now ossified) antiquity was still the key to the bourgeois concept of 'cultivation' and 'erudition', which was supported by an education system still geared towards the study of classicism. Accordingly, it continued to exercise a profound influence over the bourgeoisie's cultural endeavours. The Gewandhaus, no less drawn to the same classical ideals, could thus sustain its cultural and artistic authority unchallenged. Any attack on its artistic ideology would also have to battle against the concept of *Kultur*, especially since concert halls, unlike art galleries, remained under the direct control of the middle class rather than the more multi-layered municipal bodies or state ministries.

This persistence of traditional cultural paradigms spelled out a relative immunity to historicism – a method which stressed the transience and ephemeral nature of all moral, political, social and cultural structures previously deemed permanently legitimate. In ascendance since the 1860s throughout Europe, this approach began to undermine traditional notions concerning religion, morality, history, abstract notions of time and space, and man's place within them. The continued detachment of Leipzig's public concert from all such socio-cultural constructs, combined with the centrality of (subjective) feeling, however, very much ensured that Germany's aesthetic system remained impervious to the challenge posed by historicism. As will become evident later, the development of a specifically German variant of historicism paradoxically legitimised the cultural superiority of the German classical period within the concept of *Kultur*.

By contrast, Birmingham's music culture – legitimising itself through religious and moral truths – seemed inevitably troubled once the caustic power of historicism began to relativise moral and religious 'absolutes' upon which the Festival were originally founded and still depended. As this chapter will show, it was only the firm grip of Festival officials on Town Hall proceedings, coupled with obdurate hold of institutionalised middle-class tradition, which allowed the Festival to maintain its traditional cultural base, at least for the time being. The traditional concept of association, too, retained its validity. The true test of all music, wrote the *Birmingham Post*, 'must be its emotional effect... arousing and thrilling even the least imaginative hearer'.[5] Music was still regarded as an 'artistic union of inarticulate sounds and rhythm, exciting agreeable sensations, and raising mental images and emotions directly or indirectly pleasing. When conjoined to poetry, ... its office is then to enforce the meaning of the words and add a colouring to them'.[6] To ensure success, the artist was expected to convey effectively dramatic power to fire the imagination, to move the soul through exalted feeling or pathos, with a propriety deemed suitable to middle-class sensibility. This was further substanti-ated by the overwhelming authority of John Ruskin – Britain's foremost Victorian art critic. For him, all art had to relate to human experience which meant that the pursuit of beauty for its own sake would lead to sterile and dead art.[7] Music – conjoined with poetry as a natural expres-sion of pure human passions – should always induce proper moral feeling which can then inform a perfect social and cultural order.[8] Such sen-timents were still being articulated a decade after the Ruskin–Whistler trial[9] (1878) which, within the visual arts, at least, sorely tested the continued authority of literary, narrative and allegorical art which had dominated the Victorian art scene. This was despite the onset of Impres-sionism on the Continent and despite the aesthetic advances made since Matthew Arnold, and later, Walter Pater, that resulted in a first acceptance of English formalism.

The visual arts and music were not seen to share the same aesthetic foundations which meant that, for a while at least, the predicament affecting art did not seem to have any bearing on concert halls. Also, music and the musician had always been far more dependent on bourgeois patronage than was the painter or sculptor – especially in Birmingham, where musical performances required considerable finan-cial backing and organisational support. This meant that, despite artistic and aesthetic advances, public performances were still required to satisfy the cultural wants and needs of Birmingham's middle class. As these were still based on traditional concepts, a certain incongruity between the Festival and the wider cultural developments (not dissimilar to the emer-gent schism witnessed at Leipzig's Gewandhaus), arose during the 1870s and 1880s. Evidence for this can be found in the musical commissions offered during that time.

The Repertoires

Leipzig

Whatever hopes there had been in the months leading up to March 1848, by the early 1850s until the late 1880s, the overriding cultural mood was that of Biedermeier *Gemütlichkeit* which was complemented, and indeed nourished, by a huge upsurge in economic prosperity during the 1850s and 1860s. This development was further supported by the granting of unprecedented economic freedom – freedom of trade and freedom of enterprise – by individual state governments. As far as the entrepreneur, banker and merchant were concerned, Germany was at its healthiest and wealthiest. During the early years of the 1870s, further economic growth was triggered by French reparation payments following the defeat at the hands of the Prussian army and the unification of Germany.

This dramatic transformation in economic fortunes inevitably rocked nineteenth-century society to its core. In a town such as Leipzig – still a centre of the publishing and textile industries – the social structure of civic life was altered considerably. New factories, roads, railways emerged and new working-class slums rose alongside them. A new social reality, characterised by widespread poverty, pauperism, prostitution and child labour changed the civic landscape beyond all recognition. The city faced accusations of moral corruption, and it was in literature – realist and later naturalist plays and novels – that the problems arising from that new social and economic reality were first publicly raised.[10] Nothing, however, could awaken the Gewandhaus from its metaphysical dream world. This was inevitable given that there is little which could have reconciled the new social reality with the classical ideals still propagated in Leipzig's concert hall.

If anything, the mid-nineteenth century rise of a specifically German variant of historicism gave further impetus to the primacy of classicism. As the previous chapter explained, in an attempt to legitimise its own cultural ethos, the *AMZ* began to argue that no single historic epoch could claim a monopoly on classicism but that such an accolade was determined by the healthiness of the cultural condition which, in turn, nurtured classical works. Leipzig during the early nineteenth century, it was argued, was one such epoch. The mid-century advance of historicism legitimised this further: the scientific approach to studying the past demonstrated that, like other artistic and literary movements such as the late eighteenth century *Sturm and Drang*, the German musical classical age, spanning the decades between the young Haydn and the mature Beethoven, now had a beginning and a definite end, with clearly perceptible characteristics which separated it from the preceding and subsequent cultural ages. As such it could be treated as a cultural epoch which, under the vanguard of Leipzig's bourgeoisie, was particularly rich in cultural achievements. This past, however, was not left to simmer in the past but was appropriated to serve an important purpose in the present. By making the past much more relevant to the modern, mid-nineteenth century bourgeois, the achievements of the past could be used to legitimise the cultural, political and artistic customs and rituals of the present. Thus, the notion of 'beginning' and 'end' paradoxically underlined the immutability of the Gewandhaus view of *Kultur*. The main patrons of this approach were historians/parliamentarians such as Johann Gustav Droysen, Heinrich von Sybel and later Heinrich von Treitschke who proposed that history was not only of immediate contemporary relevance, but that it was the tool with which one could understand and guide the present situation. In that respect, history creates identity; without an historical view of the past, no creative orientation towards the future was possible. With little to contribute by itself, the present was thought to offer no coherent *idea* from which a common and shared identity could be drawn. As far as the Gewandhaus was concerned, only the past was capable of doing this.

That Leipzig's premier concert institute, supported by the *AMZ* which resurfaced in 1863, would continue to hail the German classical period and legitimise its present cultural practices through its achievements has already been pointed out. The drawback of the preoccupation with the past was that it did not really say anything about the essence of music any more. The absolute confidence in the literary (Goethe and Schiller), philosophical (Herder, Kant, Humboldt) and musical (Haydn, Mozart, Beethoven) achievements might have informed Germany's ambition to become a *Kulturnation*, the 'land of thinkers and poets', but it provided little by way of musical understanding. It was Friedrich Nietzsche who first drew attention to the problematic correlation between the worship of great figures of the past and the current state of art: the tunnel-vision view of the past, detracting from the present and the future, made the public merely content to philosophise about and imitate the past's achievements. This was, according to Nietzsche, 'not a real culture at all, but only a kind of knowledge about culture… only by filling and over-filling ourselves with alien ages, customs, arts, philosophies, religions and knowledge do we become something worthy of notice, namely walking encyclopaedias…'.[11] This form of excessive consciousness or cultural insight became a typical Nietzschean charge.

For Nietzsche, Germany was particularly prone to this kind of neurotic obsession with past achievements since its swift military triumph over France and the ensuing formation of the first German nation state. As his opening paragraph of his *Unzeitgemässe Betrachtungen* (*Untimely Meditations*, 1873) affirmed, military and political success, rather than having a positive effect on the well-being of Germany's national culture, only fostered cultural complacency and uncritical self-righteousness. This cultural complacency combined with excessive consciousness, fostered by the persistence of classical values such as the Apolline principles of order and restraint, could only but subvert any form of vitality.[12] As a result, he accused his own age of being trivial, mediocre, exhausted, conventional and prosaic. Lacking in substance and authenticity, contemporary art, culture, aesthetics and beliefs in civilisations, humanity and progress must subsequently be in decay, but were continually propped up by epigonism, routinised education, convention and complacent conformity.[13] Accordingly, such concepts of culture (and art) could no longer represent the value of life, something which could only be achieved by a new art which is spontaneous and creative – driven by pre-rational powers and instincts. To counter the shortcomings of the present cultural situation which was based on an Apolline concern with order, form and belief in the permanence of greatness and nobility, Nietzsche thus introduced Dionysus – the god of orgies, chaos, instinct, darkness, destruction and intoxication. Only a balance between the Apolline desire for order and the Dionysian spirit which could bypass man's rational side, allowing him to enjoy the play of the senses without feeling the need or desire to analyse them, could ever represent the ideal of art. This ideal was, according to Nietzsche, best represented by Schopenhauer's philosophy and Wagner's music.

Whatever the individual might have made of Nietzsche's Dionysus, there can be no doubt Apollo ruled in the Gewandhaus. For one thing, until the mid-1890s the repertoire was dominated by the great classical composers and their successors: Beethoven, Schumann, Brahms, Haydn, Mozart, Schubert, Rubinstein, Mendelssohn, Lachner and Volkmann, with occasional symphonic performances of Gade, Reinecke and Spohr – 'all very much in tune with the dignity thought congruent to the Gewandhaus'.[14] Table 4.1 lists the average performances of symphonies

Table 4.1   Average Performance of Symphonies per Season in the Gewandhaus

Composer	Number of performance of symphonies per season	Notes
Beethoven	6–7	(during the seasons of 1883/1884 and 1888/1889, eight symphonies were performed)
Schumann	3	(during the seasons of 1883/1884 and 1887/1888, all four symphonies were performed)
Brahms	1	
Haydn	1–2	
Mozart	1–2	
Mendelssohn	1–2	
Schubert	1	(it would almost always be the ninth Symphony)
Rubinstein	1	
Lachner	1	(Performances stopped in 1884)
Volkmann	1	(consistently performed until 1900, afterwards rather sporadically)

Table 4.2 Premières of Brahms' Symphonies and their First Performance in the Gewandhaus

Symphony No.	Place and time of first performance	First performance in Leipzig
1	Karlsruhe, November 1876	January 1877
2	Vienna, December 1877	January 1878
3	Vienna, December 1883	February 1884
4	Meiningen, October 1885	February 1886

within each season during the 1850s, 1860s and 1870s. Every concert either began or ended with a symphony; all of the composers listed were performed consistently over the period outlined above. As can be deduced from the table, notable additions to the early nineteenth century Gewandhaus repertoire were Robert Schumann's four symphonies as well as *Das Paradies und die Peri* and Schubert's Great C-major symphony (occasionally complemented by the eighth). Except in 1883, Schubert's ninth was performed at least once a year. Since the 1870s, at least two of Schumann's symphonies were performed in any concert season. Above all, however, it was Johannes Brahms who succeeded in Leipzig. Arriving during the 1850s with his concerti, by the 1870s, Brahms had conquered the Gewandhaus with his symphonies. Table 4.2 demonstrates the short time span between Brahms' symphony premières and their first performance in Leipzig.[15]

Gone were the days when his piano concertos were ridiculed and his violin concerto popularly derided as 'a concerto against the violin'. Along with his four symphonies, they became a staple component of the Gewandhaus repertoire. Although designated 'Brahms Evenings', which led to the performance of all his symphonic works in one concert season, were not held until the first decade of the twentieth century, by the mid-1890s his position was strong enough for him to make his return to Leipzig dependent on changes in the artistic leadership.[16] The underlying reason for his acceptance is easily ascertained:

Im schroffsten Gegensatz zum heutigen decadenten Feminismus in der Kunst, Brahms war eine durchaus männliche Natur. Ein wurzelfester, echter Norddeutscher, allem Schein und äusserlichen Wesen abhold, Feind aller leeren Phrasen, grundvornehm, voll Charakterkraft, so Willens- wie Gefühlsstark etc.: die Grundbedingung künstlerischer Echtheit war bei ihm von Vornherein erfüllt, Mensch und Künstler waren Eines bei Brahms.[17]

The Goethean association of classicism, with its attributes of health and strength versus romanticism's effeminate infirmity, the Protestant north versus the Catholic south, elegance and grace versus degeneration and chronic lack of propriety – in all these Brahms posed the perfect counterpart to the *Neudeutschen* by virtue of his firm classical characteristics. Brahms' use of the grand symphonic form, strict, logical and symmetrical, further evoked, after almost 20 years of symphonic drought, a new age of the symphony. With Brahms, Leipzig again was provided with a living composer espousing artistic values which were congruent with Leipzig's cultural ideals.

However, not even Brahms was able to slow down what many decried as the decline of the Gewandhaus for which its stubborn insistence on a particular cultural system was blamed. Firstly, the stringent restriction imposed upon the repertoire meant that very little in terms of premières was achieved. Barring the first appearances in Germany of Brahms's *Ein Deutsches Requiem* (1869), Tchaikovsky's Fifth Symphony, Dvořák's *New World Symphony*, Smetana's *Bartered Bride* in 1893 (Smetana had died in 1884) and Rachmaninov's *C Sharp Minor Prelude for Piano* (from his opus 3), not much else received its first performance in the Gewandhaus. Even though Anton Bruckner saw his seventh Symphony premièred in 1884 in Leipzig with Arthur Nikisch as conductor, the performance was held at the theatre. He was not admitted to the Gewandhaus canon until the first decade of the twentieth century. Secondly, the concert format itself began to be seen as problematic. Whilst during the early nineteenth century, the concert consisted of an overture, a concerto, an aria and a full symphony, by the 1870s, concerts consisted of a symphony and an overture/instrumental concerto flanking an assortment of songs, arias, minuets, single concerto movements,[18] dances, nocturnes, serenades, romances, operatic scenes and solos of various descriptions. Such concerts, often dismissively referred to as kaleidoscopic, comprised ten or more different compositions and as such were the embodiment of Biedermeier concert culture. Compared to the early nineteenth century, the Gewandhaus concerts of the 1870s and 1880s had degenerated into one of Biedermeier comfort and drawing-room complacency. Its classical heritage and resultant cultural prestige was nominally preserved by the consistent use of symphonic works by composers listed in the table above. Except for Brahms and Rubinstein, no living composer of note contributed to Leipzig's staple symphonic diet. Instead, the fashionable artists of the day dominated the repertoire with their seemingly endless supply of epigonal études, romances and fantasias. Compared to other towns, Leipzig's declining concert standards were painfully felt and publicly deplored – even by the *AMZ*:

> Es wird in Leipzig viel, unter Umständen auch gut musiziert, aber es hat sich in unserem vornehmsten Concertinstitute eine Einseitigkeit der musikalischen Anschauung herausgebildet, die nur noch von der Selbstgefälligkeit der tonangebenden Kreise überboten wird. Wie die Berliner Oper, so zehren die Gewandhausconcerte thatsächlich heute von dem Ruhme längst vergangener Zeiten, nicht, weil man nicht etwa das Beste will, sondern weil man es nicht kann. Die Absperrung gegen die neuere Kunst, der man sich seit Jahrzehnten schuldig gemacht hat, ist nicht ohne gewaltigen Rückschlag auf unsere Kunstzustände geblieben. Leipzig dictirt heute nicht mehr, wir früher, den Geschmack in der musikalischen Welt.[19]

The new concert ventures, such as the ones formed in Weimar under Liszt in 1842 and later in Meiningen under Hans von Bülow in 1880, were now dictating the taste of the musical world. Liszt's Weimar *Hofkapelle*, in particular, was committed to the performing of the progressives: Wagner, Berlioz, Peter Cornelius. When Richard Strauss ascended the rostrum there in 1889, the small residential town had already acquired cultural renown throughout Europe (in the same way that the Gewandhaus had done during the early nineteenth century).

It was not that Leipzig was against contemporary music *per se*. A glance at Leipzig's theatre during the second half of the nineteenth century reveals a stark contrast to the Gewandhaus. Not only did members of the *Neudeutsche Schule*, particularly Wagner, dominate, Leipzig's opera premièred Wagnerian operas: *Tannhäuser* in 1853, *Lohengrin* in 1854, *Der Fliegende Holländer* in 1862, *Die Meistersinger von Nürnberg* in 1870. Two years after the Bayreuth première, it performed the *Ring des Nibelungen* (1878); in 1880, *Tristan und Isolde* followed. During the season 1887/1888, of the 54 works performed, five were national premières; of all the 214 performances at the opera, 48 were works by Wagner.[20] Verdi, too, became a favourite amongst theatre audiences. In the Gewandhaus, by contrast, following Liszt's death in 1886, only *Héroide Funèbre* was performed, while the theatre opened its doors for a 3-day concert series in honour of the deceased.

Whilst the theatre was clearly at the forefront of musical innovation, the Gewandhaus still regarded itself as the temple of pure and noble art. Except for the intermittent performances of Wagnerian overtures, arias and songs, Liszt's piano concerti, polonaises, sonnets, études and fantasias, as well as sporadic dances from Berlioz' *Damnation of Faust*, the overture *Le carnaval romain* or the *Queen Mab* scherzo from *Roméo et Juliette*, very little opportunity for performance was given to them in Leipzig's flagship concerts until the mid-1890s. It was only in extra concerts held in aid of Leipzig's poor or the orchestra pension fund concerts that contemporary music was performed. Thus, in 1857, Hans von Bülow appeared as pianist performing Liszt, and Liszt himself performed a duet from *Der Fliegende Holländer* as well as some of his own compositions. Although this event was referred to as 'a turning point in the annals of Leipzig's music life',[21] Franz Brendel's exclamation of hope was premature. An annual review of the Gewandhaus concerts published in the *AMZ* in 1867 indicated that the *Neudeutsche Schule* still had no part in concert hall culture *per se*.

It was not that Leipzig was against contemporary music; it was only that Wagner et al. could not, as yet, be granted a permanent status within the concept of bourgeois *Kultur* as it had been constructed during the early nineteenth century. The institutionalisation of Winckelmann's classicist idiom of 'noble simplicity and serene greatness' as embodiment of this ideal naturally prefigured the opposition to the *Neudeutschen* in whose works the classical harmony of 'hellenische Formschönheit and christlichen Geist, plastische Ruhe und moderne Beseelung' was thought all but lost.[22] Twenty years after the first performance of Wagner's *Die Meistersinger*, the *AMZ* scorned it once again for its predisposition towards sensual, vague, formless and intoxicating melodisation at the expense of serene, autonomous and structured melodies:

> Die Musik ist ohne merklichen Absatz oder Einschnitt, ohne bestimmte Form und Tonart, zahllose Motive drängen, häufen und verwirren sich, geschlechtslose Harmonien rauschen vorüber, bekannte, an frühere Opern anklingende Sätze für Blechinstrumente erschüttern jeden Augenblick für das Ohr.[23]

Such music, declared Eduard Hanslick, could only but 'spell the end of art'.[24] Like the Ossian world,[25] it was deemed gloomy, melancholic, aberrant and amorphous; yet for any artistic perfection as defined by the *AMZ*, art was required to portray the wholeness and simplicity of existence, free from the artist's inchoate will and force. Only through compositions which were free from individualistic, confused and obscure emotions (with which only a few could empathise) could art contribute to the ennoblement of the individual's spirit (*Geist*).[26] This was something the *Neudeutschen*, with their 'infantile interplay of tones and feelings', were thought incapable of accomplishing.[27] Like Nietzsche's Dionysus, the *Neudeutschen* could not be granted entry into the sanctum of Leipzig's premier musical institution. The writings of the *AMZ*, as well as repertoire statistics, show they would not do so until the 1890s. In order to maintain this policy of exclusion, the Board of Directors opted for a *Kapellmeister* who would comply with, rather than challenge, the artistic ideology of the Gewandhaus. His name was Carl Reinecke.

Carl Reinecke and the Gewandhaus, 1860–1895

Biedermeier *Gemütlichkeit* reached its apogée with the appointment of Carl Reinecke in 1860, a gentle, pedantic and meticulous conductor, who, however, possessed neither the charisma and reputation of a Mendelssohn nor the authority, passion and asperity of a Hans von Bülow. Indicative of his own character, Reinecke referred to Mendelssohn as 'the representative of the straightforward compositional craftsmanship, of clear form, of neo-classical style rather than the brave active fighter, the organiser and creator of a future-oriented music life'.[28] The will of the composer was deemed paramount; the musical score was sacred and thus immune from subjective interpretation. As the *Leipziger Volkzeitung* reported:

> Reineckes Schaffen zeichnet sich durch Adel und Form, melodischen Wohllaut und geistvoll-künstlerische Mache aus. Doch ist seine Erfindung wenig bedeutend, seinem Werk fehlt das grosszügige elementar wirkende. Beethovens bekannter Ausspruch, die Musik muss in dem Manne Feuer aus dem Geist schlagen, findet bei Prof Reinecke keine Gnade. Was er kann, präsentiert er uns in verbindlicher Form, doch fühlt man das konventionelle.[29]

Reinecke's rather conventional approach to conducting was becoming ever more apparent when compared with the new generation of conductors, such as Bülow, Liszt, Wagner and Richter, in whom the fire Prometheus stole from the gods was ablaze. Speaking a language which is only known to the creative genius, the conductor, in order to translate and convey this subjectivity to the audience, was necessarily forced to go beyond the confines of traditional interpretation, which were defined by classical restraint and artistic submission. In doing so, the conductor assumed centre stage, or, as Liszt proclaimed: *Le concert c'est moi*. With it, they proposed an entirely different sort of attraction such as 'the seductive motoric stimulus of the visible effect which, often informed by vain self-representation on the rostrum, forces the audience in their spell and often diverts them from what they should be listening to'.[30] Thus, it was not primarily the music which dictated concert practice, but the will of the conductor.

Such expressions of artistic individuality was very much in line with the cultural discourses of the time, first instigated by the posthumous works of Schopenhauer, but even more so by Nietzsche. In all his works published in the decade between 1879 and 1889 – *Menschliches, Allzumenschliches, Die Fröhliche Wissenschaft, Jenseits von Gut und Böse, Zur Genealogie der Moral* and *Götzen-Dämmerung* – Nietzsche had, as mentioned earlier, attacked the values of bourgeois culture at its very core by insisting that all values, norms and standards had been fashioned according to temporary needs which meant they were little more than artificial values which stifled rather than invigorated the onward progress of art. Only the *Übermensch*, by rising above social and cultural conventions, could overcome stultified tradition and procure the '*Umwertung aller Werte*' (re-evaluation of all values) – an adage that reached common currency during the last decades of the nineteenth century. Thus, the artist was hailed as representing the new vanguard of humanity, a notion which proved to furnish the modern artist (as well as 'the young and the disaffected, the self-styled rebels, martyrs and prophets, the wannabe *Übermenschen*'[31]) with a whole new concept of artistic responsibility.

Such artistic responsibility was a direct attack on the traditional tenets of *Kultur* as practised in the Gewandhaus since the early nineteenth century. Here, the ideal of the artist, first defined by E. T. A. Hoffmann, was still valid. The *AMZ*, now on a cultural mission to halt this process of 'artistic vandalism', argued that such artistic despotism and chauvinism could only flourish where critical understanding and education of the audience was wanting:

> Da solch Despotie . . . überhaupt nur da möglich ist, wo es keine gebil
> deten Hörer giebt, wo der Musikdirector als Autokrat gebieten kann,
> wo das Publicum, wie ein Herde Schafe, willenlos dem Führer folgt,
> weil es ohne den kritischen Maasstab gelassen ist, welche erst die
> genauere Bekanntschaft mit den Meisterwerken gewährt.[32]

Thus, it was not the performing artist who held the key to the ethereal kingdom. This privilege, according to the *AMZ*, could only rest with the music itself; as was proclaimed during the 1848 debates, a thorough understanding of the master works was still the key to all cultural advancement. The conductor was there to perform them in an appropriate manner.

Although Reinecke's calmness and composure was unable to procure any excitement amongst audiences, at least he remained true to the Gewandhaus' cultural ideal. Given the prominence of the classical canon, little else was expected of him other than to obey the canon dutifully and to conduct in a sober and dignified manner. By doing so, however, he inadvertently confirmed Leipzig's reputation as a stifling *Biedermeier* town and his own reputation as a mere *Biedermeier* artisan.[33] The resultant indifference to, or lack of appreciation of, Reinecke can be determined by the treatment he received. Whilst Bülow and Liszt were fairly much at liberty to perform and conduct as they pleased, Reinecke was told what to do every step of the way. While Bülow's sarcasm and frequent histrionics were well-known at home and abroad – his staging of Beethoven's Ninth twice in the same concert[34] being one, his utilising pre-concert space for political rallies[35] being another example – Reinecke was submissive, obedient and dutiful. Any attempts on his part to introduce musical novelties were crushed before they could take root. When, for example, in 1859, the Board of Directors discovered that a number of composers had sent compositions directly to the conductor rather than to the directors, they decreed that no composition would ever be accepted unless it was addressed to the Board first. The decision as to what was and what was not played in the Gewandhaus was thus still entirely left with the directors, along with those it appointed as consultants (*Sachverständige*). Quite often Reinecke complained that concert programmes were erroneous because the directors had not consulted the conductor before they were sent to be printed ('a serenade is, after all, not a symphony'[36]). Far from what any of the new conductors would accept, Reinecke was, furthermore, contractually obliged to conduct public rehearsals, to perform at chamber music evenings and, whenever asked to do so, order scores and new instruments, make overnight sleeping arrangements for soloists, convey to the directors public reactions to concerts and apply for holidays for members of the orchestra.[37] Only after 29 years of service did Reinecke ask for and receive a salary increase.[38] Disliked and mistrusted by other members of his profession across the Board from Bülow and Wagner to Brahms, Reinecke's undistinguished period of office came to an even more inglorious end in 1895 when Arthur Nikisch was approached by the Board of Directors to take over the Gewandhaus concerts. Because Nikisch could not take up his new appointment immediately, Reinecke, much to his disdain, was asked to cover for him in the interim.

Totally subservient to the will of the directors, Reinecke was in no way able to assert his own artistic authority. The Reinecke incumbency was indicative of a music culture which was immersed in the ethos of classicism, first codified by Winckelmann, and in his wake presented to the world by Herder, Goethe, Schiller and Beethoven. Carl Reinecke was expected both to conform to that ideal and to represent himself as its physical manifestation without letting his own artistic personality interfere. Yet ideals, however potent, could not retain their hold on bourgeois music culture forever. The long engagement of Carl Reinecke demonstrates the flaws that were inevitably inherent in the preponderance of abstract ideals at the expense of social reality. Reinecke was no Mendelssohn and certainly no Bülow or Wagner. The growing dissatisfaction directed at him can be interpreted as an indication of the increasing discomfort with the dominant presence of a rigid idealism at the expense of art as a breathing and active constituent of human existence. Indeed, by the end of the nineteenth century, personality and artistic individuality finally claimed their place within Leipzig's music culture. Arthur Nikisch's arrival in 1895 was, in fact, greeted with a sigh of relief.

For the most part of the second half of the nineteenth century, however, the Gewandhaus together with the *AMZ* insisted on a cultural propriety defined by traditional classicism and its non-referential and universal properties. Resolutely contemptuous of Schopenhauer's irrational will, Nietzsche's individual hero and his call for a *Umwertung aller Werte*, as well as modern concert practices, the Gewandhaus and the *AMZ* held onto their belief that the music of past masters was still the key to all cultural refinement. The persistence of its conviction can be demonstrated by the cultural attitudes demonstrated by the Gewandhaus and the *AMZ* during a time of monumental changes before and after the unification of Germany under Bismarck.

The Franco–Prussian War and Reichsgründung

Culture rather than politics or religion had always been singled out as the only medium by which the 'German nation' could be conceptualised and identified, especially so as *Kultur* could exist without a constitutional framework secured by political unity. Not surprisingly, therefore, after 1871, culture seemed the obvious vehicle through which imperial unity, identity and overall legitimisation could be achieved. Supported by a number of new and established music journals dedicated to promoting a new and all-embracing national consensus, it was the cultural icons such as Goethe and Beethoven, in particular, which were to spearhead the campaign for Germany's national awakening. Both had lived and worked at the time when 'Germany' first sought to liberate itself from the French yoke during the 'wars of liberation'. Now a new rhetorical device crafted the line of continuity – linking 1813–1815 and 1870/1871 – with retrospective force. Within this concept, the German nation state was the result of inevitable historical progress with Goethe and Beethoven serving as its cultural scaffold.

The fact that the 100th anniversary of Beethoven's birth (1870) and the formation of Germany as a political entity occurred within quick succession was indeed a fortunate circumstance. Beethoven's iconic and symbolic importance could be, and was, efficaciously utilised in the myth-making process which was designed both to magnify Germany's greatness as a cultured nation and to use its perceived cultural supremacy as the foundation stone for the new German nation state. What was particularly beneficial to the nationalist cause was the abiding assumption that Beethoven's compositions embodied purity, health, strength and moral soundness. These qualities could easily be pitched against the moral decline, debilitated health and 'resultant' military defeat of France and French decadence. Thus, part of the nationalist endeavour was to extract from traditional classicism the ethical attributes whilst dispensing with its insistence on the non-referential, universal and timeless properties. The war against France was thus a war of sturdy German art against scandalous French art. With the benefit of hindsight, victory, it seemed, had been certain from the start, given the divine alliance of military prowess and artistic strength, both presumed intrinsic to German *Geist* and *Kultur*:

> Gewiss ist: der Reinigungsprocess wird, so weit er dem deutschen Volke obliegt, gründlich vollzogen werden. Unsere tapferen Armeen werden, Dank ihrer sicheren Führung und dem ihnen inwohnenden Geiste, siegreich die materiellen Waffen, wir Anderen werden die geistigen Waffen führen. Alles, was an die moderne Ungesittung des Pariser Lebens erinnert … werden wir auszurotten trachten. […] "Offenbach hinaus aus Deutschland!" – das müsste unser Grundsatz sein und bleiben.[39]

This nationalistic view attributed the same level of importance to the artistic achievements of the Weimar and Viennese classics as it did to the military victories gained over Napoleon or the Battle of Sedan.[40] National stereotyping further supplied a common denominator during a time when disparate elements needed to be unified in a common identity.[41] Anti-French sentiments were common to all parties. In all, as in most of the other arts, the nationalist camp began to associate music with militarist–realist sentiments, thus tearing down the transcendental veil which had shrouded music since the early nineteenth century. This new national awakening was supposed to banish the proverbial lethargic and apolitical '*deutschen Michel*' [German Michael] which so defined Biedermeier culture, from Germany's cultural sphere.

Whilst such attitudes dominated some journals, particularly the *NZfM* and the *Musikalische Wochenblatt*, the Gewandhaus and the *AMZ* remained ever more steadfast in their defence of the traditional idea of classicism. This meant that neither was able, or willing, to endorse the nationalist cause, since the association of music with any non-aesthetic and referential phenomena would have violated their idea of art. Thus, whether 1866 or 1871, the *AMZ* refrained from such argumentation. Music was a kingdom, access to which gave a privileged view of what was eternal, perfect and beyond the ravages of time, whether it was placed in the past, the present or the future. Indeed, if the Gewandhaus was to be taken as a prototypical example, one would not even have noticed that major military victories had been secured and political unification achieved. The concert repertoire did nothing to acknowledge one of the most important events in modern German history. The reasons for this appear threefold.

Firstly, bourgeois concert culture was still based on non-referential qualities – a phenomenon which, during the second half of the nineteenth century, was efficaciously exploited to its natural ends. Music, more than ever before, served as a deliberate counter-force to the ills incurred during the *Gründerzeit*: rapid industrialisation, suburbanisation and unprecedented anonymity. Against such phenomena, the concert hall was supposed to invoke 'the noble spirit for the elevation and edification of humanity and for the beautification of existence'.[42] For one critic, in a curious parallel with prostitution, music, like love-making, lost its sacred aura when dragged into the everyday sphere, that is, when it was reduced to a craft or trade.[43] Music's association with transcendental idealism made the Gewandhaus a perfect sanctuary from Max Weber's disenchanted, ordered, mechanised, bureaucratic, regimented and rational world of modern life. Within this sanctuary, people could 'turn for relief from regimentation and predictable tedium to those very realms of social life, those zones of solace, wherein rationality has the least play and the least likely impact on the future'.[44] By way of 'cultivating a posture of redemption from mechanisation', the Gewandhaus retained its privileged place within the upper altitudes of Leipzig.[45] In this way, it offered little opportunity to promote modern notions of national identity which meant that the Gewandhaus was deemed doubly unsuitable for any political, state-building ventures.

Secondly, there was very little support from the composers and practising musicians themselves. Apart from the brief upheavals of 1848/1849, composers generally refrained from any direct political involvement. The classical model of the ideal bourgeois artist precluded active political involvement since 'to participate in politics or even to write about it was a derogation of his calling'.[46] 1848 really seemed to have been the last time that musicians in Germany had exercised their political conscience. Furthermore, the generation that had erected barricades in 1848, constituted a firmly established bourgeoisie by the 1870s. Even though Richard Wagner once had hoped that this new German culture could vitalise Germany, indeed rescue it from the fossilised culture of antiquity which so permeated bourgeois culture, he eventually succumbed, following spells in exile, to the temptations of aristocratic patronage. Even though Wagner's writings certainly exuded political messages, his compositions decidedly refrained from doing so – showing 'only the remotest connection with society in which he lived'.[47] His *Bayreuther Schauspielhaus*, rather than representing the aspirations of the German nation, turned to glorifying a pagan culture to an exclusive circle of devoted Wagnerians. Not even Wilhelm II, the Prussian King, was willing to grant Wagner's opera house national status. He also refrained from attending any of the opening ceremonies.

Thirdly, many composers who had made up the cultural canon of the Gewandhaus did not fit the Empire as it stood in 1871, that is, Bismarck's *kleindeutsche Lösung* that excluded Austria and its imperial satellites Hungary and Bohemia. Removing Austrian composers from the terrain of German (rather than bourgeois) culture would have radically reduced Germany's cultural heritage to Beethoven and Schumann. Mozart, Haydn and Schubert would have had to be returned to their original country. More than anything, this circumstance highlights the disparity, even incompatibility, between bourgeois notions of *Kultur* and national/political necessity. Cultural institutions such as the Gewandhaus along with the *AMZ* were simply not inclined to endorse Germany's national awakening. Instead, it aimed to maintain the correlative relationship of music with civilised and cultivated humanity as a whole as this extract may demonstrate:

Der Name 'Beethoven' vereinigt alle gebildeten Nationen, wie kaum ein zweiter in der Kunstgeschichte, zu dem gemeinsamen Bekenntnis der Bewunderung und der Ehrfurcht vor der Hoheit des Genies.... Noch ist der Beethoven'sche Geist der Maasstab, nach dem Alle

gemessen werden.... Der hundertste Geburtstag wird die Feier geisti-
ger Grösse und Hoheit für alle civilisirten Nationen des Erdkreises
sein, von der nicht allein die Kunstgeschichte, sondern auch die Cul-
turgeschichte der Menschheit mit Befriedigung Kenntnis nehmen.[48]

Beethoven stood for all who espoused culture and education, rather than
mere 'Germaness'. It was an anathema to presume that just anyone –
by virtue of being German – should claim a prerogative on Beethoven,
because any appreciation of his music still necessitated primary knowledge in order to recognise beauty and the sublime: 'Do not let someone
who is not acquainted with music listen to Beethoven's Ninth! Given
his educational deficiencies, he will and cannot understand the beautiful; even if he may not regard it as ugly, at least he will not appreciate
its beauty; his judgement will be disparaging (*abfällig*)'.[49] Politics might
have developed a dependency on the masses, *Kultur* certainly had not.
Here, only a small (initiated) minority was still deemed able to enter into
the 'most holy' place of musical art. Thus concert hall music could not, at
least in Leipzig, serve as a means to generate imperial identity, national
legitimacy or international recognition, something the Empire sought
in the wake of political unification. Rather, Leipzig's aesthetic culture –
the conscious separation of art from politics – ensured the Gewandhaus
had indeed little to offer so far as actively boosting the German Empire's
credibility was concerned. The construction of a second Gewandhaus
in 1884 sheds further light upon Leipzig's reluctance to relinquish its
bourgeois ethos, in exchange for a national one.

The Second Gewandhaus[50]

The numerous extensions to the old Gewandhaus made throughout the
century could not in the end keep pace with the demand as subscriptions
increased.[51] Brahms, when asking for extra tickets for one of his concerts,
was told that nothing could be done. 'All good seats have been, since the
commencement of the Gewandhaus concerts, subscribed and reserved
as family property. The only way is to marry into it'.[52] Only artistic or
political luminaries could (to account for the slight exaggeration of the
previous quotation) still receive their tickets through a reserve held by
the Gewandhaus Board of Directors. The average bourgeois, however,
was hard pressed to gain access to the sanctum; despite the explosion
in the number of potential consumers of *Kultur*, access to the Gewandhaus was still reserved to the affluent, traditional town élite. This did not
change with the opening of the new, more spacious concert hall in 1884
(Figure 4.1).[53]

Figure 4.1   Leipzig's New Gewandhaus, 1936 (BA 1977/2496, printed with kind permission of *Stadtarchiv Leipzig*)

The construction of the new Gewandhaus came at a time which witnessed an explosion in the number of new concert halls and opera houses throughout Europe: for example, the *Musikvereinssaal* in Vienna (1870), the Royal Albert Hall in London (1871), the *Casino* in Basel (1876), the *Festspielhaus* in Bayreuth (1876), St Andrew's Hall in Glasgow (1877) and the New Opera House in Dresden (1878). All these buildings resulted from a prosperity brought about by unprecedented economic growth. So too in Leipzig. In 1880, the Gewandhaus Board of Directors called for an architectural competition which was only open to German and Austrian architects.[54] Out of 75 entries received, the Berlin architects, Martin Gropius and Heino Schmieden won the contract. To fund the planning and construction of the new concert hall, the Board of Directors did not ask for government subsidies as was the case with Semper's new opera house in Dresden where the Finance Ministry, acting as *Bauherr* (client), contributed considerably.[55] Rather, the Board of Directors relied on donations and private loans such as that by the Leipzig merchant and banker, Franz Dominic Grassi, according to whose will the Board of Directors were granted a loan of 400,000 Goldmarks.[56] The Board further issued *Stiftungsanteile* (foundation shares) of 500 Goldmarks and sold *Anlehnsscheine* (loan shares) at 1000 Goldmarks each. For the loans, a 2 per cent interest rate was paid, some of which could be redeemed against the subscription.[57] The right to a subscription in the Gewandhaus (deemed valid so long as the concerts existed) was thus effectively bought by those possessing considerable financial assets – the wealthiest of Leipzig's *Bürgertum*. Whilst in Dresden, the King of Saxony (first Johann then Albert) was to retain absolute authority in all matters regarding the opera house, in Leipzig, all power rested, as usual, with the bourgeoisie represented by the Board of Directors and Leipzig's Town Council.[58] Thus, the type and shape of the architecture was conceived in accordance with bourgeois, rather than any notion of broader national representations (Figure 4.2).

Like the first Gewandhaus, the interior was constructed in the (neo-)classical style: symmetrical, orderly and clear. The difference from its predecessor lay in its sheer opulence. Richly ornamented, complete with chandeliers, pilasters, columns and framed medallions of portraits of famous composers in bronze which were attached to the front of the galleries, the new Gewandhaus demonstrated the desire for representational architecture which could express not nationalism, but the wealth

Figure 4.2   Interior of Leipzig's New Gewandhaus about 1900 (BA 1983/16640, printed with kind permission of *Stadtarchiv Leipzig*)

and success of Leipzig's *Bürgertum*. Despite this additional opulence, the important point is that the Gewandhaus was still, both outwardly and inwardly, identifiable through its adherence to a classical ethos. The maintenance of this cultural ethos not only ensured cultural continuity but demonstrated an insistence on a bourgeois, rather than specifically German, identity. Three issues may be highlighted in order to demonstrate Leipzig's deliberate attempt to maintain its cultural stance along traditional lines. The first issue concerns the placing of a 3-metre high bronze statue depicting Mendelssohn outside the main doors of the Gewandhaus in 1892 (Figure 4.3).

Figure 4.3 Statue of Felix Mendelssohn outside Leipzig's New Gewandhaus (BA 1983/16428, printed with kind permission of *Stadtarchiv* Leipzig)

His right elbow is leaning against the conductor's rostrum, a baton held in his right hand while his left hand is holding a rolled up musical score. His eyes are fixed on the town centre. On the three front steps leading up to the statue sits Euterpe, the muse, and on the side steps three naked cherubs, each one holding a violin, flute and a musical score. A golden inscription above the laurel decoration facing the main entrance of the Gewandhaus reads typically: *'Edles nur kündet die Sprache der Musik'*.[59] As is indicated by the auxiliary subjects, the statue of Mendelssohn complied with the very ideal of Winckelmann's idea of a Greek masterpiece: 'its noble simplicity and serene greatness' captured in the pose, dress as well as in the expression. The resemblance to the great philosophers and scholars of classical antiquity is evident. Thus the primary incentive for Leipzig's concert culture was still linked to the humanistic ideals emanating from the Renaissance and through the centuries that followed. Leipzig's *Bürgertum* still regarded itself as the 'legitimate heir of centuries of history, and attempted to express this optimistic faith in *progress* by demonstrating a proprietorial control over the past'.[60] As far as the Gewandhaus was concerned, the individual who personified this past most adequately was *Gewandhauskapellmeister* Felix Mendelssohn. By choosing him, the Board of Directors had clearly demonstrated where the Gewandhaus belonged culturally. The statue, as did the concert hall itself, represented Leipzig, its cultural achievements and history, rather than those of Germany. The latter might have been served more adequately by Beethoven who had outstripped Mendelssohn in the Gewandhaus regarding the frequency of performances by a long way. So far as Mendelssohn's general reputation within the Germany's cultural narrative was concerned, his popularity had suffered a steady decline since the 1860s, but clearly not in Leipzig.

Secondly, the two-day opening ceremony further supported Leipzig's traditional cultural stance. With the sole addition of J. S. Bach,[61] the cast of composers whose works were performed is all too familiar: Bach, Handel, Haydn, Mozart, Beethoven, Weber, Schumann and Spohr. Beethoven's Ninth symphony and Handel's *Messiah* comprised the two main performances. In stark contrast to the opening of the first Gewandhaus in 1781, not a single composition by a living artist was used in the opening ceremony of 1884 – not even Brahms. The same composers who inspired the middle-class cultural creed then, now confirmed it.

Thirdly, the opening ceremony was attended by King Albert of Saxony in the company of his wife (rather than a representative of the Hohenzoller House). It seems, for the first time, that, paradoxically, the Gewandhaus made a point of deliberately associating itself with one political entity (Saxony) and distancing itself from the other (Germany). Such an association was, perhaps, made easier after the military defeat in 1866 at the hands of the Prussians, when the Wettiner House swore an oath of allegiance to the North German confederation which effectively ended Saxony's political sovereignty. Thus, whilst feelings of pride in Saxon peculiarities rose perceptively, they did so at the time when Saxony was no longer an independent political entity. With the ascent of the Hohenzoller House as Germany's royal representatives, Saxony's royal family, the Wettiner, became an excellent, though temperate, means of signifying Leipzig's standing in Saxony's enduring history. After all, in the same way that Berlin could hardly outshine the literary achievements of Weimar, so the capital was unlikely to better the musical successes of the Gewandhaus.

Thus, whilst the national camp, supported by a number of longstanding and new music journals, aimed at furthering its cultural ambitions by way of exalting the iconic status of Beethoven et al as national treasures, Leipzig utilised its position as the original patron of classical music within Germany to further its reputation as the principal proprietor of *Kultur*. However, as the artistic reign of Reinecke as well as the repertoire patterns during his reign have shown, the flaws inherent in such an insistence on traditional cultural patterns at the expense of progress were beginning to be felt.

Birmingham

Britain in mid-century was a land of economic prosperity and possessed a stable political system. Chartism and food shortages, so prevalent during the 1840s, had been overcome or at least kept under control. The idea of 'progress' through railroads, free trade and the 1851 Great Exhibition was edging its way into the mindset of provincial England. With the exception of the Crimean War (1854–1856) and remote disturbances such as the Indian Mutiny and the Chinese War, it was a period of peace.[62] Free trade and *laissez-faire*, the acme of economic liberalism best represented in the Cobden–Chevalier Treaty of 1860,[63] exemplified the political and economic philosophy of the time in which governments must, above all according to John Stuart Mill's *On Liberty* (1959), ensure the free development of the individual. Vigorously endorsed by Mill, Britain's foremost liberal philosopher and economist, the sovereignty of the individual was to be defended on the grounds that utilitarian action was justified whenever the ennoblement of character followed as a result (*Utilitarianism*, 1863).[64] Samuel Smiles' *Self-help* (1859) provided the most positive incentive for individualistic ambition to date in that every individual is responsible for his social and economic advancement. The economic boom spanning the 1850s and early 1870s seemed to confirm the superior ethos emanating from British liberalism.

Economic liberalism was complemented in the political sphere by the electoral dominance of the Liberal Party which governed the country between 1846 and 1874. Locally, political self-regulation was the dominant practice until the 1880s. Independent of Whitehall, local politics was conducted by those who contributed to it financially, namely, the urban middle class. This progress, as well as the material prosperity it brought with it, was achieved by way of physical, moral and intellectual improvements naturally suited to a middle class which had long since regarded itself as the standard-bearers of morality and industry.[65] Lord Macaulay outlined the historical foundations for 'progress' in association with the nonconformist and liberal-minded middle class by bestowing a specifically bourgeois character upon the Glorious Revolution of 1688 and the Reform Act of 1832. The post-Darwin torrent of publications, spearheaded by Herbert Spencer, which attempted to fuse progress achieved in the intellectual, moral and social spheres with the theory of evolution, provided seemingly sound scientific foundations for what could only have been asserted hitherto. In short, mid-century England was the grand age of the Victorian middle class which as 'an example for mankind'[66] was '... conscious of no weakness, no inferiority ... believing that the freedom and prosperity of England are their work, and that the future belongs to them'.[67]

Such self-confidence required public manifestations that could equally espouse the cultural pretensions of the urban middle class. The language used to describe the Triennial Festival in daily newspapers clearly demonstrates the function and role of culture in middle-class society. It was, the *Birmingham Post* declared, 'the one redeeming quality of Birmingham',[68] 'periodically shedding a kindly refining influence over the hard rough work-day experience of the toilers in the "hardware village" and goes far to prevent the horny casing of our hands from enveloping our hearts, and the iron of our forges and factories from penetrating our souls'.[69] Just as in the early nineteenth century, the Festival was supposed to elevate the mind of the practically orientated industrialist habitually guided by less compassionate philosophies such as *laissez-faire*. The financial profits arising from the Triennial Festival were, as always, transferred to the General Hospital, which owed its continued existence to the Festival. More than any other cultural event, the Festival, by way of its sheer dimensions, was thought to publicly enhance the sobriety, dignity and nobility of Birmingham's inhabitants to equal the town's material growth. Fully resourced, Birmingham did not hold back: despite some resentment expressed in some corners, Charles Gounod, for example, received an astounding £4000 for bequeathing *The Redemption*, the first part of his sacred trilogy, to the Festival. Art was evidently worth investing in.

As the generously financed commission of Gounod's *Redemption* shows, the Festival continued its association with religion – its conventions and language, and by way of religion, with morality. This was underpinned by a mid-Victorian religiosity which was as potent as it had been during the early nineteenth century. The difference from the early nineteenth century was that religious attitudes had now created an all-consuming reality centred on moral development, self-conquest, strictness of conscience and the 'overcoming of the wicked one'. According to Matthew Arnold's *Culture and Anarchy* (1869), the reason behind this persistence was that in religion, the middle class had found 'a sufficient basis for the whole of their life fixed and certain for ever, a full law of conduct, . . . a law of unexampled power for enabling them to war against the law of sin in their members. . . . The book which contains this invaluable law they call the Word of God. . . .'[70] Given its all-pervasive reality, religion could not but subsume art too into its sphere. Evidence can be found in the Festival programme itself; the vast majority of commissioned works were of a sacred rather than secular nature: for example, William Sterndale Bennett's Sacred Cantata, *The Woman of Samaria* (1867), Julius Benedict's *St Peter* (1870), Arthur Sullivan's *The Light of the World* (1873), G. A. Macfarren's *The Resurrection* (1876), C. Villiers Stanford's *Three Holy Children* (1885) and *Eden* (1891) as well as Parry's *King Saul* (1894) and *Job* (1897). As mentioned above, of special importance was the sacred trilogy composed by Charles Gounod comprising *The Redemption* (1882), *Mors et Vita* (1885) and *Messe des Morts* (1888), to which should be added Antonin Dvořák's *Requiem Mass* (1891).

As can be deduced from this list, the major difference from all the previous choral productions was that religion in art was no longer dependent on Protestantism in itself. Although religious symbolism and language in choral productions were still a prerequisite, Catholic elements were now also tolerated. This development can be explained through the different role which religion was supposed to perform. Whilst during the eighteenth and early nineteenth centuries, English national identity had defined itself against Catholicism by Anglicans as well as Dissenters alike, thus enabling the middle classes to view themselves as the 'national guardians of the Protestant conscience',[71] by the second half, anti-Catholicism as a way to construct national identity, was slowly eroded. Rather than through Protestantism, 'the nation was conceived in more secular terms, such as *empire* and *race*, the latter having the advantage over religion on the grounds of 'empirical' validation'.[72] In other words, the need for Protestantism in middle-class culture became obsolete; other types of Christianity could just as well be suited to the task of promoting cultural respectability so long as they moved within the familiar confines of English aesthetics. Catholicism, with its particularly rich cultural and artistic heritage, was now looked upon favourably, appearing, given its long absence, acceptably exotic. As the *Birmingham Post* explained: 'The three previous mornings being reserved for oratorio and other forms of sacred music familiar to Church and concert-goers in this country, it is well that the fourth should be devoted to the illustration of the rich stores of Roman Catholic ritual music, which must otherwise be a sealed book for the great mass of the British public'.[73]

Gounod's sacred trilogy is a case in point. Although Part 1 – *The Redemption* – espoused a content which centred on man's Fall and Redemption, presenting a series of detached episodes such as the Creation, Fall, the divine Promise of Redemption, the Passion, Resurrection, Ascension and Pentecost, it also featured phenomena previously not heard in traditional choral writings such as Gregorian chant and the liturgical chant of the Stabat Mater – the meditation of the suffering Mary at the sight of her son's crucifixion – prominent within Catholic liturgical practice. (In *Mors et Vita*, the sequel to *The Redemption*, Gounod even included a Requiem. The concluding part – the *Messe des Morts* – is a traditional Requiem for the faithful departed without added prose and textual material as can be found in *Mors et Vita*.) What made *The Redemption*, however, appear familiar to the Festival public was its gigantic proportions, which had become a prerequisite for all choral writings particularly since Mendelssohn's *Elijah*. To fulfil its intentions – to bring the great truths of Christian Revelation vividly before the mental eye and conscience of his public – Gounod planned on a 'very large and comprehensive scale, for a band and chorus of full proportions, with supplementary band and choir for certain specific effects, and a numerous array of principal vocalists, comprising two sopranos, a contralto, two tenors, two baritones, and a bass'.[74] This was thought conducive to the dramatic content of the story. Apart from this, Gounod left ample scope for the communication of sympathy – a necessary component of English aesthetics: Gounod's dramatic treatment of Mary's distress at the sight of her son's crucifixion was done in a way that could be appreciated as much as Mendelssohn's Elijah saving the widow's son. And indeed, as the *Birmingham Post* commented, Gounod was so successful in dramatic representation of the music alone, that 'even without the choir certain scenes were vividly brought before the mental eye of the spectator'.[75]

The sheer volume and magnitude of the work was 'deemed worthy of the town', its local newspapers devoting column upon column to the occasion which had transformed Birmingham into 'a sort of Mecca for musical pilgrims from all parts of the world'.[76] Birmingham, the 'centre of the Empire', was reaching confidently beyond British shores: there was little disagreement when it transpired that Gounod had dedicated *Mors et Vita* not to Queen Victoria but to 'the Pontiff, his Holiness Pope Leo XIII', despite the fact that it was the Festival Committee which had authorised Gounod's remuneration. The enthusiastic acceptance of Gounod's Sacred Trilogy is indicative of a slow but steady transformation in the perception of what constituted provincial middle-class culture. The natural conclusion to this change was Dvořák's *Requiem Mass* and, particularly, Edward Elgar's *Dream of Gerontius*, a work based on a poem by Cardinal Newman, which was first performed in Birmingham in 1900.[77] Both composer and 'poet' were Roman Catholics; John Henry Newman was (before his conversion to Catholicism) a prominent member of the (High Church) Oxford Movement which, during the 1830s, sought to return the Anglican Church to its Catholic roots. Non-Protestant elements previously deemed detrimental, even threatening to the concept of middle-class culture, had now become acceptable.

Although this digression is important to note, the largest proportion of all choral commissions was still very much in line with traditional oratorio compositions in that they set classical biblical stories to music. Bennett's *The Woman of Samaria*, Benedict's *St Peter*, Sullivan's *The Light of the World*, Stanford's *Eden* or Parry's *King Saul* and *Job* bear evidence to this. All these works were based on familiar biblical stories with an accompanying moral lesson. In all of them, the overtly religious tenets of penitence and faith as keys to salvation and personal success were still given overwhelming centrality. For example, in his oratorio *St Peter*, the three incidents chosen by Benedict – Peter's obeying of his calling by John the Baptist (part one), his failing faith out on the stormy sea but subsequent return to faith (part two) and his denial of Jesus, subsequent repentance and deliverance from certain death under Herod the King (part three) – map out three stations in the life of Jesus' disciple. In all three sections, the message of absolute faith in God's omnipresence and omnipotence is conveyed. The same central concern is voiced by way of the familiar biblical story of the woman of Samaria and Job in Bennett's and Parry's respective eponymous oratorios. Stanford's *Three Holy Children* in which the refusal of three Jews to engage in idolatrous worship, as commanded by the heathen king, ends with each being cast into the furnace. By trusting in God's ability to deliver them from any harm, each of the captives steps forward into the flames which are, however, extinguished by an angel. In line with the original story in the Book of Daniel, the king, now realising the true power of God 'who hath sent His Angel, and delivered His servants that trusted him' confirms that 'there is no other God that can deliver after this sort' and all join in the collective glorification of God. Assisted by the Very Rev. the Dean of Chester and the Rev. Canon Percy Hudson, Stanford created an oratorio in which God's existence is demonstrated through the conversion of a non-believer. The story-telling aspect of a leading biblical protagonist was also maintained by Arthur Sullivan in *The Light of the World*. Here, the central character is Christ himself. Unlike Handel's *Messiah*, however, where the spiritual idea of Christ is conveyed or Bach's Passions where the suffering of Christ on the cross is accounted for, Sullivan's oratorio sought to capture the human aspects of Christ's life on earth. Beginning with the Annunciation, the escape to Egypt and later Nazareth and his ministry in Jerusalem, the oratorio ends with Jesus' betrayal, death and resurrection.

The primacy given to oratorios during an age of less dogmatic, less denominational Christianity is, perhaps, surprising unless, of course, oratorios were deemed to have lost their primary duty to inculcate basic religious and moral lessons in the listener and thus rise above denominational differences. They existed because tradition demanded it. Every Victorian spectator and listener was still equipped with an impeccable moral sense which was essential to comprehend the moral and religious ideals portrayed in a work of art. A common knowledge of biblical stories was still widespread. The symbolism, language, liturgical passages and favourite biblical excerpts were familiar to everyone: they were still commonly found within the literature of the day and formed part of everyday conversation even among those professing no, or very little, religiosity of their own.

Such an instinctive appropriation of religion can also be detected in the oratorios commissioned during the second half of the nineteenth century. Most were saturated with familiar liturgical passages such as the *Magnificat* or the beatitudes, as can be found in Sullivan's *Light of the World*. Macfarren's *The Resurrection* was introduced in the Festival programme as comprising Chapter 20 of St John's Gospel interspersed with other passages of the Bible, the Book of Common Prayer and from popular hymnology. Bennett's *Woman of Samaria* even includes a rendition of Henry Francis Lyte's *Abide with Me*, a poem which was written in 1847 and set to music by William H. Monk in 1861, and one that is still today a firm favourite. Although conveying none of the sadness in which the words were originally conceived (in the oratorio, the Samaritans have just become believers and are rejoicing therein), the words would have struck a familiar chord with the audience. Apart from common liturgical passages, most oratorios were also replete with classical quotations from the Bible: 'Daughters of Jerusalem, weep not for Me, but weep for yourselves and for your children' (Luke 23:28); 'The Lord will not turn His face from them that seek Him' (II Chronicles 30:9), 'Judge not, that ye be not judged; condemn not, and ye shall not be condemned; forgive and ye shall be forgiven' (Luke 6:37). 'I am the resurrection and the life' (John 11:25) and so on. Some of these can be found in virtually every libretto, provoking accusations of blasphemy even by John Ruskin who deemed oratorios to wither 'the life of religion into dead bones on the siren-sands'.[78] Whenever the *Sanctus* appeared in a sacred composition (for example, the *Holy, Holy, Holy* chorus in *Elijah*), the audience would still rise *en masse* throughout its duration. (This practice caused some confusion at the performance of Schubert's Mass which 'it should be remembered forms part of the Roman Catholic mass, at which the worshipper invariably kneels down'[79]). Whether the individual professed some kind of religiosity or not was beside the point – the observance of customary cultural practice was paramount. A religious content in music, even if only maintained nominally, still offered considerably more respectable points of references than could secular topics usually associated with an operatic culture. In addition, a secular music culture could never justify the charitable funds which the Festival was still expected to grant; and religiously inspired charity was one of the cornerstones of the Festival.

As in Leipzig, the persistence of a very potent cultural tradition effectively negated the acceptance of intellectual advances made since the nineteenth century. For the time being, the constitutional framework of the Festival was able to uphold Birmingham's music tradition regardless of whether the original sentiments which gave rise to it in the first place were still commonly extant. Changes in the socio-cultural, religious and philosophical make-up of Victorian Birmingham could not yet sufficiently challenge traditional cultural practice; this was only achieved at the beginning of the twentieth century. The separation of culture from the wider intellectual currents led to its entering a period of languorous existence as the analysis of the repertoires has demonstrated. This cultural stagnation, as the case of Leipzig has shown, created, however, a cosy niche which tended to nurture the complacent admiration of one's own cultural achievement. One of the first to recognise and criticise such developments was Matthew Arnold. To him culture must be a study of perfection which 'consists in becoming something rather than in having something'.[80] Culture was supposed to humanise and broaden the basis of life, thus fulfilling a function which is vital to the development of mankind. Failure to do this would only lead to culture which is dead and stagnant, valued only (and here Arnold predates Pierre Bourdieu's *Distinction* by almost a century) 'as an engine of social and class distinction, separating its holder, like a badge or title, from other people who have not got it. No serious man would call this *culture*, or attach any value to it, as culture, at all.'[81]

To Birmingham's middle class, however, such criticism meant little when compared to the cultural reputation which the Festival had bequeathed to Birmingham. With 'nearly every musical notability in London [contriving] to find his way to Birmingham',[82] there were, besides a good number of representatives of art, science, music and literature, peers, members of parliament, county magnates, the Mayor, High Sheriffs as well as religious dignitaries such as Cardinal Newman in attendance. This list of the 'distinguished company' was always published in local newspapers as part of the Festival reviews, and gave visible evidence of the esteem in which the Festival was held. The national reputation the Festival had thus acquired ensured that Birmingham's inhabitants, by virtue of their patronage, could be associated with notions of civility and erudition. Within the context of provincial British music culture, Birmingham had reached the acme of cultural maturity.

As in Leipzig, such accomplishments were not something town, hospital and Festival officials would allow to be put at risk – a decision which had far-reaching consequences as far as the musical development of Birmingham was concerned. The Triennial Festival, indeed, had become an institution deemed indispensable to Birmingham's cultural reputation within the nation. As such it was shielded and protected, allowing the Festival to become one of the wealthiest public charities in the Midlands. As a charitable foundation, it had to compete for public donations. Encouraged by a Festival Committee which comprised of members of the Town Council as well as governors of the General Hospital – the recipients of the Festival profits – the Festival adopted a sharp business ethos in order to ensure the highest possible profits. The combined efforts of local and political dignitaries working towards guaranteeing the success of the Festival meant that new cultural ventures were often opposed as soon as they were suggested. Local newspapers and music journals, on the other hand, were not holding back letters of protests against Birmingham's 'chronic lack of plentiful musical performances'.[83] When, for example, a new Music Hall was proposed, it was swiftly condemned as 'an uncalled for and impertinent opposition to the old Town Hall'.[84] The Festival committee, closely allied with the Birmingham's Town Council (then referred to as the puritanical Saint-Party or Economy party), frequently intervened whenever new musical enterprises, requiring Town Council permission, threatened to disturb the triennial enterprise. Too much exposure to the nation's favourite oratorios was thought to jeopardise the Festival's profits:

> The Hospital Committee, indeed, have never made any secret of their policy in this matter. They have always decried the frequent performance of oratorios in the town, on the assumption that the pecuniary success of their festivals would be thereby certainly damaged. In other words, music, per se, was to them nothing, unless as an apology for levying a triennial impost on the pockets of their fellow-townsmen.[85]

Birmingham's institutionalised charity commanded conservative policies which, in turn, allowed other, more progressive musical towns, particularly Manchester under Charles Hallé, to surpass Birmingham. Indeed, apart from the Festival Choral Society, providing four oratorios per year, not much else was available as far as public entertainment was concerned. Only a few short-lived concert enterprises were founded during the 1890s. The Triennial Festival enterprise kept the development of further musical institutions firmly in check, an unfortunate circumstance which Arthur Sullivan in his boa-constrictor allegory sarcastically condemned.[86]

Birmingham's protection of its music culture at all cost meant that the artistic institutions of the Festival survived the second half of the nineteenth century relatively unchanged. Below the institutional shell, however, first cracks began to appear and increased the more the extra-musical values associated with Birmingham's music culture began to lose their relevance as the twentieth century opened. Not even the most unyielding of traditions could possibly justify the subsistence of traditional religious and moral views in the light of contemporary developments. Without the sustenance of religion and morality within the wider sphere of everyday life, Birmingham's music culture lost its essential basis. What it was left with was an aesthetic disposition which still provided the framework, but one which lacked the intrinsic value which genuine religious sentiments had previously provided. For the time being, however, tradition and the ubiquitous support granted by both the authorities and the press ensured its survival. The domineering presence of the Festival conductor, Michael Costa, further reinforced the reputation of the Festival.

The Reign of Michael Costa in Birmingham

Mendelssohn and *Elijah* marked a turning point in Birmingham's cultural development. Like *Messiah*, the regular performance of *Elijah* was crucial to the maintenance of the cultural heights and commercial success Birmingham had to achieve if the town was to retain its cultural reputation. Following Mendelssohn's death in 1847, it was left to Michael Costa to further Birmingham's cultural ambitions. Nowhere near as accomplished a composer as Mendelssohn was, Costa's appointment to conduct the Triennial Festival (until 1882) was no doubt the result of the favourable and sparkling reputation he had gained from a distinguished conducting career in London which included the opera houses in Haymarket and Covent Garden, choral societies (Sacred Harmonic Society) as well as orchestral appointments at the Philharmonic Society.[87] By way of his existing authority and in stark contrast to Reinecke at the Gewandhaus, Costa was able to take absolute authority on matters concerning the Triennial Festival.

Firstly, he was able to choose the repertoire which meant that his personal likes and dislikes came to be mirrored in the concert programme. During Costa's reign and until Hans Richter's appointment, Bach, Schumann, Brahms and English composers generally, were hardly performed. Secondly, as far as the concept of authenticity was concerned, Costa appeared more than cavalier, if not actually indifferent to it: he edited scores as required and according to his own whim. Such artistic independence was further underlined by his character which was equated with puritanical and authoritarian dictators: discipline, precision and order were his maxims. He watched over his musicians like a teacher watches over a class of juvenile delinquents with punishments such as fines for lateness or scruffy appearance, imposed upon the sinner. Compared to Costa, the dominant British conductors of the time – Smart, Parry, Balfe, Benedict – appeared to be little more than neighbourly and congenial dilettantes.[88] None of this, however, diminished the cultural success of the Festival; indeed such a domineering presence, if conveyed successfully, could only but enhance the perception of the Festival in Birmingham's provincial music culture. The public and symbolic representation of artistic grandeur within the Town Hall and on the rostrum was essential to Birmingham's cultural endeavour.

The drawback with the centrality and dominance of the conductor and his artistic preferences was that the general mood of Birmingham was rarely reflected in its cultural preferences, that is, not even that most pervasive of popular creeds – imperialism. By the early 1870s, the monarchy had become the focus of the new Imperialism in the Crystal Palace speech given by Benjamin Disraeli. In 1876, this was further cemented by declaring the Queen Empress of India. At the same time, the revival of the Tory Party under Disraeli (who led the Tories to victory in the general election of 1874) and later Lord Salisbury did much to undermine the positive image of liberal free trade. Arguably, protectionism and themes of imperialism and patriotism began to dominate the mind-set of the English middle class. Certainly, Birmingham, once the centre of political and religious dissent, now came, under the mayoralty of Joseph Chamberlain – the arch-Imperialist – to see itself as the centre of the Empire from the mid-1880s onwards.[89] One would expect a music Festival such as that of Birmingham to make full use of the potential which invariably accompanies such festivities. However, similarly to the Gewandhaus, the Festival was barely able to serve any other purpose than to continue within the framework of its time-honoured cultural practice. To be sure, Hans Richter, who succeeded Costa to the post of Festival Director in 1884, encouraged the performance and commission of British music: Macfarren, Balfe, Benedict, Smart, Sullivan, Barrat, Stewart, Anderton, Bishop, all helped to conceive the notion that Britain's musical capabilities possessed a level of self-confidence and buoyancy which enabled Britain to foster its own artistic talents. The performance of symphonic works by home-grown composers, such as Parry's Symphony in G major, Mackenzie's Violin Concerto and Percy Pitt's Sinfonietta in G major marked an attempt to establish a British instrumental music tradition. But this was as far as Birmingham seemed willing or able to go.

For a start, Richter's Hungarian birth and Germanic musical upbringing did not sit well within an atmosphere defined by British patriotism. Secondly, the artistic freedom granted to Richter at Birmingham meant that contemporary German as well as Slavonic music were performed with increasing frequency. Beginning with sporadic overtures, arias and duets under Costa, every Festival under Richter witnessed increasing amounts of German music, particularly the *Neudeutsche* variant.[90] This was despite the continual criticism in various music journals of modern German music and its imitation in England ('music must now be intense or nothing . . . even if [the composer] set to music the logarithmic table'[91]). Rather than bequeathing a sense of British cultural achievement to the Festival, Richter, who introduced Wagner's *Ring der Nibelungen* to London, did, in fact, much to encourage a new understanding of instrumental music in Birmingham. Even though criticism of his appointment was not wanting, particularly from Arthur Sullivan who would have preferred an Englishman ascending the Town Hall rostrum, it could not dissuade the Festival organisers from appointing a conductor of considerable cultural status and European renown.

Similarly to the Gewandhaus, during the second half of the nineteenth century, the role of the conductor developed within existing cultural parameters. The different cultural positions already taken by Mendelssohn in the two towns, found their natural conclusion in Reinecke and Costa. Whilst Reinecke continued, but ultimately failed, to uphold and embody an artistic model perfectly exemplified by Mendelssohn during the 1840s, Costa and Richter excelled in sustaining the reputation of the Festival's cultural tradition by virtue of their authority and artistic renown. From the beginning, Reinecke's artistic individuality was curbed by the institution he was meant to lead. In Birmingham, the inherent grandiosity of oratorio and opera performances, combined with the financial pressures posed by charity, ensured that the conductor enjoyed considerable freedom and prestige so long as he met expected norms. The autocratic, almost dictatorial, incumbency of Costa, in particular, was in many ways indicative of the culture he commanded. In fact, his officious presence was required as part of the Festival's *raison d'être*. The diametric opposition of Costa's artistic independence to Reinecke's rather formal, almost submissive, conductorship at the Gewandhaus is indicative of the different assumptions about culture held by their respective musical institutions.

Conclusion

For both towns, the second half of the nineteenth century was one of cultural consolidation. The artistic and aesthetic ethos which had emerged during the first part of the century had now been translated into solid cultural practice which was able to establish notions of cultural identity. As the sections on the repertoires, conductors and concert hall above have shown, they acquired permanence within the concept of bourgeois culture. This permanence was ensured even at a time when many of the traditional conceptions regarding religion, society and time were being challenged by the caustic power of historicism. However, neither music culture was greatly affected as yet, though the reasons for this were different in the two cases. In Birmingham's Triennial Festival which was impregnated with traditional values inherent to religion and morality, the cultural framework was maintained on the grounds of traditional cultural practice and the concerted efforts of town and festival officials to guarantee financial success for its charitable aims. Leipzig's Gewandhaus remained unaffected because of its aloofness from extra-musical and non-aesthetic values such as those inherent in religion and morality – the main targets of historicism. This insistence on traditional cultural patterns in the face of different social, political and religious questions inevitably raised suspicions of cultural anachronism and subsequent stagnation and complacency in both towns. These charges were raised again with increasing urgency during the last decade of the nineteenth century when bourgeois culture faced its most threatening challenge yet. This time, it was the consuming sense of *fin-de-siècle* which, with its compulsive ideas of relativism and powered by *avant-garde* vigour, formed the greatest threat to bourgeois culture. The denigration of bourgeois culture as divorced from breathing humanity now became a popular theme despite, paradoxically, the tendency towards world-weary decadence in the works of the young rebels of the *avant-garde*, especially in Vienna, at the turn of the century. Nevertheless, the traditional concepts and ideals embodied by Mendelssohn, Brahms and Reinecke were no longer sustainable and began to falter. Autonomy of art became the new leitmotif. The responses from Leipzig and Birmingham are the subject of the following chapter.

Notes

1. Contrary to Hegel, Schopenhauer argued that an aimless and irrational will is the essential reality in the universe. Taking as his point of departure the Kantian notion of external objects being mere products of our cognitive faculties, Schopenhauer proposes that the world is a phenomenon, a *wesenloser Schein*, an illusion in the minds of sentient beings. Rather than through cognition and reason, therefore, access to this inner world can only be achieved through the irrational and limitless will within ourselves. Since this irrational will is dominated by strife and conflict, the individual can never rest, but is condemned to a life of want, boredom, loneliness and deprivation. It is only in art that humans have a means to escape from the tyranny of will. His chosen art was music: whilst we can recognise the *copy* of an Idea in the visual and poetic art, music alone personifies the will itself as it is most removed from the world of appearances. Music was thus a means of giving immediate access to the world of ideas behind the world of appearances. Whether yearning or excitement, there is nothing that music cannot express. See Beardsley, *Aesthetics*, p. 265f and Fubini, *Geschichte der Musikästhetik*, p. 222f.
2. Hammermeister, *The German Aesthetic Tradition*, p. 113.
3. Beardsley, *Aesthetics*, p. 274.

4. Such a method of enquiry cleared the path for musicology. Hanslick himself was appointed to an unpaid lectureship in 1856 by the University of Vienna and in 1861 promoted to the post of an associate professor (full professorship followed in 1870) on, paradoxically, the history and aesthetics of music.

5. *Birmingham Post*, 24 August 1888.

6. Extract from the *Penny Cyclopaedia* quoted in 'Essay on Music' in *The Musical Times*, Vol. 11, 1 May 1863, p. 43.

7. Buckley, *The Victorian Temper*, p. 155.

8. D. Sousa Correa, 'Goddesses of Instruction and Desire: Ruskin and Music' in D. Birch (ed.), *Ruskin and the Dawn of the Modern* (Oxford: Oxford University Press, 1999), p. 116.

9. The Grosvenor Gallery, London's first independent gallery (forever resisting the dominance of the Royal Academy), specialised in modern Art and represented the New Aesthetic movement. It was there that James McNeill Whistler exhibited his *Nocturne in Black and Gold: The Falling Rocket* (1874) which was savaged by John Ruskin in his *Fors Clavigera*. Whistler sued for libel and won but was awarded minimal damages of one farthing without costs. Although Ruskin subsequently resigned from his position as Slade Professor of Fine Arts at Oxford, contemporary observers were not convinced that Whistler had indeed won. His subsequent bankruptcy seemed to confirm this.

10. Realism is defined by the quest to render everyday characters, situations, dilemmas, and events in an accurate or mimetic manner. It was largely a reaction to romanticism with its fantastic, mythological, implausible plots. Representatives were Wilhelm Raabe, Gustav Freytag and Theodor Fontane. Naturalism is also defined by a turn away from the idealised world to the current themes of the day. The horrors of industrialisation, alienation, poverty, prostitution were central. Man is a product (and often victim) of his circumstances. In short, writers were going beyond themes hitherto deemed worthy to be used as literary subjects. The main representative of naturalism was Gerhart Hauptmann.

11. Nietzsche quoted in J. Sheehan, 'Culture' in T. C. W. Blanning, *The Nineteenth Century: Europe, 1789–1914* (Oxford: Oxford University Press, 2000), p. 126.

12. M. Beddow, *Thomas Mann – Doktor Faustus* (Cambridge: Cambridge University Press, 1994), p. 8. At the heart of Nietzsche's rejection of the permanence of values was his belief that it was man who created his idols and gods in line with his needs and interests at any given time. No eternal values, truth and objectivity could thus ever exist.

13. Nipperdey, *Deutsche Geschichte 1866–1918*, Vol. 1, p. 512.

14. Anon., 'Die Leipziger Concert-Saison 1864/65' in *AMZ*, No. 17, 26 April 1865, p. 276.

15. Forner, *Die Gewandhauskonzerte*, p. 99.

16. Forner, *Die Gewandhauskonzerte*, p. 126. Brahms was dissatisfied with the way Reinecke interpreted his C major Symphony and insisted on a different conductor.

17. C. Söhle, 'Johannes Brahms todt!' in *Musikalisches Wochenblatt*, Jg 28, No. 15, 8 April 1897, p. 210f. 'In stark contrast to the decadent femininity in today's art Brahms was of an entirely masculine nature. Firmly rooted, thoroughly north-German, averse to appearances and externalities, enemy to all empty turns of phrase, fundamentally noble, full of strength of character,

as strong of will as of feeling etc: the basic requirement of artistic genuine-
ness was fulfilled from the start, man and artist were one and the same in
Brahms.'
18. During the 1830s, the *AMZ* always congratulated the Gewandhaus for not
succumbing to the then fashionable practice of separating symphonies.
19. Quoted in Forner, *Die Gewandhauskonzerte*, p. 107. 'Leipzig makes a lot, and
sometimes also good, music but there has emerged a certain one-sidedness
regarding the musical perception in Leipzig's most noble concert institute
which is only surpassed by the smugness exhibited by its predominant circles.
Like the Berlin opera, so too the Gewandhaus concerts rely on the renown
of times long past, not because one does not want the best but because one
cannot do it any other way. The resistance to modern art which Leipzig has
been found guilty of for decades has not been without mighty setbacks on
the state of our art. Leipzig no longer dictates the taste of the musical world
as it had done previously.'
20. Forner, *Die Gewandhauskonzerte*, p. 115.
21. Quoted in C. Böhm, S.-W. Staps, *Das Leipziger Stadt- und Gewandhausorchester:
Dokumente einer 250jährigen Geschichte* (Leipzig: Kunst und Touristik, 1993),
p. 124.
22. Anon., 'Die Romantische Musik, psychologisch-historisch betrachted' in
AMZ, No. 10, 4 March 1863, p. 169.
23. Anon., 'Erste Aufführung der Oper: "Die Meistersinger in Nürnberg"' in *AMZ*,
Nr 28, 8 August 1868, p. 221. 'The music is without perceptible break or decisive turns, without definite form and tonality, countless motives are wrestling,
piling up and becoming confused, sexless harmonies are roaring by, familiar
movements for brass instruments reminiscent of earlier operas, are at every
moment a shock to the ear.'
24. E. Hanslick, 'Richard Wagner's Meistersinger' in *AMZ*, Nr 29, 15 July 1868,
p. 226. The article was originally published in the *Neuen Freien Presse*,
24 June 1868.
25. James Macpherson's translation of Ossian had an immense impact on the
Sturm und Drang movement, especially on Herder and Goethe. The latter
included long passages, translated into German by himself, in *Die Leiden des
Jungen Werther* (1774). Macpherson's work was, of course, later revealed as
bogus: the 'translation' was his own invention.
26. Anon., 'Das Wesen und die vorbildliche Bedeutung der "classischen" Musik'
in *AMZ* No. 5, 28 January 1863, p. 80.
27. Anon., 'Erste Aufführung der Oper: "Die Meistersinger in Nürnberg"' in *AMZ*,
Nr 28, 8 August 1868, p. 221.
28. Forner, *Die Gewandhauskonzerte*, p. 97. '...Repräsentanten des sauberen kom-
positorischen Handwerks, der klaren Form, des klassizistischen Stils und nicht
den mutig-tätigen Streiter, den Organisator und Gestalter eines zukunftsori-
entierten Musiklebens.'
29. Review in the *Leipziger Volkszeitung*, 23 February 1895 quoted in K. Seidel,
Carl Reinecke und das Leipziger Gewandhaus (Hamburg: Reinecke Musikverlag,
1998), p. 207. 'Reinecke's activity is distinguished through nobility and form,
a melodically pleasing sound and an intellectual and artistically stimulating
manner. However, his invention is of little weight, his works lack generous
elemental force. Beethoven's famous exclamation that music has to strike

fire in man through his spirit finds no favour with Prof Reinecke. What he can do is presented to us in a polite manner, yet one cannot but feel the conventional.'

30. W. Salmen, *Das Konzert: Eine Kulturgeschichte* (München: Beck, 1988), p. 50. '… der verführerische motorische Reiz des Sichtbaren, die zuweilen von eitler Selbstpräsentation am Pult ausgehende Suggestion zwingt die Zuhörenden in ihren Bann und lenkt oft von der zu vernehmenden Sache ab.'

31. M. Jefferies, *Imperial Culture in Germany, 1871–1918* (Basingstoke: Palgrave Macmillan, 2003), p. 139.

32. Anon., 'Die Leipziger Concert-Saison 1864/65' in *AMZ*, No. 17, 26 April 1865, p. 276. 'Since such despotism is only possible where no educated listeners are present, where the music director commands like a dictator, where the audience, like a herd of weak-willed sheep, follows the leader because it is left without a critical standard that only a closer acquaintance with the masterworks can provide.'

33. F. Hennenberg, *Das Leipziger Gewandhausorchester* (Leipzig: Bibliographisches Institut, 1984 [1962]), p. 47.

34. Hanslick noted with regard to the double Ninth: 'Die Ungläubigen mit einem Feuerwehrschlauch zu taufen' [To baptise the non-believers with a fire-hose]. Quoted in H. C. Schonberg, *Die Grossen Dirigenten*, p. 152.

35. In 1892, Bülow famously devoted Beethoven's 3rd symphony to Otto von Bismarck during one of his pre-concert talks of the Berlin Philharmonia almost 2 years after the Iron Chancellor had been dismissed by Wilhelm II. The ideals of *liberté, égalité, fraternité* became *Kavallerie, Infanterie, Artillerie*.

36. Quoted in Seidel, *Carl Reinecke*, p. 57.

37. Seidel, *Carl Reinecke*, p. 46.

38. Reinecke received salary of around 5000 Marks per annum for the first 30 years which was raised to 7000 during his last 5 years at the Gewandhaus. When Nikisch first took office, he immediately received a salary of 12,000 (20,000 according to some sources) per annum. Reinecke's dismay is understandable considering that Nikisch was really only employed on a part-time basis (he also held appointments in Berlin and Hamburg) and was not obliged to perform as a soloist in the grand concerts nor at chamber evenings. See Seidel, *Carl Reinecke*, p. 188.

39. A. Dörffel, 'Aus neuester Zeit' in *Musikalisches Wochenblatt*, Jg 1, No. 39, 23 September 1870, p. 610. 'One thing is certain: the cleansing process, in as far as it is the responsibility of the German people, will be executed with thoroughness. Our brave armies will, thanks to their sure guidance and the spirit living within them, handle the material weapons, we others will handle the spiritual weapons victoriously. Everything which reminds us of the modern immorality of Parisian life we shall know how to eradicate. […] "Offenbach out of Germany!" This should be and remain our guiding principle.'

40. Hermand, *Geschichte der Germanistik*, p. 55. The Battle of Sedan on 2 September 1870 led to the Prussian victory over the French. It became a national holiday, often used to unveil national monuments.

41. R. Parr, 'Identity in Difference: Collective Symbols and the Interplay of Discourses in the Two German Unifications' in R. Speirs, J. Breuilly (eds),

Germany's Two Unifications: Anticipations, Experiences, Responses (Basingstoke: Palgrave Macmillan, 2005), p. 79.

42. J. Schucht, 'Eröffnungskonzerte des Neuen Gewandhauses' in *NZfM*, Bd 80, Vol. 49, 19 December 1884, p. 542. '. . . edler Geist zur Erhebung und Erbauung der Menschheit und zur Verschönerung des Daseins'.

43. H. Ritter, 'Ueber musikalische Erziehung' in *Musikalisches Wochenblatt*, Jg 12, No. 41, 6 October 1881, p. 482.

44. A. Sica, 'Rationalization and Culture' in S. Turner (ed.), *The Cambridge Companion to Weber* (Cambridge: Cambridge University Press, 2000), p. 57.

45. Sica, 'Rationalization and Culture' in Turner, *The Cambridge Companion to Weber*, p. 57.

46. G. A. Craig, *Germany 1866–1945* (Oxford: Oxford University Press, 1981 [1978]), p. 215.

47. Craig, *Germany*, p. 215. The great exception, of course, is *Die Meistersinger*. Even though, the action takes place in the sixteenth century, the message inherent in Hans Sachs' final appearance is clearly designed to arouse anti-French sentiments.

48. J. Alsleben, 'Zur Beethoven-Feier im Jahre 1870' in *Musikalisches Wochenblatt*, Jg 1, No. 22, 27 May 1870, p. 340. 'The name Beethoven unites all educated nations, like scarcely any other in the history of art, in the shared declaration of admiration and reverence before the sovereignty of genius. . . . Beethoven's spirit is still the standard by which everyone is judged. . . . The 100th anniversary of his birth will be the celebration of spiritual greatness and sovereignty for all civilised nations around the world, which will be acknowledged with satisfaction not only by the history of art but also by the history of the culture of humankind.'

49. F. Pohl, 'Auch ein Handwerk. Eine Kritik der Musikkritik' in *Musikalisches Wochenblatt*, Jg 17, No. 10, 4 March 1886, p. 125.

50. The last concert in the old Gewandhaus was held in 1885. The building was destroyed in 1895.

51. R. Skoda, *Neues Gewandhaus Leipzig: Baugeschichte und Gegenwart eines Konzertgebäudes* (Berlin: Verlag für Bauwesen, 1985), p. 18. Extensions and renovations include: installation of side boxes (1824), complete renovation (1833, Oeser's painting on the ceiling was destroyed), building of new second staircase (1842), installation of gas lamps and heating stoves (1852), enlargement of hall (1870), names of composers – Mendelssohn, Bach, Handel, Gluck, Haydn, Mozart, Beethoven, Cherubini, Schubert, Weber, Spohr, Schumann – inscribed (1872), installation of Galleries (1879).

52. Thomas Engelmann in a letter to Johannes Brahms dating 22.12.1876, quoted in B.Weinkauf, *Briefe das Gewandhaus zu Leipzig betreffend* (Leipzig: Mitteldeutscher Verlag, 1987), p. 23.

53. First attempts towards building a new concert hall were made in 1872 but the town rejected the specified locality (*Königsplatz*). Areas that were suggested by the town could not be financed. Renewed attempts were made in 1877. A site in the south-west part of the town near Harkort Strasse owned by Friedrich Voigt was chosen. Voigt agreed to give 4000 square metres without payment. In return, the town promised to build roads. The erection of the concert hall led to an increase of land and property prices, leaving Voigt with a handsome profit.

54. Skoda, *Neues Gewandhaus Leipzig*, p. 22. The condition was that costs would not exceed 700,000 RM (extra for the organ). The concert hall itself had to seat 1700, a stage which could accommodate 400–450 musicians and singers, an organ, open galleries and boxes, changing rooms for soloists (with wardrobes and toilets), separate room for the Board of Directors with extra study, a meeting room for 100 orchestra members, a library, a home for the house administrator and it was to have wardrobes (separate for musicians). To ensure the same sound quality as in the old Gewandhaus, the new concert hall was built with the same materials.

55. H. Magirius, *Die Semperoper Dresden: Baugeschichte, Ausstattung, Ikonographie* (Leipzig: Edition Leipzig, 2004), p. 29.

56. Grassi had left 2,327,423 Goldmarks to Leipzig's Town Council which was charged with the responsibility of investing this large sum in a number of causes. These included the funding of 20 new posts in the Gewandhaus orchestra, a number of museums as well as statues in honour of Goethe, Bach and the *Völkerschlacht*.

57. Weinkauf, *Briefe*, p. 56.

58. Given the Empire's federal structure, the construction of public buildings was, like all cultural institutions, the responsibility of individual states or municipal authorities. Cultural policy was one of the last remaining areas where individual states could exercise their autonomy.

59. The statue was demolished at night in 1936 by orders of Nazi authorities. Description taken from Weinkauf, *Briefe*, p. 44. 'Noble things are proclaimed only by the Language of Music.'

60. Jefferies, *Imperial Culture*, p. 101.

61. The Bach revival since the 1850s led to a re-evaluation of Bach's status within Leipzig's music culture. No longer ignored, he had become, in effect, the musical son of Leipzig.

62. Between 1815 and 1914, Britain took no part in European conflicts (except in the Crimean War).

63. It was a Free Trade agreement between Britain and France which reduced duties on British coal and other manufacturing goods in return for reductions in brandy and wines.

64. This was an advance on the Utilitarianism as espoused by his godfather Jeremy Bentham and his father James Mill who claimed that an individual's action can be deemed morally and ethically sound so long as it was useful.

65. D. Thomson, *England in the 19th Century* (Hammondsworth: Penguin, 1961 [1950]), p. 101.

66. Anon., 'To the Editor' in *The Quarterly Musical Magazin and Review*, No. 13, Vol. 4, 10 December 1821.

67. M. Arnold, 'Democracy' in S. Collini (ed.), *Culture and Anarchy and Other Writings* (Cambridge: Cambridge University Press, 2002 [1993]), p. 19f.

68. *Birmingham Post*, 21 August 1858.

69. *Birmingham Post*, 28 August 1861.

70. Arnold, 'Culture and Anarchy' in Collini, *Culture and Anarchy*, p. 139.

71. A. Briggs, *The Age of Improvement, 1783–1867* (Harlow: Longman, 2000 [1959]), p. 467.

72. McLeod, *Secularisation*, p. 235. The reason for this change is the decline of ultra-evangelicalism, the growing force of Anglo-Catholicism, the rise of a more liberal theology within nonconformism in which anti-Catholicism was not deemed central and the respect commanded by people such as J. H. Newman.

73. *Birmingham Post*, 6 October 1894.

74. *Birmingham Post*, 24 August 1882.

75. *Birmingham Post*, 24 August 1882.

76. *Birmingham Post*, 30 August 1882.

77. Elgar's *Dream of Gerontius* will be considered in Chapter 5.

78. Ruskin quoted in Correa, 'Goddesses of Instruction and Desire' in Birch (ed.) *Ruskin*, p. 116.

79. *Birmingham Post*, 9 October 1897.

80. Arnold, *Culture and Anarchy* in Collini (ed.) 'Culture and Anarchy', p. 62.

81. Arnold, *Culture and Anarchy* in Collini (ed.) 'Culture and Anarchy', p. 58.

82. Anon., 'Birmingham Festival' in *The Musical World*, No. 35, Vol. 33, 1 September 1855, p. 558.

83. Anon., 'The New Music Hall' in *The Musical World*, No. 36, Vol. 34, 6 September 1856, p. 568. '[Birmingham's] festivals, to be sure, are the finest things of their kind in the world; but they occur but once in three years, and the interval between them is all but an utter blank so far as music is concerned.'

84. Anon., 'The New Music Hall' in *The Musical World*, No. 36, Vol. 34, 6 September 1856, p. 568.

85. Anon., 'The New Music Hall' in *The Musical World*, No. 36, Vol. 34, 6 September 1856, p. 568. It also transpired that members of the Festival Committee 'gentlemen by position and affluence – could condescend to the undignified course of personally canvassing their friends against the very spirited attempt on behalf of good music'. Another such incident occurred when Mr Tonks, a manufacturer, applied to the Town Council to stage a concert of sacred music on the evening of Christmas Day in the Town Hall. After a successful performance in 1855, the second staging of 1856 was halted at the last minute after the council members 'had taken tea with a parcel of old women', resulting in a reversal of the initial decision.

86. 'Birmingham's musical life is like a boa-constrictor which gorges itself every three years and fasts in between – now, of course, the situation has completely changed'. Arthur Sullivan lecturing to members of the Clef Club in Birmingham 1883.

87. M. Musgrave, 'Changing Values in 19th Century Performance: The Works of Michael Costa and August Mann' in C. Bashford, L. Langley (eds) *Music and British Culture, 1785–1914: Essays in Honor of Cyril Ehrlich* (Oxford: Oxford University Press, 2000), p. 169.

88. Schonberg, *Die grossen Dirigenten*, p. 132.

89. In 1895, Chamberlain was offered a number of cabinet offices, including Chancellor of the Exchequer, but chose the relatively minor office of Imperial Secretary.

90. The performance of a march, an aria and a prelude to Act Three of Wagner's *Tannhäuser* during the 1876 Festival marked the first hearing of Wagner. Liszt followed with his Hungarian Rhapsody No. 1 during the 1885 Festival.

91. Anon., 'Reminiscences of the Birmingham Festival' in *The Musical World*, No. 36, Vol. 57, 6 September 1879, p. 567. 'Our composers [will] devise combinations more and more thrilling, till the nerves can respond no longer, and someone discovers that the real purpose of music is to affect the mind and heart rather than the ganglionic centres ... '.

5

Transformations and Approaches to War: *Fin-de-Siècle* to 1914

Introduction

By 1900, both the Gewandhaus and the Triennial Festival had been in existence for more than a century. During that time, they had assumed a role which made them indispensable to the reputation of the towns' civic culture. By way of the artistic institutions within the Gewandhaus and the Festival – the repertoires, artists and concert halls – art had assumed particular connotations, values and norms which had stood for many decades at the centre of bourgeois culture. Previous chapters have demonstrated how and why these phenomena differed in Birmingham and Leipzig, and that neither town had been willing to surrender its established cultural configurations. Although both music cultures slowly broadened the definitions of their artistic canons, the cultural paradigms established during the first half of the nineteenth century were too inextricably linked to middle-class concepts of cultural respectability. As such, they proved remarkably resistant to change for much of the second half of the nineteenth century.

By the end of the nineteenth century, however, bourgeois culture faced an entirely new challenge, namely a powerful phenomenon which pervaded the arts as well as the social and natural sciences: the relativisation of values. In going beyond the subversion of religious and moral values as historicism had done, this latest development undermined the universality of single-value systems and demanded that everything, including cultural values, can only be but relative to its time and space. Such advances filtered through the intellectual and cultural spheres in England and in Germany although the differences in their respective aesthetic developments necessarily invoked different responses to the new opportunities which presented themselves. Whilst relativism, with accompanying features of decadence, was more prominent in Germany, France and above all Austria, it was aestheticism which began to make itself felt in England's artistic circles. This chapter aims to establish how far and in what ways the cultural disposition of the Gewandhaus and the Triennial Festival was affected. It proceeds by providing a general introduction to the advances made; these developments then provide the background against which Gewandhaus and Festival practices are measured.

Relativism and its Impact on Culture

The assertion that everything is relative was part of a general phenomenon that appeared to challenge all traditional values and norms, whether in art, science, moral philosophy, history, psychology or philology. In the wake of Nietzsche, the desire for such a fundamental upheaval began to exert its full influence especially in France and Germany during the last decade of the nineteenth century when a generation of intellectuals, artists and scientists, to whom the cultural, social, scientific and moral orientations of the time had become increasingly questionable, began to respond radically to the impact of new ideas. Deeply influenced by Nietzsche's appeal for the '*Umwertung aller Werte*', Max Weber, one of the founders of Sociology, for example, called for the acceptance of a polytheism of values. With this concept, he, like Nietzsche, emphasised the brittle nature of moral and philosophical values which had been the foundation of Western culture hitherto. Instead he advocated 'moral decisionism' – a concept which stipulated that every individual should make his/her own choices rather than base his/her moral behaviour and ethical standards on some supposed universal or natural law. A determined rejection of Enlightenment rationality and the positivist practice of searching for and establishing natural (or scientific) laws from which a universal order could be derived, is characteristic of this attitude.

What became known as *Lebensphilosophie*, was not, however, a philosophical concept but should be seen as a cultural attitude which began to touch every discipline: Weber's advocacy of 'moral decisionism' was as characteristic as Wilhelm Dilthey's emphasis on the subjective conception of historical knowledge: 'meaning in history was not fixed, but changed with the situation in time and culture of the historian himself and with the active decisions he took in his personal world'.[1] Countering the one-sided emphasis on rationality and universalism, knowledge, Dilthey argued, could only be comprehended through cognitive thought in conjunction with non-rational, creative and dynamic elements. Intrinsic to this development was the (neo-Kantian) turn towards the inner, 'subjective' world of the observer, something which was further advanced with the works of the French philosopher Henri Bergson and, most notably, Sigmund Freud. Whilst the first promoted the status of intuition by arguing that it complements rather than negates intelligence, Freud's discovery of the Unconscious gave prominence to man's hidden motivations (drives and instincts) over and above 'free will' or the rational, emancipated 'self', as the determining agencies of human behaviour and action. Following in the wake of Nietzsche, Weber, Dilthey and Freud each in his own discipline, helped to initiate the revolt against the apparent certainties held by the previous generation of writers, scientists, philosophers, moralists and many others. No longer susceptible to a cut-and-dried final analysis, any discovery and the conclusions drawn from it were essentially dependent on the disposition of the observer. The notion of single, all-embracing constants underpinning moral or philosophical truths, seemed equally lost.

These new, indeed revolutionary, ideas appeared to offer art an escape route from its hide-bound bourgeois conventions that until now had been firmly underpinned by single-value systems. Ever since art's inception into the bourgeois world during the second half of the eighteenth century, fixed cultural values had always provided audiences with clear reference points for the understanding and appreciation of a work of art. Now relativism was seen to undermine the previous certainty of such values in art. As a result, 'isms' followed fast upon one another: after the dead end of naturalism came neo-romanticism, *fin-de-siècle* decadence, impressionism and later, its antipode, expressionism.[2] The new expressive possibilities allowed the artist of whichever vocation to venture beyond the representation of nature or external objects in a realistic, mimetic manner, and instead search behind the surface images for emotional, and in the case of expressionism, visionary meanings via expressive distortion. Art turned, as Walter Muschg put it, 'to the representation of psychological and intellectual contents and created meditations, hallucinations and visions. The representational retreated or dissolved completely'.[3] Literary characters of the *fin-de-siècle*, for example, are portrayed as unhealthy in body and mind, tortured by a morbid and nervous disposition and possessing little or no stability in their lives. Franck Wedekind's *Lulu* [comprising *Erdgeist* (1895) and *Die Büchse der Pandora* (1905)] and Arthur Schnitzler's *Liebelei* (1895) and *Anatol* (1888–1891), for example, exposed the hypocrisy of traditional conventions behind bourgeois morality, love, marriage and sex, and reduced them to empty, often grotesque, rituals.[4] Major novels by Robert Musil, Hermann Hesse, Heinrich Mann and Thomas Mann all revealed a bourgeois world disintegrating at its core. There was a strong premonition that the old world order was nearing its end. Art began to highlight vividly the crisis of modern man in the face of industrialisation, social anonymity and dehumanisation. However, whilst the culture of relativism affected the individual artist or scientist, it remains to be seen whether and in what ways it could influence the notion of *Kultur* in general as well as the cultural institutions through which *Kultur* was channelled.

Whilst expressionism took hold in central Europe, particularly in France, Austria and Germany, where aestheticism was a relatively brief phase, England provided fertile ground for the spread of a movement that rejected any value other than beauty as the purpose of art. Nowhere but in England were moral and religious values so dominant in art – only in England could the demand for *l'art pour l'art*, as a reaction to the moralising tone of previous art, be greeted with such enthusiasm. Taking as their point of departure the works of James McNeill Whistler, who popularised the notion of 'art for art's sake', Walter Pater and Oscar Wilde became the most prominent advocates. To them, 'the single duty of the artist was not to communicate his vision but to express his individuality, to enshrine in splendidly factitious forms the product of a prolonged self-indulgence in aesthetic appetites beyond the imagination and the means of the Philistine'.[5]

As in Germany, though from a different viewpoint, the artist in Britain was reclaiming his art from its moral and religious baggage. Such overt disdain for morality, however, naturally made the proponents of aestheticism an easy target for accusations of immorality. The well-publicised trials and tribulations of Oscar Wilde certainly confirmed this commonly held view. As in Germany, the established press never failed to remind its readers of the threat to morals posed by claims for the autonomy of art and the 'resultant' undermining of cultural standards. In both Britain and Germany, press criticism often mirrored a discomfort with the *fin-de-siècle* in general, above all its supposed destructive effect on society, morality and the modern individual.

Fin-de-siècle and the Bourgeois Concert

> Welch trübseliges "grosses Sterben" in unserer Kunst im Laufe der letzten paar Jahre! Auf Tschaikowsky folgte Bülow dann Rubinstein, darauf Bruckner und schnell nach ihm Brahms. Wien ist nun völlig verwaist.... In Wien, auf classischem Boden, ist ein Johannes Brahms erloschen, die wehmüthig langsam erbleichende Abendröthe jener grössten Epoche deutscher Tonkunst, deren strahlende Mittaghöhe Beethoven war. Wem im gegenwärtigen jungen Componistengeschlecht wäre die Kraft verliehen, uns den Verlust eines Brahms zu ersetzen?[6]

Over and over again, it was the apparent dissipation of reliable artistic production, complying with cultural orthodoxy and thus serving to uphold cultural traditions, that was being lamented. To the conservative critic, contemporary concert culture was drifting with the currents of the hour with every kind of cultural authority treated with contempt. By disassociating art from its moral and educational qualities, the artist was seen as obliged solely to his art. Without bourgeois 'guidance', however, they argued that not much vitality, integrity and strength could possibly be expected: ' ...statt kraftvoll-bewusstem Vorwärtsstreben kamen nun ängstlich klügelndes Raffinement, Pessimismus;...gewisse Krankhaftigkeit, Gequältheit, Unnatürlichkeit... übertriebene Weltschmerzstimmung...'.[7] To the traditionalist, all these phenomena represented common signs of decay and enfeeblement as traditionally revered signs and symbols were rejected as meaningless. The modern concert, or the well-publicised musical 'exhibitions' witnessed in the great metropolises – Paris, Vienna and Berlin – certainly provided cause for concern for the timorous observer. In their concert halls and opera houses cultural anarchy – expressed in the rejection of traditional concepts of the laws of tonality and harmony as well as in the denial of art's association with edifying purposes – not only ruled but was positively celebrated. Such art was thought to provide little prospect of authoritative guidance and stability.

Earlier, the rationality and naturalness of the harmonic system had been a given reality; presumed to be eternally valid they provided the basis of all theoretical understanding.[8] However, there could be, Arnold Schoenberg declared, no eternal laws: 'the only artistic law which can be deemed forever valid, is that of consistent change and inexorable progression because art reflects life in its mobility'.[9] With relativism permeating the artistic sphere, new forms and ways of composition, that ignored the hallowed classical tradition with its antiquated system of tonality, order and symmetry, could be explored. Taken to the extreme, art lent itself to extreme abstraction and abjured narrative as exemplified in the music of Arnold Schoenberg, Skryabin, Stravinsky, Hindemith, Prokofiev, Honegger, Bartók, Alban Berg and Anton Webern. Igor Stravinsky's introductory note to *Le Sacre du Printemps* (1913) is indicative of this development: 'It represents pagan Russia and is unified by a single idea: the mystery and great surge of the creative power of Spring. The piece has no plot.'[10] Music was thus stressed as an abstract medium, even a jumble of symbolical sound with arbitrary meanings which could not be understood by anyone but its creator and the initiated.[11] The absolute autonomy of subjectivity replaced universal laws once rendered comprehensible through education and regular visits to the concert hall. The concert hall collective, previously bound by a common cultural heritage forging a common sense of identity, 'was now feared disjointed as the dialogue between composer and audience took place – like abstract thought-experiments – in a void with notions of history and tradition discarded for good'.[12]

Because modern music could no longer be easily comprehended, it could no longer fulfil its moral or educational purpose, nor convey a sense of shared values. In such circumstances, cultural pessimism took a firm hold amongst conservatives who deplored the loss of the 'belief in the defining narrative of one's own culture'.[13] This apparent evaporation of cultural propriety was further visibly demonstrated by the association of the concert with disreputable behaviour as well as a healthy contempt for time-honoured behavioural norms, proper etiquette and manners. As can be seen in an emblematic passage in Thomas Mann's *Doktor Faustus* (1947) where the narrator looks back at the *fin-de-siècle* concert:

> … die Gesellschaft will aufgeregt, will herausgefordert, in pro und contra auseinandergesprengt sein, für nichts ist sie so dankbar wie für den amüsanten Tumult, qui fournit le sujet für Zeitungskarikaturen und unendliches Geschwätz, – der Weg zum Ruhm führt in Paris über die Verrufenheit, – eine rechte Première muss so verlaufen, dass mehrmals während des Abends alles von den Plätzen springt und die Majorität brüllt: 'Insulte! Impudence! Bouffonnerie ignominieuse!' während sechs, sieben initiés, Erik Satie, einige Surrealisten, Virgil Thomson, aus den Logen rufen: 'Quelle précision! Quel espirit! C'est divin! C'est suprême! Bravo! Bravo![14]

Scandals and revolt were thus deemed intrinsic to the modern concert experience. Major controversies were associated with musical events such as the Paris première of Stravinsky's *Le Sacre du Printemps* and the 'scandal concert' of 1913, organised by Schoenberg, who performed his *Kammersymphonie* as well as works by his students Berg and Webern. On the latter concert, the *Wiener Chronik* noted that hissing, clapping, banging keys and whistling frequently interrupted the performance. In the second gallery, the first fight of the evening commenced between adherents of rivalling fractions. Following the performance of Berg's *Zwei Orchesterlieder nach Ansichtskartentexten* [Two Orchestral Songs According to Postcard Texts], those still remaining calm now lost their composure too. The atmosphere reached boiling point when Schoenberg himself interrupted the performance and threatened to have members of the audience removed from the concert hall. This was met with further moaning and shouting (further aggravated by Berg, who yelled at the audience from his box). When members of the agitated audience slowly approached the stage, the concert was brought to an end.[15] At both the Paris and Vienna concerts, the police had to intervene to restore order. But, as Modris Ekstein writes of the first performance of the *Le Sacre du Printemps*, such notoriety was very much part of the making of modern art:

> To have been in that audience that evening was to have participated not simply at another exhibition but in the very creation of modern art, in that the response of the audience was and is as important to the meaning of this art as the intentions of those who introduced it. Art has transcended reason, didacticism, and a moral purpose: art has become provocation and event.[16]

The press naturally focused on the spectacle, the scandal, on 'a readymade cheering section [. . .], prepared to do battle against sterility'.[17] By doing so, it undoubtedly ensured modernism's primary association with notoriety and exhibitionism, underlining the disparity between the traditional bourgeois concert and its scandalous modern counterpart. Public outbursts, such as those witnessed in Berlin, Vienna and Paris were, at best, a public demonstration of the evils of the modern age: moral and physical decline, resignation, cultural decadence and loss of all norms of decency and respectability. In Leipzig's Gewandhaus, where highly traditional cultural conventions and artistic boundaries had existed for more than a century, such cultural anarchy could not have passed without notice, even alarm. The question remains whether and in what ways they were affected by these new developments in any real terms.

The Response of the Gewandhaus

Almost 50 years had passed since the Gewandhaus was last at the forefront of artistic renown. Its artistic institutions appeared to have run their course; neither the repertoire nor the conductor could regenerate the Gewandhaus by themselves. Cultural rejuvenation could only be triggered by new artistic leadership and this came with the arrival of Arthur Nikisch in 1895. With Nikisch, a conductor of the new generation, a brighter cultural age was eagerly anticipated. His background was promising. Nikisch differed from his predecessors in that he was the only *Gewandhauskapellmeister* after Mendelssohn whose musical education was in no way influenced by Leipzig's cultural traditions. Rather, he had spent his formative years as a violinist at the Vienna *Hofoper* since 1874, performing under the batons of Wagner, Liszt, Rubinstein, Brahms and Verdi – all composers/conductors with different temperaments and artistic convictions.[18] The artistic disputes of the Reinecke era were anathema to him; the *problem* of the *Neudeutschen* did not exist. Given that he was naturally inclined towards Brahms and Schumann, the break with Leipzig's tradition appeared negligible. A mitigating circumstance, as far as Leipzig was concerned, was that Nikisch was not attracted to *bona fide* modernists – Janáček, Bartók, Stravinsky, Ravel and Webern were amongst his least favourites but neither was he much attracted to Bach and Handel.[19]

Although it did not look that way to the Gewandhaus at the time, a further advantage was that Nikisch was also appointed *Kapellmeister* with the Berlin Philharmonic Orchestra, a post previously held by Hans von Bülow. This meant that Nikisch's artistic endeavours were not focused on Leipzig alone, as was the case with his predecessor. Resultant comparisons with the concert institutions of other towns undermined the hallowed exclusivity of the Gewandhaus, but at the same time it demonstrated very clearly that whilst Nikisch could engage in a fairly cautious programming in Leipzig, only slowly acclimatising Leipzig's audiences to artistic developments of the past 50 years, in Berlin, he was able to continue with and build upon Bülow's more advanced repertoire. Unlike in previous times, Berlin's concert practice now had to be taken seriously; Nikisch's Berlin Philharmonic could no longer be accused of being substandard, as this would have rebounded negatively on his involvement in the Gewandhaus. In all, a sea-change in attitudes seemed inevitable, but to overcome institutional tradition and artistic prejudice, 100 years in the making, and to develop a sense of artistic progress, was a long-term undertaking. For this, Nikisch seemed to have employed the right strategy – that is, to let time do its wondrous work.

The concert programme of 1895/1896 – Nikisch's first season – bears evidence of this: concerts began with an overture or short symphony, followed by a concerto, solo pieces or arias, and ended with another symphonic work, with compositions by Beethoven, Schumann, Schubert, Brahms or Mendelssohn. Here, Nikisch very much emphasised the Gewandhaus tradition. Brahms, in particular, was heavily endorsed: between 1895 and 1922, he gave 86 performances of the four symphonies, the *Haydn Variationen* nine times and the *Tragische Ouvertüre* ten times. Over time, however, Nikisch also began to include the representatives of the *Neudeutsche Schule*, as well as Peter Tchaikovsky, Antonin Dvořák, Bedrich Smetana, and later Richard Strauss, Max Reger, Borodin, Rimsky-Korsakov, César Franck, Debussy, Paul Dukas, Saint-Saëns, Edward Elgar, Humperdinck, Korngold, Max von Schillings, Rachmaninov and Delius. Gustav Mahler proved problematic. Although a movement of his third Symphony was performed in 1897, his second symphony was only performed in full in 1906; his first symphony in 1918, that is 30 years after its first performance in Budapest. An important addition to the repertoire was Anton Bruckner who (along with Brahms) found in Leipzig the most enthusiastic reception of his compositions outside Vienna, albeit only due to the unrelenting pressure Nikisch placed upon the directors.[20] Whilst up to 1900 only the fifth and seventh Symphonies as well as the *Te Deum* were performed, between 1900 and 1914, his symphonies were performed 14 times with the second, third, eighth and ninth being given their premières.

As has become evident from the above, it was no longer the sole prerogative of the Board of Directors to decide upon concert programming. Nikisch's artistic views were respectfully acknowledged partly because of his European reputation and partly because they remained within the boundaries of artistic tradition and cultural respectability. Compared with the new modernist experiences bursting onto the scene in the big European cities, even Richard Strauss, now considered to be a 'pale reflection of classical clarity when one returns from a *bona fide* modern noise orgy', was thought to exert a positive influence on music's natural progression.[21] This 'natural progression', made possible by the acceptance of Berlioz, Liszt and Wagner, allowed Strauss (as well as Bruckner) to be adopted into the artistic canon of the Gewandhaus. Much of this acceptance was due to the fact that by the end of the nineteenth century, the 'war of the romantics' had come to a close.

Indeed, when the centenary celebrations for those born during the first two decades of the nineteenth century arrived – Mendelssohn's in 1909, Schumann's in 1910, Liszt's in 1911 – each was celebrated equally in the Gewandhaus with concerts devoted to their lives and works. The artistic, cultural and aesthetic differences which had driven a wedge between the classicists and the *Neudeutschen* and later set 'Brahms against Bruckner are no longer valid today. The masters are now the third and the fourth of the great B's; they are modern but without the grim accompanying taste.'[22]

Thus, Nikisch and the Board managed to merge contemporary music with traditional cultural patterns without compromising cultural respectability in any way. Thus, Leipzig retained its reputation for traditional classicism, even though the ethical attributes derived from Winckelmann's classicism were broadened out of all recognition. The restrictions as to what could be incorporated into the definition of *classical* were expanded to an extent that compositions by Berlioz, Liszt or Wagner, which 40 years earlier were deemed little more than sacrilegious, could now be deemed 'classical' as a matter of course. This same extension also granted permanence to Smetana, Tchaikovsky and, most importantly, Anton Bruckner – the monumental symphonist who employed Wagnerian tone colours – alongside the 'purely' classical trinity (Haydn, Mozart, Beethoven) and Brahms. Nikisch's quest for subjectivity in his interpretation of traditional and modern music (which the acceptance of Wagner, Strauss and Mahler necessitated without, of course, engaging in the histrionics which accompanied, for example, Bülow's performances) reinforced the subtle break from traditional classical values. The compositions of modern composers simply could no longer be adequately conducted along traditional classical concepts of objectivity, composure and submission to the score that were so prominent during Reinecke's appointment.

Nikisch's international standing meant that, for the first time, it was no longer the Gewandhaus *sui generis* which guaranteed cultural renown, but Nikisch's authority. This was something the Board of Directors could no longer ignore when deciding upon its policies. Whilst they could take advantage of Reinecke's provincialism, they could not restrain Nikisch's musical aspirations which, during the 1901/1902 season, for example, led him to conduct at Hamburg, Hanover, Berlin, London and in various Russian towns spending around 89 days of the season in Leipzig and 61 days away.[23] Except for voicing their discontent at Nikisch's repeated requests for leave, there was little that the Board could do. Nikisch made his entire artistic existence dependent on his freedom of movement.[24]

However, whilst the Board of Directors seemed unable to restrain Nikisch's quest for artistic freedom, they did not loosen their grip on the orchestra. Thus, whereas Nikisch was able to tour with the Berlin Philharmonic[25] – to Paris in 1897, to Russia in 1899, to Austria, Italy, Spain and Portugal in 1901 – the Gewandhaus Board of Directors refused offers made to the orchestra to go to Bayreuth, Halle, even South America in 1913.[26] They still argued from the point of view that if anyone wanted to see or hear the orchestra, they ought to come to Leipzig. For one thing, the tripartite work of the orchestra in concert hall, church and theatre, effectively prevented any lengthy absences from Leipzig. More importantly, however, the Board still entertained the traditional idea of music and musician be in the service of Leipzig's bourgeoisie. In 1896, following an application by the orchestra to perform at Halle's *Wagner Verein*, the Board rejected the application on the grounds that:

> ... weil zu befürchten ist, dass unser berühmtes Orchester, das bisher nur edlen Zwecken gedient hat, durch Konzertreisen auf den Standpunkt eines philharmonischen Orchesters in Berlin und derartiger Gewerbsunternehmungen herabsinken könnte. [...] Gerade die grosse und vornehme Exklusivität, welche unserem Orchester bisher gewährt wurde, hat ihm den Ernst für seine Aufgabe erhalten, und sie hat zur Erhaltung seines Ruhmes viel mit beigetragen.[27]

Art then, was not to be degraded to the level of a business or trading venture. For Leipzig's manufacturers, traders and bankers, the Gewandhaus was still inextricably linked with Leipzig's purely cultural sphere. The status of the orchestra was assured by way of 'graceful exclusivity' rather than by commercial touring. The subscriptions, town council subsidies, as well as civic pride, which secured the maintenance of all public and artistic institutions were deemed sufficient; there was no need to look for extra sources of income. Whilst art and the artist might strive towards more autonomy, the institutions (financially tied to Leipzig's civic authorities) which might have supported such autonomy, remained firmly within the purview of the *Bürgertum*. Only in 1916 (that is, almost 20 years after the Berlin Philharmonic) was the Gewandhaus orchestra allowed to tour Switzerland, thus leaving the hallowed hall of the Gewandhaus for the first time. This peculiar dual identity between the traditional and the modern within the Gewandhaus can also be witnessed before and during the First World War.

Approaching 1914

In 1870/1871, during the Franco-Prussian war, the Gewandhaus as well as the *AMZ*, largely refrained from infusing music with the patriotic and jingoistic mood prevalent at the time. The aesthetic ethos they advocated had precluded any such involvement. In August 1914, however, a greater war was unleashed on the world. Rather than Prussia, it was now a united Germany trying to assert its might. The younger generation of men now volunteered to serve the German fatherland, not the Saxon or Bavarian homeland. The Wilhelminian Empire and its idea of nationhood claimed unambiguous cultural foundations – and these were generally sought within Germany's classical age. Similar to the rhetoric espoused during unification, it was the old Goethean association of the German classical period with notions of 'health', 'vitality' and 'strength' which, by the same token, led to foreign music being invested with opposite character-istics, which was particularly emphasised by art journals across the board. In an advance on the unification rhetoric, however, the idea of *German-entum* – in which the same ideas of vitality and strength were deemed to be inherent too – now figured prominently in the discussions on music.[28]

Amongst the music journals arguing for correlation between *German-entum* and 'classicism' were the *NZfM* and the *Signale für die musikalische Welt*. Underlying their polemical and popularist assaults upon 'weak' foreign music was the association of a nation's cultural production with the moral and physical condition of the nation itself. Foreign music was thus invested with negative features which, in turn, were supposed to represent national characteristics. With the majority of art and music journals now offering themselves in the service of Germany, the associ-ation of *Germanentum* with mental and moral potency became common currency. As war approached, the *NZfM* thought it inconceivable for any concert hall to perform foreign compositions:

> Jetzt, wo fast alle europäischen Staaten von einigem Klang und Rang gegen uns im Kampfe stehen, ist es unsere Pflicht, diesem feindlichen Eindringlingen die Tür zu unseren Schaubühnen und Konzertsälen zu verschliessen...also jene russische, französische und belgische Komponisten, natürlich auch die musikalisch ganz belanglosen Engländer und Serben mit ihren paar Tonwerken. [...] Auch auf dem Gebiete der Kunst, die nun einmal nicht international ist, sondern auf gesündester Volksgrundlage beruht, haben wir das Recht und die Pflicht, unsere grossen und gütigen Geister, die Alten wie die Jungen, die Klassiker wie die Romantiker auch des jüngsten Schlages, in erster Linie zu berücksichtigen.[29]

Whether classical, romantic, *neudeutsch*, even modern – style was irrelevant so long as the music expressed the German spirit (*Geist*); and it was the spirit deemed inherent to Beethoven, which was thought to embody the moral and physical strength of the German nation at this time of national awakening:

> Feinde erstehen uns ringsum und drohen die Schätze germanischer Kultur zu vernichten. [...] Jetzt gerade wird unsere Kunst beweisen können, dass sie nicht nur oberflächlicher Unterhaltung dient, sondern dass sie sittliche und läuternde Werte in sich birgt. [...] Ja, den städtischen Verwaltungen erwächst geradezu die Pflicht, für derartige musikalische Gottesdienste im Zeichen Beethoven's zu sorgen. Im diesem Zeichen wirst du siegen! Die ethische und erhebende Macht der Musik Beethoven's ist so über allen Zweifel erhaben, dass sich umständliche Beweisführung erübrigen; sie wird aber ihre Kraft stärker denn je äussern in diesen Zeiten nationaler Erhebung.[30]

The transcendental kingdom had at last been infused with *völkisch-national* thought in which Beethoven, the embodiment of all *Germanentum*, was hailed as Germany's redeemer. Along with Goethe, Beethoven formed the cultural bulwark both on the front line as well as the home front. Even more so than in 1870, this Germanic *Kultur* came to serve as a guarantor for military victory and subsequent spiritual renewal. How did the Gewandhaus respond?

Without a doubt, changes in the Gewandhaus repertoire are noticeable, particularly with regard to French composers. The season of 1914/1915 is Germanic to the core. Only one concert in October 1914 (3 months after the outbreak of war), performed non-Germanic music in the strictest sense: *Vyšehrad* by Smetana as well as Dvořák's cello concerto, flanked by a couple of his German songs. Their Bohemian origins, however, had always secured them a place within the Gewandhaus canon. Also, Bohemia, by virtue of its association with the Habsburg Empire, was now allied with Germany against Britain, France, Russia and America. French and Russian composers, by contrast, are noticeably absent during the first 2 years of the war. Tchaikovsky's Sixth Symphony was only performed again in March 1917, his First Piano Concerto in October of that year. Berlioz' overture *Le Roi Lear* was not performed until November 1917.

The rejection of Tchaikovsky during the first 2 years, in particular, was a sure indicator that the Gewandhaus did not remain immune from the nationalistic current of the day. Whilst still refraining from allowing the

Gewandhaus to be used for visible and laudable demonstrations of patriotism, the performance of Wilhelm Berger's *An die Grossen Toten* [To the Great Dead] and the *Schicksalslied*[31] [Song of Destiny] by Brahms in December 1914 proved to be expressions of contemporary sentiments within the Gewandhaus. A further noticeable change is that the final concert of the 1914/1915 season ended not with Beethoven's indomitable hymn for universal brotherhood – his Ninth symphony – (as had been standard practice for decades) but with Handel's Anthem No 1: *Gross ist der Herr* [Great is the Lord]. These Protestant-inspired nationalist sentiments were continued in the first concert of the 1915 season which opened with a chorale from J. S. Bach's cantata *Ein feste Burg ist unser Gott*[32] which was followed by Beethoven's Fifth. The overtly Germanic tone conveyed by this opening concert proved to be the standard as far as the rest of 1915/1916 season, perhaps the most Germanic of all thus far, was concerned. Given the situation at the fronts, the positive exclusion of composers from nations poised against Germany and her allies and the increasing prominence of Germanic and Protestant ingredients is, perhaps, hardly surprising. Despite the lack of overt patriotism during the concerts in the form of speeches or marked commissions, this clandestine use of specifically selected music was a sure indication that the non-referential characteristics inherent to idealism and classicism, which had always insisted on the universality of music, had been finally acknowledged to be out of date, perhaps even a fallacy.

However, this digression constituted only a brief episode in the Gewandhaus. With the cessation of hostilities, foreign composers were again included in the Gewandhaus repertoire. Although French composers were slow to follow, Tchaikovsky's return during the 1918/1919 season, which witnessed the performance of his fifth and sixth symphonies, his First Piano Concerto and *Romeo and Juliet* fantasy overture is indicative of this. The post-war season further heralded a new era which witnessed both the consolidation of Bruckner's position and the increasing acceptance of Mahler[33] and Strauss[34] within the Gewandhaus canon. As the Gewandhaus turned more and more towards traditional and modern symphonists, vocal music, which had resurfaced from the doldrums of the 1860s, was finally done away with. In its place, the traditional three-piece concert comprising an overture, instrumental concerto and a symphony was reinstated.

Thus, the impact of *fin-de-siècle* movements on the Gewandhaus is ambiguous. On the one hand, the Board was forced to relinquish some of its artistic authority as Nikisch's quest for artistic freedom could no longer be subdued. Nikisch was able to secure enough authority, not only to follow through his own artistic ideology, but to make the cultural prestige of the Gewandhaus dependent on his reputation. With it, he liberated the role of the *Kapellmeister* from the restrictions imposed by 100 years of bourgeois self-determination which had been channelled through the institutions it had created. The redefinition of the term 'classicism' meant that it could no longer feasibly remain divorced from contemporary concerns, including notions of Germany's nationalist awakening. On the other hand, however, the *avant-garde* was still a far cry from even beginning to destabilise the established cultural order, let alone laying the 'foundations for future orthodoxies'.[35] If anything, given the extension of 'classicism' beyond its original definition to include a vast number of contemporary compositions, the traditional cultural order was greatly reinforced, even enriched, following the war.

The Response of Birmingham's Festival

Similar to Germany, there was no shortage of commentators deploring contemporary developments in the arts. Joseph Bennett, one of Britain's most ardent guardians of the traditional cultural order never failed to remind his readers that moral cleanliness was paramount in the appropriation and appreciation of music. Sadly, according to Bennett, modernity provided little by way of ensuring the maintenance of such standards:

> Never has [music] so much lacked the leadership of genius and commanding power as now. [...] From Bach and Handel to Brahms, through 150 years of astonishing development, genius has influenced, if not ostensibly guided, the course of music; setting the mass of devotees an example backed by authority, overcoming all opposition, and finally being accepted as law-giver. But now the highest seats in the temple are vacant, the living voice of authority is silent, and, like a swarm of bees without a queen, the neophytes are pursuing their own devices, unguided and unchecked. [...] At present, music is in the power of the uncultured, who are ready to welcome every form of extravagance, and to determine matters of art by reference to considerations very much other than those to which the commanding voice rightfully belongs.[36]

Birmingham's Triennial Festival should have given contemporary critics such as Bennett little cause for concern, although interesting changes were inevitably being felt. Despite the fact that the Festival continued to provide its audience with the usual staple diet of oratorio-greats, the performance of newly commissioned oratorios indicates a shift in cultural expectations in that they demonstrate a move away from the didactic and moralistic concerns so paramount in traditional works. Now, a narrative *per se*, 'cut and pasted' from the Bible, however edifying, could no longer vouch for the value of art and biblical characters, however flawless, could no longer guarantee the intrinsic worth of a composition. The music to which the text was set had to demonstrate artistic value by itself: '... the colourless characters in Elgar's *The Apostles* and *The Kingdom*, such as John, Peter, Mary and Magdalen, were still less worthy of art than one Carmen or Isolde because a fascinating sinner is better than a tiresome saint'.[37]

The lack of a didactic purpose did not mean, however, that religious themes ceased to be central to choral productions. Unless art encouraged an *ideal*, it was condemned as a manifestation of cultural and national degeneration. This prefigured the rejection of *l'art pour l'art* at the Festival. For any art to be deemed worthy of the name, it had to affect the intelligence as well as the sensory nerves, for this would allow 'sensuousness, but never sensuality; [...] sentiment, but not sentimentality'.[38] To the traditional-minded observer, mere sentimentalism – a theme commonly attributed to modern art – was deemed injurious to the individual's strength of character, as it was feared to encourage a 'weak, maudlin, and ignoble temperament', thus producing 'a nation of effeminate and hysterical erotomaniacs'.[39] Thus, the need for a readily comprehensible purpose was still deemed intrinsic to any definition of art. The compositions performed at the 1900 Festival – Elgar's *Dream of Gerontius* (1900) and Brahms' *A German Requiem* (1868) – are indicative of this. At the same time, both point towards different cultural and religious contexts in which these could be received. Whilst the Handelian (and Mendelssohnian) oratorios of the early and mid-century suggested the need for explicitly moral instruction, transmitted through the trials and tribulations of biblical characters, both Elgar's and Brahms' sacred works dispensed with such time-honoured practice. Instead, they played upon the contemplative nature of more abstract ideas such as death, resurrection or the afterlife, thus playing upon the poetic treatment of religious themes. This allowed for the grounds upon which English aestheticism could, in part, develop, to be fertilised.

For one thing, Brahms' *Requiem* complied neither with the Catholic liturgy nor with the oratorio tradition. Whereas traditional Requiems were sung on behalf of the faithful departed dwelling in purgatory and to aid their speedy entry into heaven, Brahms' *Requiem* put the emphasis on the comfort of the living, now bereft. He further dispensed with the traditional liturgical sequence which comprises the Introit, Kyrie Eleison, Dies Irae, Offertorium, Sanctus, Agnus Dei and Communio. He dispensed, too, with Latin in favour of German – that is, Lutheran German.[40] His 16 biblical extracts, taken from the Lutheran Bible (from the Old Testament: Psalms, Isaiah, Solomon, Ecclesiastes and Hebrews, as well as texts from the New Testament: Matthew, Peter, James, John, Corinthians and Revelations) describe no plot, no characters, no rights and wrongs. It thus required no personalised speech, recitatives and arias, all of which were common to traditional Protestant oratorios. On the other hand, whereas traditional Requiems consisted of a prayer for the dead as well as a prayer for mercy and redemption on behalf of the dead (the day of wrath – the *Dies Irae* – was of central importance in the Requiem Mass), Brahms' *Requiem* makes no mention of divine revenge or punishment of the sinner on Judgement Day. Brahms also dispensed with the Catholic emphasis on Christ's sacrifice on the cross to redeem humankind. Instead, he attempts to articulate the inarticulable and reconcile the irreconcilable: the transience of all there is, on the one hand, and the everlasting life of the soul on the other. By suggesting the infinity and eternity of God and by providing glimpses into the glory of the coming kingdom, Brahms conveys hope and the word of God spoken to the living in need of comfort: 'Blessed are they that mourn; for they shall be comforted' (Matthew 5:4).

Similarly, the *Dream of Gerontius* does not follow the model of any previous musical settings. It narrates a soul's journey through death, providing a meditation on the unseen world of Roman Catholic theology (including angels, archangels and purgatory). It describes the story of a dying man of infallible faith. In his last hours, Gerontius dreams that he is dead and that his soul wanders into the everlasting: 'The pain has wearied me...Into thy hands, O Lord, into Thy hands...'. When the soul awakes, it is watched over by his guardian Angel. It is the Angel, the 'father gave in charge to me...e'en from its birth to save and serve', who now accompanies Gerontius to God's judgement throne where after a 'night of trial' in the lake of purgatory, Gerontius is promised a re-awakening in glory: 'Farewell, but not for ever!'. As in Brahms' *Requiem*, Elgar's *Dream* offers no explicitly didactic plot but provides, with impressive poetic power, a glimpse of the joys of the afterlife: 'I went to sleep; and now I am refreshed...for I feel in me an inexpressive lightness, and a sense of freedom, as I were at length myself, and ne'er had been before...'. Such tones had never before been heard at Birmingham's

Festival. In line with its predecessors, however, the *Dream* provides plenty of opportunity for dramatic representation, a prerequisite still central to all Festival commissions. Like Gounod's *Redemption*, it was planned on a massive scale: 'Mr Elgar out-Wagners Wagner in heavy scoring, and even comes near the aspirations of Hector Berlioz. So far as mere effectiveness is concerned there would seem to be nothing left to wish for'.[41] Despite the disappointing première, the desired effect was, according to *Aris' Birmingham Gazette*, achieved beyond doubt, as 'the straining eye of the hungering fancy discloses its idea of the maybe of the soul's future'.[42]

To judge from these examples, rather than discarding its traditional cultural ethos, the Triennial Festival resurrected and reinvented its oratorio culture. Although the obligation to instruct the listener was dispensed with, the essence of religion – its beautifying and inspiring qualities – was still required in Birmingham's Festival culture. Such was made clear in the review of Granville Bantock's setting of Omar Khayyam – the eleventh-century Persian astronomer. From the outset it faced 'certain disadvantages' because Bantock did not rely on religious, and therefore respectable, themes. By doing so, he laid himself open to accusations of cosmic ignorance as far as public middle-class cultural expectations were concerned. After all, 'the words of the Holy Writ wedded to music come to us with ten times the effect of equally good music wedded to secular words. But when, instead of the angels harping on the harps in Hallelujahs..., we have commendations to eat and drink and love for tomorrow we die, we English are apt to pause in doubt'.[43] That Bantock was, in fact, an outspoken atheist was irrelevant; his personal standpoint was of no consequence as far as his compositional output was concerned. Art was still primarily consumed by the middle class; its values and norms, rather than those of the artist, were still deemed paramount in all artistic productions.

The evening sessions too underwent profound changes. The lack of a clearly defined instrumental tradition at the Festival combined with the absence of requisite musical styles (romanticism, classicism) meant that Hans Richter, who had succeeded Costa as Festival conductor in 1885, was fairly much at liberty to follow his own artistic impulses. A direct result was that instrumental music was given far more attention than hitherto. One of Richard Wagner's former pupils and most loyal disciples at Bayreuth (where he conducted the first performance of Wagner's *Ring des Nibelungen*), Richter was *Kapellmeister* at the *Hofoper* in Vienna (where he premièred Brahms' second and third symphonies as well as Bruckner's fourth symphony) and conducted the Philharmonic

Concerts in London, where he also established the *'Richter'schen Konzerte'* at St James Hall. In London, Richter conducted the first performance of Elgar's *Variations on an Original Theme* (Enigma) as well as his first symphony which the composer had dedicated to the conductor. An important circumstance was that Richter also conducted Manchester's Hallé Orchestra from 1899 to 1911 where he did much to support English composers as well as Bartock and Sibelius. This sheer variety of composers which Richter championed is reflected in the evening sessions of Birmingham's Festival. Apart from routine performances of Beethoven's Violin Concerto and symphonies, particularly the Fifth, Seventh and Ninth, as well as numerous Wagner overtures, Richter also added Brahms' symphonic works, Schubert's Ninth and later Tchaikovsky's Sixth Symphony as well as his Violin Concerto to the Festival repertoire. Interestingly, too, Richard Strauss' symphonic poems received an extensive hearing.

This new appreciation of purely instrumental music meant that the evenings were freed from the dominance of the seemingly endless number of isolated operatic scenes and arias. Whereas previously all evening performances were devoted to 'the lighter class of music'[44] (which meant that the orchestra did little beyond accompanying the selections from Italian opera with an occasional Rossini overture thrown in[45]), orchestral music was now receiving greater attention and recognition. The repertoire was filled with longer, symphonic works which were performed in their entirety. A typical evening session under Richter thus comprised the following: Egmont overture by Beethoven, the Stabat Mater by G. Hensche, Schubert's Ninth Symphony, a recitative and aria from Gounod's *Faust*, the Alto Rhapsody by Brahms and the *Husitska* overture by Dvořák. By reducing the number of compositions during the evening session to predominantly instrumental music, Richter undoubtedly helped to create a new and better understanding of purely orchestral music which had been impossible hitherto. This new appreciation for instrumental music, however, had to be sustained without the aesthetic foundations which had been present in Germany for the last 100 years. The institution of Germany's 'transcendental kingdom' was literally unthinkable in the context of Britain's more mimetic tradition. Whilst Germany had in place a language which could rationalise the intricacies of instrumental music and a ready set of values to match, this was not the case in Britain. Britain's aesthetic framework had not developed a critical discourse with which instrumental music could be substantiated. Thus, whenever a critic reviewed a symphony, for example, it often sufficed to say that 'Richter conducted it'. Critics would rarely venture beyond a general description of the structural characteristics of an instrumental composition.

The demise of the moral requirement of art to instruct the audience during the morning sessions and the rise of non-referential music during the evening session was made possible by the decline of practical Christianity, that is, religious-inspired charity as part of the musical festivities. Although Festival Committee members were still associated with the General Hospital and accounts were still published in newspapers, the overall understanding of charity as a fundamental component of the Triennial Festival – as an exonerating counterpart to musical enjoyment – was diminishing. Charity had become a nominal adjunct necessitated by tradition. A combination of factors was responsible.

Firstly, towards the end of the century, Birmingham experienced massive economic growth; side by side with the older industries, new ones sprang into existence and brought their pioneers to great affluence. To this new social group, that distinctly Victorian middle-class notion of art uniting the 'brotherhood of men' to alleviate the suffering of humanity, bore relatively little meaning. The old Festival institution with its established rituals and character was no longer relevant to them as it had been to the traditional middle class, to whom these rituals had been part of more universal philosophy. As the *Birmingham Post* noted:

> [The Festival] has been largely dependent in the past upon well-to-do people in the town and the neighbourhood, to whom Festival week was one of the social delights of the year. Today the rich have many other toys to play with; some of them have fallen away from the festival, while others continue to support it partly for the sake of the charity and partly from family tradition, but, as I can testify, not without some grumbling in private.[46]

Secondly, it was to this Victorian generation that philanthropy and charity still conveyed a symbolic power and means of public recognition which formed part of the criteria for acquiring and maintaining social leadership.[47] In the light of late nineteenth-century suburbanisation, amalgamation of enterprise and the coming of mass society, however, charity had lost this attribute – there was little that charity could do as far as maintaining class relations and local authority was concerned. Rather than voluntary associations, public welfare provisions fell now more and more under the jurisdiction of central or local government agencies, which meant that personal philanthropy and charity provided far less of an incentive to raise the individual's standing within the community.[48]

Thirdly, the decline of philanthropic action as part of the Festival proceedings was furthered by modern investigative studies on the causes and workings behind working-class poverty and deprivation. The early nineteenth century belief that proper moral behaviour, diligence and propriety necessarily secured personal prosperity, thus associating working-class pauperism with immorality and indolence, had now given way to a conviction that poverty (no longer called pauperism) was involuntarily thrust upon the working class by economic competition rather than by a lack of personal morality. Since the publication of Charles Booth's *Life and Labour of the People of London* (1889–1903), Seebohm Rowntree's *Poverty: A Study of Town Life* (1901) and Jack London's *People of the Abyss* (1903), poverty was recognised as a social phenomenon which could be investigated and remedied with suitable reforms. Such reforms could not, however, be any longer adequately put through by traditional, voluntary efforts. As Jack London exclaimed: 'These people who try to help! Their college settlements, missions, charities, and what not, are failures. In the nature of things they cannot but be failures. They are wrongly, though sincerely, conceived. [...] They do not understand the simple sociology of Christ, yet they come to the miserable and the despised with the pomp of social redeemers'.[49] The misery caused by poverty could not be alleviated by 'begetting in the poor yearnings of the Beautiful and True and Good'.[50] Rather, it was local government policies which could assuage the misery of the labouring poor.

Nowhere was this conviction more apparent than in Birmingham, where Joseph Chamberlain proposed urban renewal schemes which could properly force through much-needed civic improvement. Never one to withhold his disdain for the evangelical notions of 'saving souls', Chamberlain used his Unitarian proclivity for practical social analysis in order to implement social changes beyond personal philanthropy. According to his secular religious outlook, Chamberlain's improvement schemes epitomised the view in which 'social conditions were the source of sin and legislation the basis for salvation'.[51] As local governments were seizing middle-class philanthropy by transferring it into the realms of political action, middle-class culture lost one of the pillars that supported its existence. This development spelled the end of the view 'in which all the love of our neighbour, the impulses towards action, help, and beneficence...diminishing human misery, the noble aspiration to leave the world better and happier than we found it...come in as part of the grounds of culture'.[52] Matthew Arnold, for one, would have seen the criticism he voiced of the association of religious-inspired charity and middle-class culture finally justified more than 20 years after the publication of his *Culture and Anarchy* (1869).

The demise of philanthropic action ultimately effected the Festival's original *raison d'être*. This became particularly evident in the precarious balance sheet which demonstrated just how charity grew to matter less and less to Festival proceedings. Its long history of success obliged the Festival Committee to seek constantly to exceed previous musical triumphs. (After all, the hope to discover yet another *Elijah* was never given up.) This obligation, however, raised levels of expenditure with each succeeding Festival, whilst the number of seats in the Town Hall, by contrast, could not but remain the same. The result was a steady decline in net profits: whilst during the late eighteenth century, it remained at a steady 50 per cent, dropping slowly to around 30 per cent in 1900, it arrived at an all-time low of 14 per cent in 1912. Of the £10,900 taken from ticket prices and donations £9400 were paid out in fees and other kinds of expenditure leaving a meagre donation of £1500 to the General Hospital. The last time it had managed to raise this amount of money was in 1799, the difference being that expenditure then was as low as £2500 leaving a profit margin of 57 per cent.[53] The numbers indicated what many long suspected, namely, that the Festival had lost sight of its charitable obligations. The huge expenditure – caused by advertisements plastered around the town as well as placed in local and national newspapers, prospectuses, refurbishment and decorations which were required for the occasion, and excessive payments which had to be made to artists commissioned to compose works specifically for the occasion – had long been accepted as necessary pre-requisites to the Festival. Along with the steady collapse of traditional socio-economic, demographic, religious and cultural patterns, this abandonment of traditionally fundamental constituents began to tear apart the Festival's structural foundations. The discontinuation of the Festival in 1915 and the discussion held about it in the press reveal how much the Festival had outgrown its original purpose and how little it did to make itself acceptable to the needs of Birmingham's early twentieth-century music culture.

The End of the Festival

Some argued that it was Richter's (Germanic) heavy-handed treatment of monumentally serious music that led to a steady decline in audience numbers. Far more blamed the early twentieth-century depression in trade as well as rising competition from other festivals. The 1909 Festival might have provided the evidence if the Norwich Festival held in the same year had not proven the opposite to be true. There, despite the slump in trade, attendance figures and profits had, in fact, increased. According to *The Musical Times*, the reasons for the success in Norwich were to be found in the complete 'restructuring' of the festival programme which was ordered by its new advisor, Henry Wood. Unlike in previous years, the programme was now filled with more popular works according to what the public desired and which 'reflected the musical spirit of the day'.[54] The greatest support was, in fact, given to Berlioz's *Damnation of Faust*. As far as Birmingham was concerned, it once and for all brought home what critics suspected for a long time: that the music itself, even if it failed to edify the soul of the listeners, had become acceptable within the public culture of the middle class and that the Triennial Festival had simply not kept up with this change in taste.

Accordingly, Birmingham, in an effort to emulate Norwich's financial success, appointed Henry Wood to conduct the 1912 Festival. His programme featured familiar works, *Messiah*, *Elijah*, *St Matthew Passion*, *German Requiem*, but also the less familiar, such as Verdi's *Requiem* and Dvořák's *Te Deum*. As far as the evening sessions were concerned, Richter's preference for Brahms', Schubert's and Tchaikovsky's symphonic works was not congruent with Wood's taste. Although performing Beethoven's Seventh, Wood returned to the more familiar works such as Rossini's *William Tell* overture, Bach's *Brandenburg Concerto No 3*, Haydn's *Concerto for Cello and Orchestra* in D-major, Bach's *In dulci jubilo*, Wagner's *Tannhäuser* overture, as well as arias by Purcell and Mozart. In returning to more anodyne artistic grounds, the purely instrumental advances made under Richter (as demonstrated, for example, by the frequent performance of Richard Strauss' tone poems) were halted. Skryabin's *Prometheus*, the performance of which would have been a UK première, was abandoned at the last minute, something which was sorely deplored in the *Birmingham Post* as *Prometheus* would have given Birmingham a 'notion of what is being attempted in music by the minds that have won their freedom from the great Wagnerian fatherhouse'.[55] In all, Wood's appointment did not produce the promised results; financially, the 1912 Festival ran at a loss.

Similarly important was the increasing dissatisfaction voiced by prominent music critics such as Ernest Newman (William Roberts), then writing for the *Birmingham Post*. His satirical assaults are indicative of how little equivalence there was left between early twentieth-century musical ideals and the Festival with its incessant performances of time-honoured oratorio-greats. Newman's favoured target was Birmingham's *Holiness Week* – the perpetual harping on sin and death during the festivities. Within this, even *Elijah* and *Messiah* were no longer spared savage ridicule. For the first time, their hallowed immunity to criticism was undermined as both were dragged into the arena of critical scrutiny. 'It might be asked', said Newman, 'why begin a Christian Festival, held for the greatest of Christian virtues, charity, with an oratorio that is neither Christian nor charitable'?[56] The answer was, of course, that *Elijah* belonged to Birmingham. The oratorio's association with Birmingham's pride and joy, her 'foster-child', Felix Mendelssohn, was still deemed essential to Birmingham's cultural reputation. Although that was not going to change, what Newman did achieve was that he publicly exposed Birmingham's obsession with Handel and Mendelssohn for what it was: a species of ancestor worship:

> And when to the pain of listening to *Baal, we cry to thee* or *All we like Sheep* for the five-hundredth time, is added the reflection that this unreasoning attachment to Elijah and Messiah is a source of a great deal of our English backwardness in music, even the greatest admirer of Handel and Mendelssohn must admit that the critic has some reason for feeling a little out of tune at times.[57]

By removing Handel and Mendelssohn from the shelter of the middle-class cultural protection, Newman inevitably challenged the intrinsic artistic merits of their works. Even *Messiah* could now no longer be held up as an exemplary work that was above criticism by virtue of its subject matter, as had previously been the case:

> It they were exercising their critical faculty upon it they would see how hopelessly antiquated much of the music is, and what is worse, how insincere. In the chorus *All we like Sheep have gone astray, we have turned every one to his own way*, the most overwhelming sense of remorse for sin – sin so great that the Saviour had to take upon Him the burden of the iniquity of the whole world. And how does Handel do it? In a chorus of free-and-easy jollity that would be more appropriate in some merry-making in the village green![58]

Related to this was the conflict between such music and modern conducting technique. To the critic accustomed to Wagner, Strauss, perhaps even Mahler, Henry Wood's performance of *Messiah* at the 1912 Festival epitomised everything that was deemed wrong with the Festival. An awareness of different muso-historical epochs and the resultant differences in the performance and reception of music were seemingly absent in Wood's rendition of *Messiah* when he conducted it with an intensity which was more typical of the post-Wagnerian age, but one quite unsuitable for eighteenth-century compositions. It became apparent that passion could not be put into suave platitudes: to perform pre-Wagnerian and pre-Straussian compositions 'with all the paraphernalia of dramatic expression that Wagner and Strauss have familiarised us with is as absurd as shedding bitter tears over the concussion of Humpty Dumpty'.[59] Newman likened it to Wood demolishing Stonehenge to build *bijou villas* with stucco fronts and pink wall paper. English music culture had simply moved on, practices and taste had changed. To Newman, it was now time for the Festival Committee to realise this fact and act upon it. As it turned out, the Festival's entrenched cultural tradition meant that there was little which could be changed.

Newman's second line of attack was the dominance of the Festival in Birmingham's cultural sphere. Without this dominance, the ubiquitous presence of *Messiah* and *Elijah* at the Festival might just have been tolerated. With the Festival running itself ever deeper into an artistic *cul-de-sac*, signs of cultural paralysis, judged by the absence of other concert institutions, were becoming increasingly apparent – and this could no longer be tolerated. On the announcement of the Festival's suspension in 1915, letters of approval and disapproval were published in *The Musical Times*, with Charles Villiers Stanford, supported by Walter Parratt and Frederick Bridge, standing at the forefront of the protest against abandonment. They did so because of the pecuniary losses incurred to both charity and (London) performers who had stood loyally by Birmingham for decades. Those arguing in favour of abandonment did so out of concern for the musical well-being of Birmingham, which stood to suffer under the dull weight of the Festival and its conventions: 'Birmingham', complained Ernest Newman 'is the least musical large town in Europe – perhaps, we may say, in the world. It has few good concerts; it has no real orchestra; it is ignorant not merely of music as a whole and of new music in particular, but of many works that have within the last few years become more or less familiar to London, Liverpool, Manchester and Glasgow'.[60] Combined with both the now commonly held assumption that Festivals drained a town of the financial resources available (usually for the mere benefit of around 2000 concert-goers out of the million inhabitants then living in Birmingham) and the bleak prophecies following the anticipated financial collapse in view of the 1912 Festival balance sheet, the Festival's detrimental effect on Birmingham's cultural sphere henceforth dominated the rhetoric of the anti-Festival faction. Thus, as far as Newman et al.

were concerned, Birmingham had two choices: either having a Festival or modernising its whole musical foundations. The solution seemed simple: like other towns, Birmingham needed organised financial effort which would secure a permanent local orchestra headed by a competent conductor.[61]

And then, of course, there was the war. The fact that the Festival was unable to unite all its resources once more in 1915, if only to rouse support for Britain's war effort, indicated that the Festival had run its course. Reasons for its demise have been dealt with above, but there was also something peculiar about the relationship of Britain, war and music which contributed to it. A basic exposition is attempted below.

Approaching 1914

If there was ever a cultural platform able to rouse an audience towards a common goal, it surely would have been a grand musical Festival such as Birmingham's. The first difficulty, of course, was that many musicians were conscripted into active front-line service and were thus difficult to find, particularly in the large numbers required by the Festival and its monumental choral productions. Secondly, the Festival's peculiarly outdated *raison d'être* which had always been to support the General Hospital and to provide ennobling entertainment for Birmingham's middle class, has to be considered. As mentioned previously, the Festival had not been able to adapt to the needs of a middle class which, during the early twentieth century, bore little resemblance to the one under which the Festival once flourished. Now it seemed doubly ill-equipped to deal with either national or local patriotic needs. Thirdly, whilst Germany's nationalistically oriented music journals and newspapers could incessantly exploit a seemingly endless repertoire of home-grown music for its patriotic ends, Britain, in comparison, had indeed little to show. There was, as yet, no obvious musical force which could be used to represent the perceived values and strengths of Britain in the way that Beethoven (as well as Goethe and Schiller) had done for Germany. To be sure, particularly under Richter's baton, a generation of British composers – Cowen, Goring Thomas, Stanford, Sullivan, Parry, Prout, Mackenzie, Elgar – was no longer deemed inferior by Birmingham's Festival managers. The Festival of 1906, for example, featured works almost exclusively by British composers: Edward Elgar, Joseph Holbrooke, Percy Pitt and Granville Bantock. The public too, *The Musical Times* declared, 'is throwing off its distrust of native music, and the coldness which was shown to native composers is rapidly giving way to a strong desire to welcome every honest effort'.[62] The free trade policy which governed English festivals since their earliest days had given way to pride in British artistic achievements, something which found its most decisive expression in Edward Elgar, whose descent 'from a fine old yeoman stock of Weston, Herefordshire, and [is] therefore intensely English' was deliberately pointed out as being particularly felicitous.[63]

But even Elgar could not be held up to the British soldier in the same way as Beethoven could to his German counterpart. Since the early nineteenth century, Germany's emergent aesthetic system provided a plethora of ways and means by which Beethoven could be valorised. Since unification he had been hailed as Germany's redeemer; along with Goethe and Humboldt, he had been declared a foundation stone upon which Germany could build its idea of the *Kulturnation*. During the war, Beethoven's compositions were thought to exude the German Geist through which the soldier was to absorb the strength and vitality deemed inherent in the German character. Britain's aesthetic system, by comparison, simply provided little or no relevant endorsement for art and artists to be used in this way. As a result, the Festival was not equipped, either in its aesthetic requirements or artistic institutions, to enhance the patriotic needs of Birmingham.

Leading on from that, whilst the artistic productions of a highly active and publicised faction of Germany's musical and literary élite were nourished by political upheavals such as the revolutions of 1848 (and/or were utilised for patriotic ends from the 1870s onwards with retrospective force), no such artistic élite had developed in England. In fact, there had not been a tradition of investing music with political or national sentiments since the eighteenth century. At that time, however, the common enemy was Catholicism; now it was Germany. Whilst Handel had provided England and Birmingham with suitable Protestant compositions against the common foe, there was little by way of English music which could do the same for England against Germany. Worse still for Birmingham, what would the 4-day festivities consist of without its traditional repertoire, replete with the mighty Haydn, Handel (whom Germany had long claimed back), Beethoven, Mendelssohn – even Wagner? Perhaps because of all this, there were a sizeable number of people who, despite calls for a boycott, argued for the continued performances of German music in British town and concert halls. The Birmingham Post's most prominent music critic spelled out what many suspected, namely that eradicating German music from British concert halls would be, in fact, a futile, even ridiculous undertaking:

> If you do [boycott German music] than you have to be logical and ban
> all published German music. It moral corruption lurks in the Beeth-
> oven symphony that we hear in the concert room, why expose the
> tender maiden in the privacy of her own drawing room to the corrup-
> tion of a Beethoven sonata? Mothers, look to it! Guard your girls from
> the monsters of iniquity who wrote the Matthew Passion, the B minor
> Mass, the Ninth Symphony, the Jupiter and the Creation. We must
> even go further: why stop at music? Should not pressure be put upon
> the Medici Society and other reproducers of pictures to burn all the
> plates they may have of Dürer and Holbein? If Bach and Beethoven
> are to be cast out, why should Lessing and Schiller and Goethe and
> Kant be allowed to stay in. [...] Then, if it is to be all or nothing and
> rather all than nothing, let us delete from our hymn-books and banish
> from our church services the beautiful hymn tunes that have come
> to us from the German Protestant Church. Let the Protestant revert
> to Catholicism, for was not Luther a German? Let us, finally, deny
> ourselves books in toto, for was not the inventor of printing a Ger-
> man? Let us be wise men if we can; but if we are going to be fools let
> there be no limit to our foolishness.[64]

To many Britons and to as many Germans, Bach, Beethoven and Brahms
were still the epitome of civilisation and cultivation. To reject them was
to let go of that association. Furthermore, taking away all the composers
of German origins would have meant the near depletion of the Festival
repertoire.

Conclusion

Thus, the Triennial Festival was abandoned at the beginning of the war
owing to a combination of reasons, all of which point to one central issue: that the Festival, whose founding principles had crystallised
out of eighteenth-century concerns gradually ceased to relate to the
social, cultural, political and economic conditions that rapidly re-defined
Birmingham's early twentieth-century public sphere. Even though a
more aesthetic and poetic musical culture was allowed to rise, the Festival's link to the traditional philanthropic task of supporting the General
Hospital, and above all its insistence on time-honoured cultural, religious and aesthetic practices, meant that the Festival's structure was no
longer able to serve a purpose that fitted a different time, generation
and context. The edifying benefits once sought in and drawn from the
performance of oratorios were no longer held in the same high regard;

because welfare support had come progressively under the auspices of local government agencies, independent charity had lost ground as far as supporting an important institution like the General Hospital was concerned; finally, the vitality of music culture itself had begun to suffer under what came to be perceived as the overwhelming power of the Festival, and widespread protests in favour of different, and more varied, concert ventures were voiced. In short, one by one, the values that once underpinned the Festival became obsolete. Because it was unable to change or adapt its original purpose, because it was unable to rid itself of its baggage of traditional middle-class norms and values, the Triennial Festival finally lost its *raison d'être*. Thus, as in Leipzig, it was not so much the predominance of modernist – indeed, decadent – ideas during the *fin-de-siècle* that rocked the Festival's foundations. Rather, it was the undermining of the middle-class religiously inspired moral and charitable purpose that was the ultimate cause of the Festival's demise.

Leipzig's Gewandhaus, by contrast, with its far more ethereal and intangible values continued to withstand the cultural vicissitudes of time. This meant that, as in 1848 and 1871, the Gewandhaus remained immune to the tumultuous ideas of both the *fin-de-siècle avant-garde* and the cataclysm of 1914. In stark contrast to Birmingham's Festival, Leipzig's adherence to 'timeless' and 'universal' classicism proved in fact flexible enough simply to absorb the challenge of artistic advances without allowing them to change the fundamental tenets of German idealism that its middle class had so long espoused and in which it had found and continued to find its confident identity.

Notes

1. H. S. Hughes, *Consciousness and Society: The Reorientation of European Social Thought, 1890–1930* (Brighton: Harvester Press, 1979 [1959]), p. 195.
2. None of these movements must be too sharply identified. They tended to be rather incoherent and diffuse and were not necessarily espousing a 'programme' as was the case with the *Neudeutschen* during the 1840s. One must be careful not to assume that changes were inevitable, planned and thought-out only because the historian has detected historical patterns and located the *Zeitgeist* within them.
3. Muschg, *Studien zur tragischen Literaturgeschichte*, p. 19.
4. P. J. Brenner, *Neue deutsche Literaturgeschichte: vom 'Ackermann' zu Günter Grass* (Tübingen: Max Niemeyer Verlag, 2004), p. 198.
5. Buckley, *The Victorian Temper*, p. 218.
6. C. Söhle, 'Johannes Brahms todt!' in *Musikalisches Wochenblatt*, Jg 28, No. 15, 8 April 1897, p. 210f. 'What depressing "great dying" has emerged in our art

during the course of the last few years. Upon Tchaikovsky followed Bülow then Rubinstein, then Bruckner and swiftly after him Brahms. Vienna is now entirely orphaned.... In Vienna, on classical soil, a Johannes Brahms expired, the melancholic slow paling sunset of this greatest of epochs of German music, whose shining midday light was Beethoven. Who amidst today's generation of young composers has been granted the power to compensate for the loss of Brahms?'

7. R. von Mojsisovics, 'Neue Bahnen III: Dekadenz in der Musik' in *Musikalisches Wochenblatt*, Jg 37, No. 9, 1 March 1906, p.173f. 'Instead of powerful forward striving, there came only timorously intellectualising refinement, pessimism;... a certain morbidity, agony, unnaturalness,... and exaggerated sense of world-weariness.'

8. Fubini, *Geschichte der Musikästhetik*, p. 359.

9. Fubini, *Geschichte der Musikästhetik*, p. 365. 'Das einzige künstlerische Gesetz, das als ewig gelten kann, ist das des beständigen Wechsels und der unaufhaltsamen Weiterentwicklung, denn die Kunst reflektiert das Leben in seiner Beweglichkeit.'

10. Quoted in Eksteins, *Rites of Spring*, p. 9.

11. E. A. Baughan, 'On the Modern Language of Music' in *The Musical Times*, Vol. 55, 1 April 1914, p. 234.

12. R. Scruton, 'True Authority: Janáček, Schoenberg and us' in P. Davison, *Reviving the Muse: Essays on Music after Modernism* (Brinkworth: Claridge, 2001), p. 21.

13. Arthur Danto quoted in Sheehan, *Museums*, p. 148.

14. Mann, T., *Dr Faustus: Das Leben des deutschen Tonsetzers Adrian Leverkühn erzählt von einem Freunde* (Frankfurt/Main: Fischer Taschenbuch Verlag, 2003), p. 531. 'Society demands to be excited, challenged, torn in sunder for and against; it is grateful more than anything, for the diversion and the turmoil qui fournit le sujet for caricatures in the papers and endless chatter. The way to fame, in Paris, leads through notoriety – at a proper première people jump up several times during the evening and yell "Insulte! Impudence! Bouffonerie ignominieuse!" while six or seven initiates, Erik Satie, a few surréalistes, Virgil Thomson, shout from the balconies: "Quelle précision! Quel esprit! C'est divin! C'est suprême! Bravo! Bravo!"' Thomas Mann, *Doctor Faustus: The Life of the German Composer Adrian Leverkühn as Told by a Friend* (London: Secker & Warburg, 1949). Translated by H. T. Lowe-Porter.

15. See www.wiener-symphoniker.at/gesch/ge010405_d.htm.

16. Eksteins, *Rites of Spring*, p. 15.

17. Eksteins, *Rites of Spring*, p. 15.

18. Forner, *Die Gewandhauskonzerte*, p. 138.

19. Forner, *Die Gewandhauskonzerte*, p. 169.

20. In 1884, Nikisch performed Bruckner's Symphony Nr 7 in Leipzig's *Stadttheater*.

21. A. Spanuth, 'Der fünfzigjährige Richard Strauss' in *Signale für die Musikalische Welt*, Jg 72, No. 23, 10 June 1914, p. 966. '...fast wie ein Abglanz klassizistischer Klarheit wenn man gerade von einer richtigen modernen Geräuschorgie kommt. Bei Strauss lag das verblüffend Neue vor allem in der Handhabung, in der Anwendung des von Berlioz, Liszt und Wagner Vorbereiteten; bei Debussy, Skryabin und Schoenberg dagegen lernen wir

etwas wesentlich Neues kennen, wie zum Beispiel die totale Emanzipation vom Tonalitätsbegriff.'

22. #, 'Zehntes Gewandhauskonzert' in *NZfM*, Jg 79, No. 51/52, 19 December 1912, p. 726.

23. *SAL Gewandhaus zu Leipzig,* Briefe Arthur Nikisch 382–430, Letter No. 414, 14 February 1902.

24. *SAL Gewandhaus zu Leipzig*, Briefe Arthur Nikisch 431–475, Letter No. 471, 7 January 1904. '...nachdem 12 Jahre hindurch die Gewandhaus Concerten durch meine auswärtige Thätigkeit nicht geschädigt wurden und auch in Zukunft nicht geschädigt werden können, darf ich wohl die Hoffnung hegen, dass die geehrte Concert-Direction nicht plötzlich Schwierigkeiten sieht, wo solche tatsächlich nicht vorhanden sind und das bisherige freundliche Entgegenkommen nicht unnötigerweise einschränken wird. Nicht nur meine materielle, auch meine künstlerische Existenz hängt davon ab.' ['Since throughout the last 12 years the Gewandhaus concerts were not impaired through my out-of-town engagements and will not be so in the future, may I cherish the hope that the revered Board of Directors does not suddenly see difficulties where there are none and that the friendly co-operation between us thus far is not unnecessarily curbed. Not only my material existence but also my artistic existence depends on it.']

25. Touring orchestras became a familiar sight. The *Meininger Hofkapelle*, for example, visited 108 European towns performing 371 concerts out of town between 1880 and 1914.

26. Forner, *Die Gewandhauskonzerte*, p. 131.

27. Böhm, Staps, *Das Leipziger Stadt- und Gewandhausorchester*, p. 165. 'Because it is feared that our famous orchestra which so far has only served the noblest of purposes might be reduced to the level of a philharmonic orchestra in Berlin and such business ventures through concert tours. [...] It is precisely the great and noble exclusivity which has been granted to our orchestra thus far, which has preserved for it the serious commitment to its duty and has contributed much to the maintenance of its glory.'

28. Music again seems to lag behind its sister arts. For an account of literature during the Second Empire see R. Speirs, 'German Literature and the Foundation of the Second Empire' in Speirs, Breuilly, *Germany's Two Unifications*, pp. 185–208.

29. W. Tappert, 'Unsere Musikprogramme und Deutschlands Feinde' in *NZfM*, Jg 81, No. 37/38, 17 September 1914, p. 487. 'Now that almost all European states of any name and rank stand against us in combat, it is our duty to shut the doors of our theatres and concert halls to these enemy intruders...all these Russian, French and Belgian composers, naturally also to the musically trivial English and Serbs with their few odd musical works. [...] In the sphere of art too, which is just not international but rests on the healthiest ethnic basis, we have the right and obligation to consider in the first place our great and gracious spirits, the old as well as young, the classical as well as romantic, even those of the youngest generation.'

30. R. Birgfeld, 'Ehrt eure deutschen Meister' in *Signale für die Musikalische Welt*, Jg 72, No. 34, 26 August 1914, p. 1254. 'Enemies surround us and threaten to destroy the treasures of Germanic culture. [...] Especially now, our art can prove that it does not just serve superficial entertainment but that it harbours

within itself moral purifying values. [. . .] Indeed, the civic authorities acquire nothing less than the obligation to ensure such musical services under the sign of Beethoven. Under this sign you will triumph! The ethical and elevating power of Beethoven's music is so beyond all doubt that elaborate proof is superfluous; in these times of national elevation, it will express its power more strongly than it did ever before.'

31. Brahms' *Schicksalslied* was composed in 1871. The three verses were taken from Friedrich Hölderlin's *Hyperion*, which deals with the Greek wars of liberation from Turkish oppression. The three verses emphasised the contrast between the carefree life of the ancient gods (verses one and two) and the constant and eternal suffering of mankind under Destiny's unrelenting force (verse three). Brahms' repetition of the introduction to verses one and two, however, changes the meaning of Hölderlin's poem in that the fatalistic vision of human existence is now turned into a reconciliation between humankind and the gods and thus into a belief of man's sharing of divine peace.

32. Apart from being one of the Lutheran Church's most prominent anthems (bequeathed to it by Martin Luther himself) the final line which ends with '*Sie haben's kein Gewinn, Dass Reich muss uns doch bleiben*', is often interpreted as exuding both religious and nationalistic sentiments.

33. Mahler's *Kindertotenlieder, Das Lied von der Erde, Lieder eines fahrenden Gesellen* as well as the symphonies were already increasingly performed towards the end of the war.

34. Straus' *Eine Alpensymphonie, Tod und Verklärung, Also sprach Zarathustra, Don Juan, Till Eulenspiegel, Ein Heldenleben* and other works became noticeably more popular during the post-war concert seasons.

35. Jefferies, *Imperial Germany*, p. 7.

36. J. Bennett, 'Some Present Aspects of Music' in *The Musical Times*, Vol. 39, No. 661, 1 March 1898, p. 159.

37. *Birmingham Post*, 3 October 1906. Although reviews were still written anonymously, the language suggests that it was probably penned by Ernest Newman.

38. F. C. Baker, 'The Function of Art' in *The Musical Times*, Vol. 51, No. 809, p. 435.

39. Baker, 'The Function of Art' in *The Musical Times*, Vol. 51, No. 809, p. 435.

40. Again, whilst Handel uses excerpts from the burial service within the Anglican *Book of Common Prayer* (1662) such as *I am the Resurrection and the Life, I know that my Redeemer liveth, The Lord giveth and the Lord taketh away*, Brahms' use of the Lutheran bible within a Catholic setting further demonstrates how English Protestantism had ceased to be the sole guiding force for British cultural production.

41. *Aris Birmingham Gazette*, 4 October 1900.

42. *Aris Birmingham Gazette*, 4 October 1900.

43. *Aris Birmingham Gazette*, 8 October 1909.

44. *Birmingham Post*, 29 August 1861.

45. *Birmingham Post*, 3 October 1900.

46. *Birmingham Post*, 7 October 1912.

47. P. Shapely, *Charity and Power in Victorian Manchester* (Manchester: Smith Settle on Behalf of the Chetham Society, 2000), p. 19.

48. As already mentioned, Birmingham was comparatively late in its founding of Voluntary Associations, a development which was further exacerbated by

the existence of a 'puritanical Saint Party' during the 1850 and 1860. By the 1880s, Chamberlain's reform project put governmental agencies in control of civic and welfare matters. Thus one could argue that Birmingham missed out on the golden age of élite voluntary associations.
49. J. London, *People of the Abyss* (New York: Lawrence Hill Books, 1995 [1903]), p. 306.
50. London, *People of the Abyss*, p. 306.
51. Marsh, *Joseph Chamberlain*, p. 95f. 'We bring up a population in the dank, dark, dreary, filthy courts and alleys such as are to be found throughout the area which we have selected; we surround them with noxious influences of every kind, and place them under conditions in which the observance of even ordinary decency is impossible; and what is the result? [...] The fact is, it is no more the fault of these people that they are vicious and intemperate than it is their fault that they are stunted, deformed, debilitated and diseased. The one is due to the physical atmosphere – the moral atmosphere as necessarily and surely produces the other. Let us remove the conditions, and we may hope to see disease and crime removed' (Chamberlain speech to the Town Council, 12 October 1875).
52. Arnold, 'Culture and Anarchy' in Collini (ed.) *Culture and Anarchy*, p. 59.
53. All data taken from Handford, *Sounds Unlikely*, p. 204.
54. Anon., 'Birmingham Musical Festival' in *The Musical Times*, Vol. 50, No. 801, 1 November 1909, p. 735.
55. *Birmingham Post*, 26 September 1912.
56. *Birmingham Post*, 14 October 1903. 'Elijah begins with the proclamation of a dire affliction. Of the national life we have on the one side idolatrous fanaticism, on the other, stern unyielding justice; the charity that thinketh no evil is absent.'
57. *Birmingham Post*, 3 October 1906.
58. *Birmingham Post*, 5 October 1906.
59. *Birmingham Post*, 2 October 1912.
60. E. Newman, 'The Question of the Birmingham Festival' in *The Musical Times*, Vol. 56, 1 February 1915, p. 77.
61. Following the demise of various concert ventures, such a proposition was, in fact, finally accomplished in 1921 with the founding of the Birmingham Symphony Orchestra, the first municipally funded orchestra in the country.
62. Anon., 'A. C. Mackenzie on the Aspects and Prospects of Music in England' in *The Musical Times*, Vol. 28, No. 527, 1 January 1887, p. 15.
63. Anon., 'Edward Elgar' in *The Musical Times*, Vol. 41, No. 692, 1 October 1900, p. 641.
64. E. Newman, 'On the Boycotting of German Music' in *Birmingham Post*, 16 August 1915.

Conclusion

The principal aim of this study has been to understand the ways and means by which two important urban centres formed particular cultural ideals and fashioned or re-fashioned the institutions that sustained them. Whilst institutional frameworks had been in existence since the early and mid-eighteenth centuries, it was the aesthetic, philosophical and religious ideas, developed during and after the Enlightenment, that furnished the norms and values through which a rising middle-class consciousness could flourish. These norms and values, imposed upon to existing institutions, helped to develop the particular identity of the Triennial Festival and the Gewandhaus. Both institutions, in turn, ensured a level of propriety deemed necessary to the sustenance of the public culture of the middle class, the main consumers and benefactors of culture. This development occurred in Leipzig and Birmingham alike. In both, the dominating presence of the middle class in the cultural sphere was particularly important as a compensation for the political representation that at the time still eluded them.

However, given that there can be no universal laws concerning cultural or artistic propriety, each middle class developed its own cultural ideals in accordance with its needs and the means available to them. As we have seen in Chapter 1, on a basic level, the disparity in Birmingham's religious, economic and political spheres necessitated a type of culture which could help to unify its middle class and establish a class-identity that transcended individual loyalties. Thus, the Triennial Festival was grounded in commonly accepted notions of philanthropy and morality. In Leipzig, by contrast, no such potential fissures existed. Practical considerations of this kind therefore did not impinge on a bourgeois music culture that was considered in any case to exist in a sphere far beyond the constraints of the everyday reality. As Chapter 2 has demonstrated, the more practical aspirations of Birmingham's Festival thus stand in sharp contrast to the more ethereal nature of the philosophical system of transcendental idealism, favoured by Leipzig. The aesthetic consequences for the development of the public concert in the two towns – the emphasis on instrumental music in Leipzig and the oratorio tradition in Birmingham – are clear.

By concentrating on repertoire preferences, attitudes towards composers and the construction of concert space, Chapter 3 sought to provide empirical evidence for the developments described in the previous two chapters. Despite the inevitable disparity between the Gewandhaus and the Festival, both relied equally on foundations afforded by a powerful process of canonisation. Once accepted and internalised, these canons developed into rigid socio-cultural constructs that commanded absolute legitimacy. As such, cultural canons provided continuity and stability for the establishment and maintenance of middle-class cultural identity for much of the remaining decades of the nineteenth century. The efficacy of these canons was demonstrated in Chapter 4 which highlighted a schism between the now established cultural values of the middle class and the aspirations of radically innovative philosophers (Nietzsche, Arnold) and artists (Wagner).

Chapter 5 dealt with the late nineteenth and early twentieth centuries, during which time cultural institutions either re-oriented themselves or faltered. Their fate, however, was not so much determined by the new artistic or philosophical currents which pervaded the *fin-de-siècle*. More important was the question as to whether the aesthetic and socio-cultural norms, which for so long had provided the scaffolding of the respective musical institutions, had retained their validity in the face of the wider social, cultural, political and economic changes that arose around the turn of the century. It is here that the advantages provided by comparative analysis become evident. Comparative analysis curbs the dangers of assuming that there is such a phenomenon as a *normal* or *anomalous* development. For the comparative approach allows not only for greater flexibility than is commonly the case in single-focused studies, but also enriches the subject of enquiry via the exploration of dissimilarities and congruencies. Notions of 'normality' are thus properly relativised as contrasting contexts are examined. Throughout this study it has been argued that within each locality, cultural ideals were formed in accordance with the relevant social, cultural, economic, political and philosophical conditions. Viewed from within its own local context, therefore, the development of culture necessarily follows a 'normal' path. It is the recognition of this fact which curtails the trend to extrapolate from what is 'normal' in one case and to extend the result to all others. Instead, comparative history allows the observer to identify and accept, as in the case of Leipzig and Birmingham, two different kinds of 'normality'.

The demise of the Festival in 1915 can thus not be used to conclude that Birmingham's cultural sphere developed 'abnormally'. Rather, it seemed a 'normal' conclusion for its time and context. The carefully nurtured association of the Festival with non-musical values such as morality, religion and philanthropy – all time-specific and referential – meant that the values and norms which had once been a means of underpinning bourgeois culture, giving it stability and a sense of purpose, slowly lost their relevance as time and context changed. Whilst the increasingly obvious schism between time-honoured practice and contemporary values could still be safeguarded by tradition during the 1880s, this was no longer possible in 1915. Conversely, the survival of the Gewandhaus is not indicative of a 'right' path to cultural development. Rather, this survival was conditioned by its proclivity towards a 'timeless' idealism and classicism and its consequent divorce from time-specific and referential qualities. Whilst this phenomenon would have been entirely incompatible within Birmingham's musical tradition, it allowed Leipzig's public music culture to withstand many of the socio-cultural, political, artistic and philosophical challenges launched by the progress of time. Thus, Leipzig's Gewandhaus represented one of the few remaining sanctuaries to provide stability during a time of rapid change. Whereas Birmingham's outmoded cultural patterns were eventually discarded and replaced by new ones, classicism's ability to appear in different guises and to serve under different pretexts meant that it continued to dominate the cultural ideology of the Gewandhaus. Here, despite the excitement in all the other arts, music remained deeply conservative, both in its artistic norms and cultural elitism.

Bibliography

Ameriks, K. (ed.), *The Cambridge Companion to German Idealism* (Cambridge: Cambridge University Press, 2000).

Anderson, B., *Imagined Communities: Reflections on the Origins and Spread of Nationalism* (London: Verso, 1991 [1983]).

Applegate, C., Potter, P. (eds), *Music and German National Identity* (Chicago: University of Chicago Press, 2002).

Baker, N. K., Christensen, T., *Aesthetics and the Art of Musical Composition in the German Enlightenment: Selected Writings of Johann Georg Sulzer und Heinrich Christoph Koch* (Cambridge: Cambridge University Press, 1995).

Bashford, C., Langley, L. (eds), *Music and British Culture 1785–1914: Essays in Honor of Cyril Ehrlich* (Oxford: Oxford University Press, 2000).

Bate, W. J., *From Classics to Romantic: Premises of Taste in Eighteenth-Century England* (New York: Harper & Row, 1961 [1946]).

Batsche, Z., Garber, J. (eds), *Von der Ständischen zur Bürgerlichen Gesellschaft. Politisch-soziale Theorien in Deutschland der Zweiten Hälfte des 18. Jahrhunderts* (Frankfurt/Main: Suhrkamp, 1981).

Beardsley, M. C., *Aesthetics from Classical Greece to the Present: A Short History* (New York: The Macmillan Company, 1966).

Beddow, M., *Thomas Mann – Doktor Faustus*, Landmarks of World Literature (Cambridge: Cambridge University Press, 1994).

Bergfeld, I., *Leipzig: Eine kleine Stadtgeschichte* (Erfurt: Suttonverlag, 2002).

Bimberg, S., *Handbuch der Musikästhetik* (Leipzig: Deutscher Verlag für Musik, 1979).

Birch, D. (ed.), *Ruskin and the Dawn of the Modern* (Oxford: Oxford University Press, 1999).

Bird, V., *Portrait of Birmingham* (London: Robert Hale, 1970).

Bishop, P., Stephenson, R. H., *Friedrich Nietzsche and Weimar Classicism* (New York: Boydell & Brewer [Camdon House], 2004).

Blackbourn, D., *History of Germany, 1780–1918: The Long Nineteenth Century* (Oxford: Blackwell, 2003 [1997]).

Blanning, T. C. W., *The Nineteenth Century: Europe, 1789–1914* (Oxford: Oxford University Press, 2000).

Böhm, C., Staps, S.-W., *Das Leipziger Stadt- und Gewandhausorchester* (Leipzig: Kunst und Touristik, 1993).

Bourdieu, P., *Distinction: A Social Critique of the Judgement of Taste* (London: Routledge, 2000 [1979]).

Brenner, P. J., *Neue deutsche Literaturgeschichte: vom 'Ackermann' zu Günter Grass* (Tübingen: Max Niemeyer Verlag, 1996).

Briggs, A., *History of Birmingham, Volume 2: Borough and City 1865–1938* (Oxford: Oxford University Press, 1952).

Briggs, A., *The Age of Improvement, 1783–1867* (Harlow: Longman, 2000 [1959]).

Buckley, J. H., *The Victorian Temper: A Study in Literary Culture* (Cambridge: Cambridge University Press, 1969 [1951]).

Bunce, J. T., *The Birmingham General Hospital and Triennial Music Festivals* (Birmingham: Benjamin Hall, 1858).

Bunce, J. T., *History of the Corporation of Birmingham Vol. 2* (Birmingham: Cornish, 1885).

Burns, R., Rayment-Pickard, H. (eds), *Philosophies of History: From Enlightenment to Post-Modernity* (Oxford: Blackwell Publishers, 2000).

Butler, E. M., *The Tyranny of Greece over Germany* (Cambridge: Cambridge University Press, 1935).

Butler, E. M., *The Fortunes of Faust* (Cambridge: Cambridge University Press, 1952).

Cannadine, D., *Lords and Landlords: The Aristocracy and the Towns, 1774–1967* (Leicester: Leicester University Press, 1980).

Chorley, H. F., *Music and Manners in Germany: A Series of Travelling Sketches of Art and Society* (London: Longman, 1841).

Colley, L., *Britons: Forging the Nation 1707–1838* (New Haven, London: Yale University Press, 1992).

Collini, S. (ed.), *Matthew Arnold: Culture and Anarchy and Other Writings* (Cambridge: Cambridge University Press, 1993).

Cornish's Stranger's Guide Through Birmingham (Birmingham: W Cornish, 1913).

Craig, G. A., *Germany 1866–1945* (Oxford: Oxford University Press, 1981 [1978]).

Creuzburg, E., *Die Gewandhaus-Konzerte zu Leipzig 1781–1931* (Leipzig: Breitkopf und Härtel, 1931).

Czok, C., *Das Alte Leipzig* (Leipzig: Köhler & Amelang, 1978).

Dahlhaus, C. (ed.), *Das Problem Mendelssohn* (Regensburg: Gustav Bosse Verlag, 1974).

Dahlhaus, C., *Nineteenth-Century Music* (Berkeley: University of California Press, 1988) English translation by J. Bradford Robinson.

Davidoff, L., Hall, C., *Family Fortunes: Men and Women of the English Middle Class 1780–1850* (London: Routledge, 2002 [1987]).

Davison, P. (ed.), *Reviving the Muse: Essays on Music after Modernism* (Brinkworth: Claridge, 2001).

Dean, W., *Handel's Dramatic Oratorios and Masques* (Oxford: Oxford University Press, 1959).

Doerffel, A., *Geschichte der Gewandhausconcerte zu Leipzig vom 25. November 1781 bis 25. November 1881* (Leipzig: Breitkopf & Härtel, 1884).

Duclaud, J., *Leipziger Zünfte* (Berlin: Verlag der Nation, 1990).

Eagleton, T., *The Ideology of the Aesthetics* (Oxford: Blackwell, 1990).

Eckermann, J. P., *Gespräche mit Goethe in den letzten Jahren seines Lebens.* www.gutenberg.spiegel.de/eckerman/gesprche/gesprche.htm. (Vols 1 and 2 published in 1837, Vol. 3 in 1848).

Edwards, E., *Some Account of the Origins of the Music Festival and of James Kempson, the Originator* (Birmingham: Sabin & Stockley, 1882).

Eksteins, M., *Rites of Spring: The Great War and the Birth of the Modern Age* (London: Anchor Books, 2000 [1989]).

Elias, N., *Über den Prozess der Zivilisation, Soziogenetische und phychogenetische Untersuchungen, Vol 1: Wandlungen des Verhaltens in den weltlichen Oberschichten des Abendlandes* (Amsterdam: Suhrkamp, 1997 [1939]).

Elliott, A., *The Music Makers: A Brief History of the Birmingham Triennial Festival 1784–1912* (Birmingham: Birmingham City Council, 2000).

Faulstich, W., *Die bürgerliche Mediengesellschaft 1770–1830*, Geschichte der Medien Band 4 (Göttingen: Vandenhoeck & Ruprecht, 2002).

Forchert, A., 'Textanlage und Darstellungsprinzipien in Mendelssohns Elias' in Dahlhaus, C. (ed.), *Das Problem Mendelssohn* (Regensburg: Gustav Bosse Verlag, 1974).

Forner, J., *Die Gewandhauskonzerte zu Leipzig*, Vol. 2 (Leipzig: VEB Deutscher Verlag für Musik, 1981).

Fubini, E., *Geschichte der Musikästhetik von der Antike bis zur Gegenwart* (Stuttgart: J. B. Metzler, 1997).

Fulbrook, M., *German History Since 1800* (London: Arnold, 1997).

Gilbert, A. D., *Religion and Society in Industrial England: Church, Chapel and Social Change 1740–1914* (London: Longman, 1976).

Gill, C., *History of Birmingham, Vol 1: Manor and Borough to 1865* (Oxford: Oxford University Press, 1952).

Gill, C., Robertson, C. G., *A Short History of Birmingham from its Origins to the Present Day* (Birmingham: City of Birmingham Information Bureau for the Corporation, 1938).

Gilmour, R., *The Victorian Period: The Intellectual and Cultural Context of English Literature 1830–1890* (London: Longman, 1993).

Gleich, C. C. J. von, *Die Bedeutung der Allgemeinen Musikalischen Zeitung, 1789–1848 und 1863–1882* (Amsterdam: F. Knuf, 1969).

Gleisberg, D., *Merkur und die Musen: Schätze der Weltkultur aus Leipzig. Eine Ausstellung aus der Deutschen Demokratischen Republik im Künstlerhaus Wien, 21.9.1989–18.2.1990* (Vienna: Das Künstlerhaus, 1989).

Glogau, H.-U., *Der Konzertsaal: Zur Struktur alter und neuer Konzerthäuser* (Hildesheim: Georg Olms Verlag, 1989).

Goehr, L., *The Imaginary Museum of Musical Works* (Oxford: Clarendon, 1992).

Gretschel, C. C. C., *Leipzig und seine Umgebung* (Leipzig: F. Fleischer, 1836).

Grout, D. J., Palisca, C. V., *A History of Western Music*, 4th Edition (London: J. M. Dent & Sons, 1988 [1960]), reprint 1993.

Grugel, L. E., *Society and Religion During the Age of Industrialisation: Christianity in Victorian England* (Washington: University Press of America, 1979).

Gunn, S., *The Public Culture of the Victorian Middle Class* (Manchester: Manchester University Press, 2000).

Habermas, J., *The Structural Transformation of the Public Sphere: An Inquiry into a Category of Bourgeois Society* (Cambridge: Polity Press, 2000 [1962]).

Hammermeister, K., *The German Aesthetic Tradition* (Cambridge: Cambridge University Press, 2002).

Handford, M., *Sounds Unlikely: 600 Years of Music in Birmingham, 1392–1992* (Birmingham: Birmingham Midland Institute, 1992).

Harvie, C., Matthew, H. C. G., *Nineteenth-Century Britain: A Very Short Introduction* (Oxford: Oxford University Press, 2000).

Hauschild, V., *Die Grossen Leipziger: 26 Annäherungen* (Leipzig: Insel Verlag, 1996).

Hein, D., Schulz, A. (eds), *Bürgerkultur im 19. Jahrhundert: Bildung, Kunst und Lebenswelt* (München: Beck, 1996).

Heine, H., *Florentine Nights* (London, Methuen & Co. Ltd., 1927). Translated by Charles Godfrey Leland.

Hempel, G. & I., *Musikstadt Leipzig* (Leipzig: Deutscher Verlag für Musik, 1979).

Hennenberg, F., *Das Leipziger Gewandhausorchester* (Leipzig: Bibliographisches Institut, 1984 [1962]).

Hermand, J., *Geschichte der Germanistik* (Reinbek: Rowohlt, 1994).

Hogwood, C., Luckett, R., *Music in Eighteenth-Century England: Essays in Memory of Charles Cudworth* (Cambridge: Cambridge University Press, 1983).

Hohendahl, P. U., *Literarische Kultur im Zeitalter des Liberalismus 1830–1870* (München: Beck, 1985).

Hopkins, E., *Birmingham: The First Manufacturing Town in the World 1760–1840* (London: Weidenfeld & Nicolson Ltd., 1989).

Hughes, H. S., *Consciousness and Society: The Reorientation of European Social Thought 1890–1930* (Brighton: Harvester Press, 1979 [1959]).

Illustrated Stranger's Guide to Birmingham (Birmingham: R. Wrightson, 1913).

Jefferies, M., *Imperial Culture in Germany, 1871–1918* (Basingstoke: Palgrave Macmillan, 2003).

Johnson, J., *Listening in Paris: A Cultural History* (Berkeley: University of California Press, 1995).

Kaschuba, W., 'German Bürgerlichkeit after 1800: Culture as Symbolic Practice' in Kocka, J., Mitchell, G. (eds), *Bourgeois Society in 19th Century Europe* (Oxford: Berg Publishers, 1993). Translated from *Bürgertum im 19. Jahrhundert* (Munich: Deutscher Taschenbuch Verlag, 1988).

Kennedy, M., *The Concise Oxford Dictionary of Music*, 3rd Edition (Oxford: Oxford University Press, 1980).

Kirk's Popular Guides: *What to See in Birmingham* (Birmingham: R. S. Kirk, 1887).

Kneschke, J. E., *Leipzig seit 100 Jahren: Säcularchronik einer werdenden Grossstadt* (Leipzig: Selbstverlag, 1867).

Kocka, J., *Bürgertum und Bürgerlichkeit im 19. Jahrhundert* (Göttingen: Vandenhoeck & Ruprecht, 1987).

Kocka, J., Mitchell, A. (eds), *Bourgeois Society in 19th Century Europe* (Oxford: Berg Publishers, 1993 [1988]).

Langford, P., *The Eighteenth Century, 1688–1815* (Oxford: Oxford University Press, 2002).

Leppert, R., McClary, S., *Music and Society: The Politics of Composition, Performance and Reception* (Cambridge: Cambridge University Press, 1987).

Lessing, G. E. in Hill, D. (ed.), *Nathan der Weise*. New German Studies Texts & Monographs, 9 (Hull: University of Hull Press, 1988).

London, J., *People of the Abyss* (New York: Lawrence Hill Books, 1995 [1903]).

Lundgreen, P., *Sozial-und Kulturgeschichte des Bürgertums: Eine Bilanz des Bielefelder Sonderforschungsbereichs*, Bürgertum Band 18 (Göttingen: Vandenhoeck & Ruprecht, 2000).

Maentel, T., 'Zwischen weltbürgerlicher Aufklärung' in Hein, D., Schulz, A. (eds), *Bürgerkultur im 19. Jahrhundert* (Munich: Beck, 1996).

Magirius, H., *Die Semperoper Dresden: Baugeschichte, Ausstattung, Ikonographie* (Leipzig: Edition Leipzig, 2004).

Mann, T., *Doktor Faustus: Das Leben des deutschen Tonsetzers Adrian Leverkühn erzählt von einem Freunde* (Frankfurt/Main: Fischer, 2003 [1947]). Translated as *Doctor Faustus: The Life of the German Composer Adrian Leverkühn as Told by a Friend* (London: Martin Secker & Warburg, 1949) by H. T. Lowe-Porter.

Marchand, S. L., *Down from Olympus: Archaeology and Philhellenism in Germany, 1750–1970* (Princeton: Princeton University Press, 2003).

Marsh, P. T., *Joseph Chamberlain: Entrepreneur in Politics* (New Haven and London: Yale University Press, 1994).

Martin, D., *Christian Language and its Mutations: Essays in Sociological Understanding* (Aldershot: Ashgate, 2002).

Mason, L. W., *Musical Letters from Abroad: Including Detailed Accounts of the Birmingham, Norwich, and Dusseldorf Musical Festivals of 1852* (New York: Mason Brothers, 1853).

McLeod, H., *Religion and the People of Western Europe* (Oxford: Oxford University Press, 1997).

McLeod, H., *Secularisation in Western Europe, 1848–1914* (Basingstoke: Palgrave Macmillan, 2000).

Middell, K., *Hugenotten in Leipzig: Streifzüge durch Alltag und Kultur* (Leipzig: Leipziger Universitätsverlag, 1998).

Morris, R. J., 'Voluntary Societies and British Urban Elites' in *The Historical Journal* 26/1, 1983.

Morris, R. J., *Class, Sect and Party: The Making of the British Middle Class, Leeds 1820–1850* (Manchester: Manchester University Press, 1990).

Muschg, W., *Studien zur tragischen Literaturgeschichte* (Bern: Francke, 1965).

Musgrave, M., 'Changing Values in 19th Century Performance: The Works of Michael Costa and August Mann' in Bashford, C., Langley, L. (eds), *Music and British Culture 1785–1914* (Oxford: Oxford University Press, 2000).

Nipperdey, T., *Deutsche Geschichte 1866–1918*, 2 vols (Munich: Beck, 1990–1992).

Nipperdey, T., *Germany from Napoleon to Bismarck, 1800–1866* (Dublin: Gill and Macmillan, 1996). Translated by Daniel Nolan.

Nipperdey, T., *Deutsche Geschichte 1800–1866: Bürgerwelt und starker Staat* (Munich: Beck, 1998 [1983]).

Orsini, G. N. G., *Coleridge and German Idealism: A Study in the History of Philosophy with Unpublished Materials from Coleridge's Manuscripts* (London: Carbondale, 1969).

Pikulik, L., *Frühromantik: Epoche – Werke – Wirkung* (Munich: Beck, 1992).

Prasch, D., *Vertraute Briefe über den Politischen and Moralischen Zustand von Leipzig* (London: Stendal, 1787).

Puhle, H.-J. (ed.), *Bürger in der Geschichte der Neuzeit: Bürgertum – Beiträge zur Europäischen Geschichte*, Bd 1 (Göttingen: Vandenhoeck & Ruprecht, 1991).

Richard, H., *Memoirs of Joseph Sturge* (London: S.W. Partridge, 1864).

Roth, R., 'Von Wilhelm Meister zu Hans Castorp' in Hein, D., Schulz, A. (eds), *Bürgerkultur im 19. Jahrhundert* (Munich: Beck, 1996).

Sadie, S., *New Grove Dictionary of Music and Musicians*, 2nd Edition (London: Macmillan, 2001).

Salmen, W., *Das Konzert: Eine Kulturgeschichte* (Munich: Beck, 1988).

Schering, A., Wustmann, R., *Musikgeschichte Leipzigs, Vol 3: Das Zeitalter Johann Sebastian Bachs und Johann Adam Hillers, 1725–1800* (Leipzig: Teubner, 1974 [1941]).

Schmitt, U., *Revolution im Konzertsaal: zur Beethoven-Rezeption im 19. Jahrhundert* (Mainz: Schott, 1990).

Schonberg, H. C., *Die Grossen Dirigenten: Eine Geschichte des Orchesters und der berühmtesten Dirigenten von den Anfängen bis zur Gegenwart* (München: Beck, 1973). Translated from Schonberg, *The Great Conductors* (London: Gollancz, 1968).

Schötz, S., *Städtische Mittelschichten in Leipzig während der bürgerlichen Umwälzung 1830–1870* (Unpublished PhD, Universität zu Leipzig, 1985).

Schulz, G., Doering, S., *Klassik: Geschichte und Begriff* (Munich: Beck, 2003).

Schumann, R., *Gesammelte Schriften über Musik und Musiker*, 2 Vols (Farnborough: Gregg Press, 1969 [1914]).

Scruton, R., 'True Authority: Janáček, Schoenberg and Us' in Davison, P. (ed.), *Reviving the Muse* (Brinkworth: Claridge, 2001).

Seidel, K., *Carl Reinecke und das Leipziger Gewandhaus* (Hamburg: Reinecke Musikverlag, 1998).

Seneca, *Ad Lucilium Epistulae Morales* (London: Heinemann, 1925). Translated by Richard Gummere.

Sengle, F., *Biedermeierzeit: Deutsche Literatur im Spannungsfeld zwischen Restauration und Revolution 1815–1848*, 3 Vols (Stuttgart: J. B. Metzler, 1971–1980).

Sennett, R., *The Fall of the Public Man* (London: Faber and Faber, 1986 [1977]).

Shapely, P., *Charity and Power in Victorian Manchester* (Manchester: Smith Settle on Behalf of The Chetham Society, 2000).

Sheehan, J., 'Culture' in Blanning, T. C. W. (ed.), *The Nineteenth Century: Europe, 1789–1914* (Oxford: Oxford University Press, 2000).

Sheehan, J., *Museums in the German Art World: From the End of the Old Regime to the Rise of Modernism* (Oxford: Oxford University Press, 2000).

Showell, W., *Dictionary of Birmingham – A History and Guide* (Oldbury: Walter Showell & Sons, 1887 [1885]).

Sica, A., 'Rationalization and Culture' in Turner, S. (ed.), *The Cambridge Companion to Weber* (Cambridge: Cambridge University Press, 2000).

Sievers, H.-J., *In der Mitte der Stadt: die Evangelisch-reformierte Kirche zu Leipzig von der Einwanderung der Hugenotten bis zur Friedlichen Revolution* (Leipzig: Evangelische Verlagsanstalt, 2000).

Skipp, V., *A History of Greater Birmingham: Down to 1830* (Birmingham: Brewin Books, 1980).

Skipp, V., *The Making of Victorian Birmingham* (Birmingham: Victor Skipp, 1983).

Skoda, R., *Neues Gewandhaus Leipzig: Baugeschichte und Gegenwart eines Konzertgebäudes* (Berlin: Verlag für Bauwesen, 1985).

Smith, W. H., *Birmingham and its Vicinity as a Manufacturing and Commercial District* (London, Smith 1836).

Smith, J.S., *The Story of Music in Birmingham* (Birmingham: Cornish, 1945).

Smith, D., *Conflict and Compromise: Class Formation in English Society 1830–1914 – A Comparative Study of Birmingham and Sheffield* (London: Routledge & Kegan Paul, 1982).

Smith, R., 'The Intellectual Context of Handel's English Oratorios' in Hogwood, C., Luckett, R., *Music in 18th Century England: Essays in Memory of Charles Cudworth* (Cambridge: Cambridge University Press, 1983).

Sousa Correa, D., 'Goddesses of Instruction and Desire: Ruskin and Music' in Birch, D. (ed.), *Ruskin and the Dawn of the Modern* (Oxford: Oxford University Press, 1999).

Steinberg, M., *Listening to Reason: Culture, Subjectivity, and Nineteenth-Century Music* (Princeton: Princeton University Press, 2004).

Stiller, G., *J S Bach und das gottesdienstliche Leben seiner Zeit* (Kassel: Barenreiter, 1970).

Stockley, W. C., *Fifty Years of Music in Birmingham/Being the Reminiscences of W. C. Stockley from 1850 to 1900* (Birmingham: Hudson & Son, 1913).

The Birmingham Directory (Birmingham, 1816 and 1846).

The Birmingham, Wolverhampton, Walsall, Dudley, Bilston and Willenhall Directory (Birmingham: Pearson and Rollason, 1780).

The British Association, *Handbook of Birmingham* (Birmingham, 1886).

Thomson, D., *England in the Nineteenth Century* (Harmondsworth: Penguin, 1961 [1950]).

Titel, V. (ed.), *Heinrich Brockhaus: Tagebücher Deutschland 1821 bis 1872* (Erlangen: Filos, 2004).

Todd, R. L., *Mendelssohn: A Life in Music* (Oxford: Oxford University Press, 2002).

Topfstedt, K., Zwahr, H. (eds), *Leipzig um 1800: Beiträge zur Sozial- und Kulturgeschichte* (Beucha: Sax-Verlag, 1998).

Turner, S. (ed.), *The Cambridge Companion to Weber* (Cambridge: Cambridge University Press, 2000).

Uglow, J., *The Lunar Men: The Friends who Made the Future 1730–1810* (London: Faber, 2002).

Wahrman, D., *Imagining the Middle Class: The Political Representation of Class in Britain c1780–1840* (Cambridge: Cambridge University Press, 1995).

Weber, R., *Mein Leipzig lob ich mir: Zeitgenössische Berichte von der Völkerschlacht bis zur Reichsgründung* (Berlin: Verlag der Nation, 1983).

Weber, W., *The Rise of Musical Classics in 18th Century England: A Study in Canon, Ritual, and Ideology* (Oxford: Oxford University Press, 1996 [1992]).

Weber, W., *Music and the Middle Class: The Social Structure of Concert Life in London, Paris and Vienna* (Aldershot: Ashgate, 2004 [1975]).

Weinkauf, B., *Briefe das Gewandhaus zu Leipzig betreffend* (Leipzig: Mitteldeutscher Verlag, 1987).

Werner, J., *Mendelssohn's Elijah: A Historical and Analytical Guide to the Oratorio* (London: Lowe and Brydone, 1965).

Whittall, A., *Romantic Music: A Concise History from Schubert to Sibelius* (London: Thames & Hudson, 1987).

Winckelmann, J. J., *Gedanken über die Nachahmung der griechischen Werke in der Malerei und Bildhauerkunst* (Stuttgart: Reclam, 1999 [1755]).

Young, P. M., *The Concert Tradition: From the Middle Ages to the Twentieth* (London: Routledge and Kegan Paul, 1965).

Young, P. M., *The Oratorios of Handel* (London: Dennis Dobson, 1949).
Zwahr, H., *Revolution in Sachsen – Beiträge zur Sozial- und Kulturgeschichte* (Köln, Weimar, Wien: Böhlau Verlag, 1996).

Journals and Newspapers

Britain:
Aris's Birmingham Gazette (1741–1956)
Birmingham Post (1857–today)
Birmingham Journal (1732–1741; 1825–1869)
The Harmonicon (1823–1833; monthly)
The Musical Examiner (1842–1844; weekly)
The Musical Times (1844–today)
The Musical World (1836–1865; 1866–1891)
The Quarterly Musical Magazin and Review (1818–1828)

Germany:
Allgemeine Musikalische Zeitschrift [AMZ] (1798–1848; 1863–1882)
Die Musik (1901–1943)
Musikalisches Wochenblatt (1870–1910; merged with *NZfM*)
Neue Zeitschrift für Musik [NZfM] (1834–today)
Signale für die Musikalische Welt (1843–1941)

Index

Page number(s) in **bold** indicate the pages where each entry has its fullest and most direct treatment.